PRAISE FO

Property of the R

"With heart and an acute sense of what it means to be displaced, *Property of the Revolution* explores the cost of leaving Cuba to come to America. This is a memoir filled with wisdom, history, joy, and the reverberating waves of grief. I wanted to sit with the *viejos* and all the love and chaos in their multi-generational home and hold on to Abuela and her stories forever."

—MARJAN KAMALI, *USA Today* best-selling author of
The Lion Women of Tehran and *The Stationery Shop*

". . . Hebra Flaster's memoir is rich with layers, blending personal anecdotes and political history into a seamless, engrossing narrative. It remains busy and dynamic, brimming with moments that compel the reader forward. From suspenseful accounts of political oppression to heartfelt recollections of her father's sacrifices, the book pulses with life. . . ."

—LITERARY TITAN, 5-star review

"Written with the vividness of a poet and the reflexivity of an auto-ethnographer, this page-turning family saga viscerally imparts the heart wrenching trauma of their refugee-dom and the emotional refuge they eventually find in the kindness of others, in each other's familial bonds, and in their marvelous memories that no revolution can confiscate. Though a classic story about displacement, resilience, and triumph, *Property of the Revolution* offers fresh perspectives and a deeper understanding of the intersectional meanings of home, country, and family."

—RICHARD BLANCO, 2013 Presidential Inaugural Poet, author of
The Prince of Los Cocuyos: A Miami Childhood

"Ana Hebra Flaster builds her story from memories of her family's journey, from Juanelo to Miami, from New York to Nashua, from Needham to Merrimack, with the lyricism of rootlessness. An unforgettable book about losses and encounters, by an author in great command of language."

—ARMANDO LUCAS CORREA, author of *The German Girl*

"If you think Cubans in the diaspora have only looked to Miami to find their new homes, this book will take you on a very different Cuban journey: to New Hampshire, where Hebra Flaster's family set down roots, never forgetting the barrio they left behind. A compelling and beautiful memoir, read it to gain a capacious view of what it means to be both Cuban and American and to understand the hurt and hope of those whose ideals of revolution were betrayed."

—RUTH BEHAR, author of *Across So Many Seas*

"Ana Hebra Flaster's memoir beautifully represents the journey so many people take when they leave a country they love because there is no other choice. *Property of the Revolution* reminds us of what immigrants and refugees bring to our country—a commitment to family, a burning desire to contribute to a new community, and a unique cultural identity that makes the U.S. stronger and more vibrant."

—JEFF THIELMAN, President and CEO, International Institute
of New England

"An emotionally resonant memoir, blending love, pride, and humor on every page. Hebra Flaster traces the long arc of trauma—from abruptly losing home and country as a child to the resilience required to survive and ultimately thrive as an adult. As a psychiatrist and an avid reader, I found it thoroughly engrossing, and I could not put it down!"

—ELLEN HILSINGER, MD

PROPERTY
OF THE REVOLUTION

From a Cuban Barrio to a New Hampshire Mill Town

A Memoir

Ana Hebra Flaster

SHE WRITES PRESS

Published 2025
Printed in the United States of America
Print ISBN: 978-1-64742-826-6
E-ISBN: 978-1-64742-827-3
Library of Congress Control Number: 2024920505

For information, address:
She Writes Press
1569 Solano Ave #546
Berkeley, CA 94707

Cover Design by Lindsey Cleworth
Interior Design by Kiran Spees

She Writes Press is a division of SparkPoint Studio, LLC.

La Engañadora
Words and Music by Enrique Jorrín
Copyright © 1953 by Peer International Corporation
Copyright Renewed
International Copyright Secured All Rights Reserved
Reprinted by Permission of Hal Leonard LLC

Names and identifying characteristics have been changed to protect the privacy of certain individuals.

Para
Abuela

Libertad es el derecho que todo hombre tiene
a ser honrado, y a pensar y hablar
sin hipocresía. . . .
Como el hueso al cuerpo humano,
el eje a una rueda, y el ala a un pájaro, y el aire al ala,
así es la libertad la esencia de la vida.

Freedom is the right of every person
to be honest, to think, and to speak
without hypocrisy. . . .
Like the bones to the human body,
the axle to the wheel, the wing to the bird, and the air to the wing,
so is liberty the essence of life.

José Martí

Author's note

The people and the events in this book are real. The scenes are drawn from my own lived experience or from the accounts of people who witnessed or experienced the events directly. To protect the privacy of some people, I've changed their names or physical characteristics.

1

Ponte Guapa

Juanelo, Cuba, November 1967

In our barrio, any kid worth her café con leche knew what the rumble of a motorcycle meant. Another family was about to disappear.

Until that night, I ran fast and free over Juanelo's crumbling streets, hunting crinkly brown lizards in the dusty yards, gossiping with the omnipresent *abuelas*. The old women took care of us while our parents worked at places like the school on the corner or the canning factory down by the river. Four generations of my family lived all around me. No one shut her windows or doors. Everybody knew everything about everyone.

On that last normal afternoon in the barrio, I was where I always was after school, chasing skinny hens in Abuela Cuca's yard, the smell of hot rubber wafting from my grandfather's stamping machine in the shed. I played at Abuela Cuca's house every afternoon until dinnertime, when the sky started to whisper about night and she or one of the other *viejos* (elders) scooted me out of the yard, stood at the corner, and watched me zigzag down Castillo to our lemon-yellow house on the corner.

The struggles the *viejos* endured during those early years after the 1959 revolution barely registered in my six-year-old brain. I only

1

knew what I knew. But one thing stumped me: sometimes, friends disappeared overnight.

After dinner every night, Florecita and I played *los caballitos* on the sidewalk. We searched for the biggest palm fronds we could find, straddled them—our "horses"—and raced at full speed, slapping our thighs with our free hands. Sometimes she cheated. Sometimes I cheated too. Above us on their porches, the *viejos* rocked away in their chairs, talking, talking—always talking.

Later, in my bed, I'd hear the clunk of a motorcycle as it snuck into the barrio and wonder. By morning the sound of the moto the night before would feel like a wispy thing that I'd only imagined. But the day I stood waiting for Florecita on the corner of Blume Ramos in my school uniform and she never appeared, I knew the moto had been real. My friend's shimmering green house was empty. A gray banner spread itself across the front door, sealing it shut.

Forty long and distant years later, I learned what it said: *Property of the Revolution.*

Now the moto was back, chugging slowly down Blume Ramos. I flew out of Abuela Cuca's gate, leaving the hens and lizards behind, and took a left onto Serafina and a right onto Castillo—our street. I saw a crowd forming in front of our house and more people rushing toward it from different directions. Those bodies sent out an energy I'll never forget, a current that ran up the street, buzzed through my feet, and landed, vibrating, in my chest.

I fought the urge to cry, to run back to Abuela Cuca's. I wanted to be brave. My mother had shown me how to make myself brave on this very same rise on Castillo, where she'd taught me to ride a bike. She had let me go too soon, and I'd picked up too much speed. I'd crashed where the road dipped, tangled up in the pedals and spokes, bloody and bawling. "*Ya pasó, ya pasó,*" Mami had said then, over and over.

And she was right. It *was* over—and, somehow, that bit of distance eased the pain. Then, with her eyes so close to mine I could see the thin blue ring around her black irises, she said, *"Ponte guapa"*—make yourself brave.

I ran straight through the dip in the road and into the bodies swarming in front of our house. I knew them all from the neighborhood. Some people were crying, even though they were smiling. Others were sobbing, hard. What were we feeling? What were we doing? People shouted, *"¡Se van, se van!"* But who was leaving?

They pushed me along and I bumped into the familiar belts and elbows of my waist-high world until I was on the sidewalk, next to the enormous moto at the curb. Through our open door, I saw a *guardia*.

He wore an olive-green uniform and was sitting at our kitchen table, his back to me. I stared at the gun holstered on his belt as I brushed past him. My father sat across from the *guardia*, his hands jammed under his chin, his gaze pinned to the top of the table.

The look on my father's face told me everything and nothing at the same time. It was someone else's face, someone else's father. Papi's frozen expression terrified me. I was too scared to talk, let alone ask questions. And no one seemed to notice me, anyway. I couldn't have understood, then, the horrible truth Papi was telling me without uttering a word.

Sometimes when our dreams come true, they break our hearts at the same time.

My parents had been waiting three years, since 1964, for this moment, the delivery of their *permiso*. But until this moment they hadn't known when—or if—the exit papers would arrive. The new government had created the *permiso* edict to slow the outflow of hundreds of thousands who were heading for higher, freer ground. The revolution had promised Cubans an end to Batista's dictatorship and the restoration of democracy. Instead, within months of the takeover, my parents had seen the economy, their personal freedoms, and Cuban society itself shatter around them. They'd never thought of leaving the barrio where they were born and raised, but now they began to search for a way out of Cuba, even if it meant leaving their extended families behind.

That concept—abandoning your family, especially your *viejos*—was Cuban taboo. My parents, like all *gusanos*—worms, the government's term for people who were "abandoning" the country—knew they'd have to turn over everything they owned to the government when they left Cuba. But these material losses couldn't compare to the pain of leaving their extended family behind, probably forever. That was the cost of their dream coming true.

My mother had felt the crush of that truth earlier, when she heard the moto turn down Castillo and pull up to our house. How many times had she heard the moto pass our house as the guard brought another family their *permiso*? Finally, it was our turn. She ran to the bedroom—her heart pounding, *bogobóng, bogobóng*—grabbed the box with our photos and baby albums, and rushed to the window that faced the alley, where Neri was already waiting to take it. Mami passed her most cherished possessions to her friend for safekeeping in the hopes that one day, maybe, we could get them back.

Neri was the kind of next-door neighbor you wanted after a communist revolution. She was always tuned in to Radio Big Mouth. Radio Bemba—Cuban slang for "the word on the street"—was the best source of information after the revolution, given the new government's complete control of the media. State TV wasn't going to tell you who was selling cooking oil on the black market, which bodega just got a shipment of black beans, or how to cheat on your ration book to get extra soap. Life-saving information like that was passed like pearls from mouth to mouth on Radio Bemba. The nosy widow told the new mother on the corner, who mentioned it to the old man at the park, who whispered it to the chatterbox standing next to you in line. Neri spent a lot of time on Radio Bemba. She'd call out to my mother with breaking news—"Consuelo, run! The potatoes are here!"—and the two of them would grab us kids and run to Antonio's bodega to wait in line, ration books in hand.

Neri was just as bound to her husband, a revolutionary colonel who would fight in Algiers, Angola, and a few other countries where Castro sent Cubans to fight imperialism. Orestes would return from one of those stints unrecognizable, his son eyeing him from their porch as he got out of a taxi on the corner, his uniform floating over him as he walked, barely rustling as his bony legs carried him home.

Neri would stay with her husband in Cuba, but she kept her promise: Mami's box stayed under her bed for two decades.

I didn't know about the box of photos, the plan to meet at the window, or anything else that day, but a quick look at the chaos in our house told me that someone had picked up my world and flipped it the hell over. One end of the table was half set for a dinner we'd never eat. Papers were spread at the other end, where the *guardia* and my transformed father radiated a tension so menacing it colored them both gray. My mother ran from room to room collecting a change of clothes and a second pair of shoes for each of us—the only items permitted in our suitcase. Juana, the president of our block's *comité*, and her daughter, Dulce, counted chairs and opened cupboards. They needed to verify that everything we'd had in the house when we first applied to leave the country was still there. *Gusanos* couldn't give away or sell their belongings; those were destined for revolutionary hands. Juana was a decent woman, so Mami hoped she'd understand that the few missing glasses and plates hadn't been sold for profit, only broken by accident.

As Juana counted cutlery, Papi sat still but worked hard not to react to the *guardia*'s insults. The only tranquil creature was Blanquita, our perpetually pregnant white mutt. Her tight belly kept her in her favorite spot by our kerosene stove.

Somehow, I saw Abuela Fina, my maternal grandmother—the one who lived with us—last. She stood in a corner holding my little brother, Sergito, who was banging his head against her chest in an attempt to get back on solid ground. Abuela Fina pulled me to her side and in no time all three of us were wailing in comforting solidarity.

Only then did the *guardia* notice me. He crooked his finger and called me over.

"*Niña*, is it true that you want to leave your house, and friends, and school, and never see them again?"

Knowing they had a chatterbox on their hands and exactly how I'd answer this question, Abuela Fina, Mami, and Papi jumped to answer for me, "*¡Sí, claro que sí!*"

Abuela swept Sergito and me into our bedroom, where we could disintegrate in peace while the *guardia* continued questioning Papi.

"Why do you want to leave the country?"

"My wife wants to leave."

The *guardia* rolled his eyes. He smirked and started to say something, but Mami interrupted him.

"I don't like communism," she said, trying to draw the attention away from my father.

The *guardia* looked at her for a long moment before turning back to my father. "I see who wears the pants here."

My mother reached for her chain, held the medallion of la Virgen between her index finger and thumb, and prayed Papi would stay in his chair.

The *guardia* continued flipping through his forms, asking questions, and not looking at my parents when they answered.

"What about bank accounts? Any withdrawals in the past five years?"

Mami sorted through an envelope and handed him a stash of deposit slips and a ledger. "We have this one savings account. We did take money out, but we returned it, like they told us at the Ministry." She opened the ledger. "That's when we returned the money. The balance is the same as when we applied for the *permiso*. Seventy-five pesos."

"What about jewelry? Where is it?"

"We don't have any," my father said.

The *guardia* looked at Papi. "So a *pelotero* who played baseball in the United States doesn't have any jewelry? Come on . . ."

"I sold what I had to pay for our wedding," Papi said.

The *guardia* laughed. "Well . . . she screwed you then, and she's screwing you now. Your flight leaves in two days. Finish packing."

Mami's legs started trembling uncontrollably. She looked at the stacked plates on the table, the pots drying on the counter. She wanted to put everything back where it belonged. "Can I shower before we leave?"

She didn't realize she'd actually spoken until the *guardia* replied, "Where are you sleeping tonight?"

Mami hadn't thought about that yet. "I suppose . . . at my brother-in-law's, upstairs."

"Then you can shower there." The *guardia* got up and collected the papers off the table. "Keys?"

As soon we'd finished packing the few items allowed us, the *guardia* swept us out to the porch—even Blanquita—and locked our door. We watched as he unfolded a long banner—the same one I'd noticed pasted on other houses. He stretched it across the door and over the jamb, pressing the glued backing into the surfaces. I remember the clap of his hand against the door and the stucco, making sure—very sure—no one would get back in without permission.

With the slapping and sealing over, the *guardia* handed the last of the documents to my father. "Your flight leaves the day after tomorrow. Be at the Camarioca airstrip by eight that night." He jumped on his moto and roared up Castillo toward the *calzada*.

The family and neighbors who'd gathered out on the street finally joined us on the porch, and the hugging and smiling and crying began. The muffled sobs and the laughter, the women wiping their hands on their skirts—tore the last bit of brave I had out of me. I began to cry, to my mortification, like a baby.

This was the scene that would spur my questions over the years. My cousins and brother would rarely ask about Cuba, but for the rest of my life I'd beg the *viejos* for their stories, hungry to understand what pushed each of them to the brink, how they survived as *gusanos* while they waited, exposed, with no guarantee of ever getting out.

But in that moment of upside-down happiness all I wanted was Blanquita. I found her lying down in front of our door, low to the ground, like me. I stroked her pregnant belly gently, so her puppies wouldn't wake up. I looked up at the banner stretched across our door, so crisp and powerful, and it wrecked me. Our house wanted to breathe, but that thin strip of paper was suffocating it.

2

Broken Reunion

Juanelo, November 1967

We slept apart from each other that night—the first time I remember not having Abuela beside me in bed. There wasn't enough room for all of us upstairs, in my aunt and uncle's apartment, even though only my uncle, Tío Angel, lived there now. Tía Silvia, my mother's sister, and my cousins, Angelito and Alberto, had flown away to the United States a few months before. So Abuela went down Ulacia to her father Don Manuel's house, Papi went to his mother Cuca's house, and Mami, Sergito, and I clomped up the outside stairs to Tío's apartment.

Mami slept between Sergito and me on Tía and Tío's bed, her mind spinning in all directions, searching for a place to land. What if Abuela decided to stay in Cuba after all? She had never wanted to leave, knowing she'd probably never see her older brother, Manolo, or her ninety-four-year-old father, Don Manuel, again. But Manolo had convinced his sister with his mathematician's logic: "Your daughters and Sergio will be working long days when they get to the United States. Who's going to take care of those four kids, Fina? I can handle Papá. He's a tough old Gallego, you know that. You have to be where Silvia and Consuelo are. It's the only solution."

And Papi. Would he control his fists during the interrogations at the airport? And what about after we got to the States? Should we settle in Miami, where so many Cubans had already settled? Or go as planned to Tía in New York City, where we knew almost no one? Tío was supposed to come as well; what if he decided to stay in Cuba?

Mami was the architect of this moment. Now she wondered—was she leading us into further ruin? Ten years ago, she'd risked her life to help the revolution succeed. Now its triumph had forced her to tear apart her old family in order to save her young one.

In the darkest part of the night, as we churned through sleep, I woke up panicked.

"Will the plane go near Vietnam?"

"Sh-shh," Mami said. "How do you know about Vietnam?"

"At school. They said American soldiers shoot mothers and children in Vietnam."

"No. Oh, God . . . No. We're not going to Vietnam. Go to sleep."

"I don't want to go to Vietnam—"

"*¡Sió!*"

I loved my school in Cuba, my uniform, the singing—but most of all I adored my teacher, one of the young teacher trainees, known as Makarenkas, who were replacing the many teachers who'd left the country by then. When I saw her in the crowd of teary friends who came to say goodbye in the morning, I ran and hid in Tía's bedroom. How could I face my idol in that room full of strange emotions, of crying and laughing and pretending?

Mami found me crouching next to the nightstand.

"Your teacher was very brave to come here, the house of a *gusano* family. You can make yourself brave too. *Ponte guapa.* Go and say goodbye."

I stood in front of my teacher, staring down at her familiar shoes.

She bent down and brought my hand to her curled bangs, one of the things I loved most about her. I stroked her soft hair, and when I stuck my finger inside the magical curl on her forehead, both of us began to cry. I felt an almost violent release of emotion as the weight of all the confusion I'd been carrying lifted off me. I felt lighter than air, like I would float away, as the sobs rocked me. But Mami and my teacher held on to me and kept me right there.

We arrived at the Camarioca airstrip in our best clothes the next night, but within hours my brother and I were filthy and sweaty from rolling around the gritty floor in a cluster of *gusanitos*, oblivious to the world as it clattered to the floor around us.

Our parents, grandparents, aunts, and uncles had other things on their minds. They rose dutifully each time their names rattled out of the tinny PA system and headed for their interrogations. The *guardias* had already gone through the suitcases of the two hundred or so *gusanos* waiting to leave the next morning on one of the two US-funded Freedom Flights. We'd lost our suitcase—a wedding present from my father's tío Juan—in that process.

Papi had watched as the *guardia* rummaging through our clothes started running his hands over the immaculate exterior of the aluminum case. He'd clicked the buckle closures a few times, testing them out, then kicked at an old suitcase he had on the floor to pull it closer. He'd dumped our clothes into the old suitcase, closed it, and handed it to my father. My parents had watched as he closed theirs shut and tucked it far under the table. Then they'd *thanked* him.

All night, the tedious exit interviews kept the adults focused, alert. The room buzzed with *gusano* tension and the metallic reverb of the speakers. Everyone knew of families who'd had a family member suddenly held back for any number of concocted infractions and then had to face the agony of leaving them behind or giving up their *permiso* and returning home, worse off than ever in the revolutionary society they had officially renounced.

Papi seemed to draw a lot of the *guardias'* attention that night. A former professional baseball player who'd played in the United States was now abandoning his homeland? And he looked much younger than thirty-four, they told him, over and over. What year was he born? He couldn't leave if he was of military age—a range that kept widening during the night. They'd have to look into it.

Abuela and Mami rose at one point when Papi came back from yet another interview, shaken.

"The medic said this is leprosy," he said, pointing to a bump on his chin, "so I can't leave the country."

"*Sinvergüenzas, cabro—*" Mami stopped mid-swear, trying to think. If she pleaded his case, she might make things worse. But if she let the bastards run with this new excuse, they might keep Papi in Cuba. My parents had already decided to split up if this happened. Whoever made it to the United States would work on getting the others out.

Mami never could keep her mouth shut. She walked to the desk where the medic was talking with a *guardia*. Papi and Abuela watched the medic stiffen and look away as Mami spoke. Suddenly, our timid *abuela* made *herself* brave and joined her daughter's campaign, using that old teacher's tone she could muster at will. Slowly, slowly, they wore that medic down. Finally, he relented.

We settled in for the night, rumpled bodies draped over each other, wrestling with sleep, speakers crackling, chairs creaking. I woke up late into the night, on a cot next to other kids, in a dark room washed in dim blue light. A woman was feeding a small child some crackers. She asked if I was thirsty. I guzzled the cup of water she gave me, marveling at the blueness all around me.

Decades later I told my cousin Angelito, the oldest of our generation, about this hallucination.

"You weren't dreaming," he said. "Same thing happened to us. That woman must have worked at the airport. In that blue room . . ."

We flew away the next morning, my face plastered against the window, Abuela dabbing me dry with her handkerchief. Just before takeoff, an attendant walked down the aisle and sprayed us with disinfectant. One day, from the other side of our lives, Mami and I would talk about getting sprayed and she'd laugh at the memory, but I still felt the sting.

The plane roared, and as we rose up in the sky I watched Cuba run away from me, faster and faster—flashing green fields, white sand, and a rippling blue-green sea.

Miami, Florida

America smelled soapy and cold, even inside the Opa Locka refugee center, just outside of Miami. I raked my fingers over a wall paneled in a bizarre material—nubby, wiry, and soft at the same time. *Alfombra*, Mami said. I'd never seen carpeting before.

In the United States, we were *refugiados*, not *gusanos*, but we still waited in lines for everything, just like in Cuba. Church groups interviewed us to see if we belonged to them, and if we did, they gave us money: twenty dollars per family member for Catholics, ten dollars for Protestants. Jews got the most—fifty dollars—so Papi got in that line. But the lady was too smart: *"Senor, yo no creo que usted es judío."*

Papi admitted she was right, he wasn't Jewish. But she still gave him the money.

It seemed like Papi's luck might run out later, when, after he described how hungry we'd been in the last few years, an upper-class Cuban refugee accused him of coming to the United States just for the food. The man said that Cubans like us were gluttons, not principled freedom-lovers like him. Papi smashed his fist into the man's soft face and all hell broke loose. But just like with the Jewish woman, Papi managed to wring a good outcome out of his bad behavior. When he was pulled out of the line and questioned about the fight, he discovered that he and the Cuban American official who was interviewing him had a mutual friend: Papi's sister's husband, a doctor who hadn't been able to get out of Cuba. When Papi told the official about my doctor-uncle's struggles, the man promised to help his old friend.

A few months later, the official's efforts paid off. Papi's sister and her husband got their *permiso* and out of Cuba.

The night of Papi's fistfight, we slept in a room with a three-level bunk bed. Mami had calmed Papi down and finally gotten Abuela Fina to sleep in the single women's area, despite her complaints. But in the middle of the night Abuela came back, spooked. She wanted to be with us. I heard them murmuring as they lifted Sergito away from me and Abuela Fina slid into his place.

Later, I heard Papi shouting, "They stole our money! Where did we leave it?"

Mami climbed up to the third-level bunk, where Papi was panting so hard the bunks were shaking. "*Ya pasó, ya pasó,*" she said, over and over, until his nightmare faded away.

New York City

Mami felt better once we were on the ground. Sergito and I had laughed each time the plane lifted us up and threw us down, but Mami puked the whole time. Papi took care of her and Abuela took care of us, explaining how we shouldn't breathe deeply in the northern cold because of "*neh-u-monía.*" Before we got off the plane, she bundled us up in our new coats and gloves, pinned us to her, and covered our mouths, like she was killing us and saving us at the same time.

Tía fell on top of us when she saw us, crying and smelling exactly like she always did, powdery and soft. She had three of everything in her apartment—three knives, three forks, three cups. Just enough for the three of them: Angelito, Alberto, and Tía. I thought it was cute, like she was playing house. But Tía wasn't playing at all, only teaching us how to be eight instead of nine, until Tío could come to us.

Tío had stayed behind to care for his last living relative, the aunt who'd raised him when he was orphaned at the age of nine. They'd agreed that Tía should leave the country with the boys before they reached military age and wouldn't be allowed to leave. Tía wrote to Tío almost every day, reminding him that we were waiting for him, and she always asked us to send him a message too. But our messages were all the same: *When are you coming?* We talked about Tío so much that it felt like he was there, except he wasn't. Where Tío was supposed to be there was just an outline, an empty space.

Every day, Alberto, Angelito, and I rode a gigantic bus to our new school. Alberto puked a lot in those days—even on the school bus. Only Angelito and I would sit near him. I understood why Alberto felt so sick. The school was enormous, the halls crowded with huge blond American kids shouting in their chewed-up language. Bells rang, doors slammed, heavy shoes pounded their way up and down stairs. The teachers let the Americanitos run around playing dangerous games, like climbing up to the ceiling on ropes and throwing red rubber balls right at each other's faces. But I liked my teacher, even though we mostly just looked at each other and smiled. On my first day, she gave me a box of creamy new crayons and a blue plastic apron for when we painted. The crayons smelled so good I wanted to eat them.

Coloring helped me forget that Abuela cried from the moment

she woke up to the moment we started to pray in our bed each night. After we finished, she'd wrap her arms around me and sniffle for a while.

Abuela was different now. Her eyes were always wet. She trembled—and it wasn't from the cold. Something was wrong. Even when I brought her to the window to see the snow falling and she smiled, she still looked sad. I had to keep an eye on Abuela in this new place.

Nothing smelled like Cuba in this city full of brown bricks—not the rice, not the water, not the freezing air that pinched your face before it spat out snowflakes. In America, you could see your breath. Papi and Mami didn't like this place—the crowded subways, the long walk just to get to a park where we could play. But Tía liked the city, so they argued and Abuela cried more. I watched and listened from the corners of the apartment. I wondered if Abuela would get sick and die. It felt like she might disappear at any moment.

One weekend not long after our arrival, old friends from the barrio showed up at our door. The Cernudas were a family of resourceful carpenters from Juanelo who'd somehow found us. The father, Armando, and his two sons, Pedro and Jorge, told stories about our barrio as they sat on the floor in the living room. Abuela's face changed as they talked about home, a new light in her eyes.

Then they started talking about their new home in a place called "New Hamcher." They liked it a lot, even if it snowed more than it did in New York. There were lots of factory jobs, good schools, lots of space for kids to play, and kind people.

Papi barely hesitated when they invited him to go back with them.

Just like that, Papi was gone. Mami kept telling me he'd be back soon, that he was looking for a house with a big yard for us to play in, but I didn't believe her. We were losing Papi, I thought, just like we'd lost Tío.

The new week started without my father. We only had mothers now. In the mornings, Tía went off to her job at the powder puff factory and Mami went with her to fill out job applications. Abuela fed us café con leche and tostadas, bundled up Sergito, and walked us to the bus stop. She didn't trust Angelito to keep Alberto and me safe on the icy sidewalks, so all five of us bumbled down the street, grabbing on to each other, trying to stay upright.

3

Executions

Juanelo, New Year's Eve 1958–January 1959
My hard-partying, apolitical, twenty-seven-year-old father went to bed at ten o'clock on the most important night of modern Cuban history. He was still recovering from a rum-soaked Noche Buena pig roast under the sprawling branches of Abuela Cuca's avocado trees. But for my eighteen-year-old mother, the partying on New Year's Eve 1958 stretched into the dawn and delivered nothing but pure joy.

Batista, the oppressor, had fled the country. His six years of dictatorship were over. The revolution had triumphed. Fidel Castro and his rebels, whom Mami had risked her life to support, were heading toward Havana to take power. The best days for Cuba lay ahead, Mami thought. The various rebel groups would join together and restore democracy to the country, just as they had all promised from the start. Fidel, whose group had gotten the most attention both inside and outside of Cuba, was rumored to be a communist, but he, too, had promised the restoration of the 1940 constitution and a return to democracy. Mami turned to the new year proud of her own contributions to the rebel cause.

As the first day of January dawned, Mami thought about my father, who'd just returned after playing in the Mexican baseball leagues.

She'd broken up with him before beginning to work for the rebels to keep him out of danger. No one knew she collected medicine and supplies and sold bonds for the cause. But now, all the worries and fear of the last few years felt behind her. She could return to a normal life. First up: restart her relationship with my father, a popular barrio ballplayer she'd known her whole life despite their nine-year age difference.

My father had been away a lot during the '50s, playing in the minor leagues in the United States, which at least partially explained his lack of interest in politics. But for my mother, the injustice and brutality of the Batista dictatorship had demanded action. The revolution, which had begun in the early '50s, had been fought on different fronts by different groups, all committed to ending Batista's dictatorship and restoring Cuba's democratic constitution of 1940.

The majority of active fighters had been university students, young alumni, and their supporters. The rebels had fought, bombed, shot, and sabotaged their way across the country throughout the '50s. Many had paid with their lives. The lucky ones had landed in jail or died instantly in violent shoot-outs. Others had died at the hands of Batista's torturers, their bodies often dumped on street corners as warnings. Some rebels had committed atrocities themselves, of course, killing suspected traitors and informants. Innocent Cubans had been killed. To stay in power, Batista's government had taken bribes, censored the press, and paid informants and backers through regular monthly payments of 33.33 pesos, known as *el treinta y tres, treinta y tres.*

Now the rebels had finally won. All that New Year's Eve and into the dawn of the first, my mother romped with her friends on the main avenue, the *calzada*, near Juanelo. They joined the throngs cheering Viva Cuba Libre, drank rum, and ate cod fritters. Celebratory gunfire sounded all around. Her friends draped their arms over each other as they came back into the barrio and went house to house, singing, toasting with the neighbors, and kissing the *viejos* and the kids who were still up. It was, she would say decades later, "the happiest day of my life." Juanelo's factory workers, teachers, and carpenters rejoiced with the young people in the streets, though some with less gusto than others.

One of them was Tío Manolo, Abuela's older brother. Mami adored her brilliant, timid uncle. Most nights, uncle and niece sat in the rocking chairs on Don Manuel's front porch, talking about politics, science, movies. Like everyone else in Don Manuel's family, Tío Manolo was staunchly anti-Batista and had supported the rebels almost from the beginning, believing that the corruption of the Batista regime made fair elections impossible.

The family gathered at night, closed the shutters and tuned in to Radio Rebelde, the rebels' clandestine radio broadcast. But Tío Manolo had been worrying that the young rebels were too inexperienced to run the country and that the revolution would turn Marxist. With the Cold War underway, that would cost Cuba its strong ties to the United States and bring radical economic and social changes. He'd decided that was too much change for most Cubans, who had enjoyed a rising standard of living and a strong economy throughout the '50s.

Mami thought her *tío* was too negative and completely wrong about the communists taking over. She stayed away from the house that New Year's Eve. She wanted a pure, uncomplicated celebration, not another debate with Tío Manolo.

On the first morning of 1959, four miles from Juanelo, Havana was awash in chaos. A strange mix of partying, relief, and bloodlust filled the air. While some cheered and sang the national anthem, others swarmed police stations and ran off with rifles and pistols.

Delinquents, office workers, weary mothers—everyone—released the fears and tensions that had built up in the last years of Batista's dictatorship. Some policemen simply handed over their weapons to "rebels"—everyone seemed to have adopted that title. Mobs surrounded the homes of members of Batista's government, military officials, and police.

Even my father ended up in a shoot-out at the home of a Batista officer that afternoon. His buddies had invited him along at the last minute, offering him one of the M1 rifles they'd picked up at a raid on the Columbia military camp.

"Waldo almost got me killed that day," Papi would later say of the adventure. "My jaw locked up from the stress of the *tiroteo*. I could only eat pureed foods for a week."

One night a few weeks later, Don Manuel's family—Abuela Fina, Tío Manolo, his wife, Tina, their twenty-year-old son, Alfredo, and my mother—gathered in front of the TV after dinner. Tía Silvia and Tío Angel walked over from their apartment carrying their babies, Angelito and Alberto. The verdicts would be televised. Some said that if they were convictions the executions would be immediate and televised, but no one believed it.

Mami stroked Don Manuel's bony back as he shook his head and muttered under his breath. Her grandfather blinked repeatedly behind his thick eyeglasses. He looked ancient to her. He'd arrived in Havana from Galicia, Spain, on the day the Cuban flag was raised for the first time in 1902. He often talked about the hope he felt at that moment, how he already felt more Cuban than Spanish. He didn't care that his native country had lost Cuba in the Spanish-American War. He had followed the war from his village, admiring the Cubans' fight and secretly hoping they'd win. Now his son and daughter, Tío Manolo and Abuela Fina, were witnessing a horror he couldn't have

imagined on that day—even after living through the political violence of Cuba's 1930s.

Tío Manolo broke the silence. "Cuba is about to regress twenty
years . . . more. On live television."

Mami kept her hand on Don Manuel's shoulders as a group of men
appeared on the screen. They lined up in front of a trench. The orders
were shouted; the gunshots exploded. The men's bodies crumpled
and fell backward into the trench. Don Manuel wiped his eyes behind
his glasses. The only other time Mami had seen her grandfather cry
was after her grandmother, Vicenta, died. Mami felt a strange mix
of sadness and rage. But she believed in her revolution. Maybe, she
thought, all revolutions unfolded this way, with necessary score-set-
tling that would eventually subside and lead to peace.

Juanelo, February 1959

No one in either Don Manuel or my father's immediate families had
served in Batista's army or as policemen, but my mother had a paternal uncle who had. Pablo had served in the military under a noto-
riously brutal Batista officer. He managed to stay hidden for a short
while, but the revolutionaries soon started to arrest anyone linked to
his commanding officer.

My mother's normally stoic aunt Hortensia arrived at Don
Manuel's house one evening, out of breath and trembling. She'd just
returned from the province where Pablo's trial had been held. He and
the men immediately below the comandante never had a chance, she
told my mother. The bloodlust in the packed hall had grown by the
moment, men with rifles sitting behind the accused men. A brave
woman had stood up to defend Pablo, telling of how he'd protected
her son from the comandante's fury once. She'd pleaded for Pablo's
life. But by then nothing mattered. Pablo was executed almost

immediately following the trial, along with several others who'd served with him.

Mami hugged Hortensia as she cried for her brother. "Where are they holding the body, Tía? I want to go to the funeral."

"Mija, there's no way with all this turmoil." Hortensia shook her head. "They put his body on a train and sent him a hundred miles from home."

Mami remembered Tío Manolo's explanation for this now-common tactic: "To keep the mourner count low and counterrevolutionaries under control."

Mami met Fidel, the man of the hour, by pure coincidence. In early 1959, she still considered him Cuba's savior. She was on an excursion with her fellow teachers to the Zapata Peninsula, about eighty miles to the southeast of Havana, shortly after Fidel took control. Fidel and his guards arrived on an airboat at the shoreline just after her group. People circled him, and he held court for a while. He posed for a few photos and was on his way.

"God, it was cold that day," Mami said, years later, as we studied the photo someone had taken. "Look at the coat I was wearing." She had on a mid-weight sweater—a coat to Cubans and a rare sight, even on a winter day.

"I kept buttoning and unbuttoning it. I was so nervous." She grinned. "*Mira que fui comemierda.*" She could call herself a shiteater from the safe distance of four decades and chuckle. "I stood this far from him," she said, looking at the foot-long space between her outstretched hands.

I barely notice Fidel in that photo. It's my mother's face that draws me in. Her mouth is slightly open; her eyes shine with adoration so pure that I am embarrassed for her. She is both shy and reverent in front of Fidel, two characteristics that would fall outside of her emotional repertoire for the rest of her life.

Staring at the photo, I begin to understand the depth of the betrayal she felt when the revolution failed her. She believed that blind devotion to the revolution in general, and Fidel in particular, had led her, our family, and the country to ruin. Mami never allowed herself to adore a politician, an actor, a writer—an anything—again. She refused to shy away from uncomfortable questions and wore skepticism proudly. She'd learned that a certain level of mistrust is essential in life, especially when choosing sides. Her country had over-trusted one man and then failed to stop the train as he ran it off the track. They'd paid dearly for that mistake.

For people like my parents, who had little material wealth to lose, the payments were the grandfathers, the aunts, and the lifelong friends that they left behind and never saw again.

4

Receive from Me a Warrior's Heart

Nashua, New Hampshire, December 1967

Ray Flanders liked Cubans, thank God. Papi didn't know that when he first stood in front of him, another tall American with big teeth, but it turned out to be a bit of luck that broke our way.

Papi had been hopeful on the journey north with the Cernudas, even though the roads were iced over and the trip took more than six hours instead of the expected four. The next morning, the men searched the *Nashua Telegraph* and found a promising house for rent. It was on a busy street, Armando warned, but it was directly across from an elementary school and a baseball field, which at the moment served as a community ice-skating rink. The farmhouse, with its dirt-floor basement, steam radiators, and old-fashioned wallpaper everywhere, dated back to the late 1800s, but Papi said it felt more like something from medieval times. It smelled like that, at least.

Ray, the owner, took a liking to Papi immediately, recalling how a Cuban classmate of his had disarmed a crazed, knife-wielding intruder in their dorm when he was in college. Ray said the Cuban student had known his way around machetes—he'd grown up on a sugar plantation—so a knife had been no problem.

"Thank God the guy with the knife wasn't the Cuban guy," Papi said to Armando as they drove away. "We'd still be looking for a house."

Papi felt triumphant. He didn't know if Tío would ever join us—and as the only man present, he felt responsible for both families. That day, he'd not only found a new home for us but had also gotten jobs for himself, my mother, and my aunt at Hampshire Manufacturing, the rubber boot factory where Ray was a foreman.

"Hold off on the first month's rent," Ray told Papi. "You can pay me after you get your first paychecks."

The eight of us moved into the rickety farmhouse at 62 Amherst Street—or "Amehr Estreet," as the *viejos* pronounced it—soon afterward, although Tía dragged her feet in protest. She thought a city would be better than a quiet town so far north. Why couldn't we live in Union City or Newark like all the other Cubans?

When Tía lobbied hard for us to move again, Mami pointed to New Hampshire's apt state motto and tried to convince her.

"Live Free or Die" on all those license plates looked like a good omen to everyone. And the adults all agreed that if the United States fell to communism, we'd be grateful that the Canadian border lay just a few hours north. From now on, they'd always have an exit plan. With all the anti-war demonstrations, pot-smoking hippies, and race riots of the late '60s, a revolution here seemed plausible. But they saw the upside of all that turmoil and held on to it for dear life. They were in a country that allowed its citizens to shout insults at their president without throwing them in jail. Maybe that was a country worth freezing for.

And freezing we were. The week we moved in, a blizzard dumped eighteen inches of snow and ice on us. Frost covered the windows. Three-foot icicles hung from the eaves. I studied the warped worlds inside the icicles that crashed to the ground. There was magic in that house. I pressed my hands against the drafty windows and watched the handprints that appeared and disappeared there. When the loud steam radiators hissed and spat, I stood in awe, marveling at yet another American contraption.

And we all fit. Abuela, Sergito, and I in one room, Tía in another, my parents in their own on the ground floor. Angel and Alberto got the best one: a large closet in the living room. The *viejos* found a bunk bed somewhere and squeezed it into that long, windowless space, creating a cozy, mysterious hideout for my overjoyed cousins.

Those first weeks in New Hampshire, my parents and aunt dug deep into the Cuban tradition of facing difficulty with great bluster, denial, and a smile. "*A mal tiempo, buena cara*" was Tía's favorite Spanish saying. For Tía, especially, "To a bad time, a good face" allowed her to live with the possibility that Tío might never join us. The *viejos* distracted themselves by telling funny barrio stories, remembering the past as if it was theirs to recreate at will. They kept the barrio and our lost family right there, just under the happy present they were trying to create.

My grandmother failed completely at this game. The past had her by the neck, and it was winning. She cried through those dark days and darker nights, a wet, soft, old-person scent wafting off her as she stirred soup on the stove, folded laundry, or stared through the kitchen window at the snowdrifts that were engulfing the house.

"I miss my brother and my father too much," she'd say when I asked why she was crying. I watched her out of the corner of my eye as she stirred mysterious concoctions on the stove, stews and purees of the cheap meat or vegetables Mami or Tía bought. Her cheeks felt wet whenever I kissed her. Her clothes were damp and smelled like salt and tears and grief. Abuela was melting from sorrow.

Alberto warned me once as we sat down to eat another one of her invented soups, "There's a lot of Abuela snot in this thing." That was mean, but I knew he loved her, too, and was just trying to laugh at the sadness around us.

To be fair, Abuela had little to work with in the kitchen. The adults counted each penny for the rent, food, clothing, furniture, household supplies—a mountain of expenses that built up all at once. We ate mostly eggs for dinner—fried, boiled, scrambled—with rice or toast. Alberto and I would sneak back into the kitchen after dinner and whip up a snack (ketchup on white bread) or a dessert (sugar on . . . white bread).

Alberto knew how to make a game of almost anything, and he didn't fail me on those hungry nights. He made a competition out of who could take the tiniest bites out of our creations, who could make the snack last the longest. I can still see his grinning face, snaggle tooth and all, as we nibbled our ketchup sandwiches in front of the fridge.

Years later, the adults would talk about those hungry nights and laugh at the ways they managed to stretch the food supply. But there was a serious note in their chuckles, as if they still respected the hunger of those days.

Mrs. Drew, my new first-grade teacher, proved a dependable ally from the beginning. She wore short sailor dresses, had sparkly blue eyes, and smelled like a cup of warm American coffee with cream. On my first day, she pushed a little desk against hers and pointed at it until I sat down. There, she created an island of security where we could practice making English sounds when she had extra time—where nothing bad could happen.

I was especially grateful for Mrs. Drew's protection the day a visitor—the father of one of my classmates, a Vietnam War veteran—came into our classroom. When I saw the uniformed soldier and heard "Vietnam" I froze, sure he'd kill us all, burn down the school.

The warnings at my Cuban school that American soldiers killed children came rushing back.

I wanted to run home, but the soldier was standing in front of the door. Mrs. Drew materialized by my side, led me to my desk, and sat down so close to me that I began to breathe again.

Mrs. Drew knew how to save me.

Mami, Tía, and Abuela sat at the kitchen table, drinking real café that the Cernudas had bought on their last pilgrimage to the Spanish bodega in Lawrence, Massachusetts. Sunlight filtered through the mismatched curtains and made shadows on the linoleum floor. Tía had found the curtains at the Salvation Army store. Each window had a different curtain, some printed, some plain, some long, some short. I colored on the floor while the mothers talked or read letters from Cuba to each other. The voices of their old friends rose up from the blue tissue-thin papers rustling in their hands. Neri, Ofelia, Pancha, and the others told them about their children, the food lines, something funny that happened at the bus stop, a new birth, a new death. Home. This was how Mami learned that our house had been given to a pro-Castro family from another part of Havana and that, before they moved in, officials had broken the banner and helped themselves to the clothes, shoes, and other things we'd left behind.

Most of the mothers' talk was about Tío. In his last letter, he'd told Tía that he would apply for his *permiso*, but Tía still had plenty to worry about. When would it arrive, if it arrived at all? How would Tío, who'd been so dedicated to the revolution, endure the verbal and physical harassment that came with being a *gusano*?

But their troubles seemed to fade away when talking about Juanelo. Even though I could trace the streets of our barrio on paper, a project that always drew Abuela to my side, I found myself wondering who "Juanelo" was. To me, the name of our barrio was in the four magical street names Abuela would write on my maps: Castillo, Serafina, Ulacia, Blume Ramos. I made Abuela say the names out loud as she wrote them down, listened as she breathed our home back into existence. "Juanelo" sounded like my mother's name, Consuelo, and the way the mothers spoke of it—that wistful tone—gave the name a human quality, something far more powerful than sidewalks, houses, streets. I decided Juanelo must be a special friend, and I hoped she'd visit us soon so the *viejos* would be happy.

Tía stopped talking about Tío and started reading a letter that had arrived from Cuba. Tío Manolo and Don Manuel had taken turns writing it. When she got to Don Manuel's part, Tía wiped her eyes and passed the letter to Mami.

"*Para Josefina, Silvia, Consuelo y toda la familia.*" Mami followed her grandfather's script as it veered across the thin paper. "I wish you all complete health and peace. I live now to eat and nothing else. Deaf and blind, and with little spirit, I can't see what I am writing. Forgive me. I received several letters from you. In them, much good news, which makes me happy. I am very happy you are all working together. Kisses for all of you, especially you three. Receive from me a warrior's heart. Tell the children I wish them much success in their studies. Always stay together."

After Mami finished, she and Tía walked away, each to her own room. Abuela stayed at the table, her eyes scanning side to side as she read and read and read.

I left the crayons and my papers on the floor and looked for Mami. She'd locked her bedroom door, so I knocked again and again until she finally cracked the door open. She wiped her face when I asked her what was wrong.

"My back hurts a little. I need to lie down for a while."

Mami always spoke, as we say in Spanish, *sin pelos en la lengua*— without hairs on her tongue—but I knew she was lying, standing in that doorway, makeup smeared, fighting back sobs, blocking the dark room behind her.

"I'll get you an aspirin," I said.

"Mija, I don't need one. I just need to sleep. It's okay." She smiled and shut the door.

I ran upstairs to the bathroom cabinet and got an aspirin anyway.

I was about to knock on her door, the single aspirin in my palm, when I heard moaning on the other side. I rested my head against the door and listened to the hurt pouring out of my mother.

Deep into one icy night, Abuela and I woke up to blaring sirens from the fire station down the street. We looked out the window as fire trucks raced up Amherst Street, their flashing red lights sweeping across the room. We held on to each other, Abuela praying as she always did when we heard sirens.

The next morning, I saw the cause for all those sirens. Just across from our school, a house had burned down, leaving a charred skeleton of crackled timbers and ash. The acrid smell of smoke hung in the air, menacing and ugly, a reminder that we were only seeing the end of a horror.

In my classroom, kids were whispering about the fire at Barbara's house. Her desk was empty. Someone had died, they said. Was it Barbara? She was a nice girl with satiny, long blonde hair. I couldn't understand the hushed words, and I couldn't stop looking at Barbara's desk.

That night, Mami translated the *Nashua Telegraph*'s report of the fire. The older brother had woken up to what he thought was sleet hitting the windows. When he realized it was the crackling of flames, he tried to wake everyone up, threw blankets out a window and then a baby brother, hoping the blankets would shield his fall.

My classmates had been right. Someone had died. One of Barbara's brothers, a boy who'd been in Alberto's class.

A child had died. A house had burned down. Ours could too. The image of the older brother throwing the baby out the window—the flames behind them—stuck in my mind. Of course the fire sounded like icy rain to him! Even I could understand why he'd been fooled. If it rained, how would anyone really know if there was a fire?

Every day, as we got close to school, the wet smell of the charred house told me that danger and death were right there next to us. And every night, I worried—who would wake us up if a fire started? Someone needed to be awake and listening in case the rain tricked us.

Bedtime became the portal to a fearful place. Once asleep, bad things could happen, and no one would know until it was too late. Abuela was teaching me new prayers, and we always ended with the Guardian Angel's Prayer. Every night, I asked my angel to please wake us if the house was burning. Abuela comforted me, but the fear of fire had taken hold.

I'd listen to Abuela's sighs, feel her chest rising and falling under the arm I draped over her waist. Her breathing slowed as she fell asleep. It was up to me now. The wild arcs of light that swept the walls as cars drove down Amherst Street helped keep me awake. I counted the seconds between Abuela's breaths to make sure she was still alive. When she took too long to inhale—or when I couldn't keep myself awake any longer—I'd shake her. She'd mumble complaints or scold me, still half asleep. But someone needed to be awake in case a fire started.

The nights of sleet and freezing rain wrecked me. Was the clicking at the window icy rain or was it a fire downstairs? I'd pinch myself or bite my tongue to stay awake. Sometimes the red wallpaper kept me awake as it bloomed into strange shapes in the dim light.

One night, as I fought to stay awake, I heard them—voices that started soft from far away but ended up loud and right over me. Men and women spoke in a strange, metallic language I couldn't understand. The voices grew so loud and angry that I covered my ears with my hands or my pillow to block them out. Nothing worked. I had to wait until they got tired and decided to leave me alone.

Night after night the voices crashed inside my head. I couldn't tell anyone about them. I knew only I could hear them. I was afraid and ashamed. I wanted to be brave, like Tía and Mami, who were strong even when they were weak—like when they cried in their rooms by themselves so we wouldn't be scared. But I wasn't brave; I was scared. So every night, I fought to stay downstairs at bedtime, angering Mami, who lacked patience in those days.

Abuela aided and abetted me, since she herself couldn't sleep and always sided with us kids anytime we were in trouble. But my stalling couldn't put off the inevitable. I knew I would wake up in the dark, terrified, sure the voices and the icy rain and the fire were coming. Panicked, I'd shake Abuela awake so I could go back to sleep—someone needed to make sure the house didn't burn down. And I had to fall asleep quickly. If I remembered the voices, they'd sneak into my ears. I had to be careful not to think about them.

5
Radio Big Mouth

Cuba, 1959–1961

Tía Silvia always knew how to block out the noise, how to think her way out of almost any problem and get the job done. In the '50s, that job was finishing her education, getting married, and starting a family.

Tuition at the University of Havana in the '50s was a reasonable sixty pesos a year, but even that was a stretch for Don Manuel. So Tía helped her grandfather by tutoring her classmates in her favorite subjects: physics, mathematics, and chemistry. She ignored the political turmoil of the Batista years, the student uprisings, the shoot-outs on campus, and studied her way around a three-year shutdown of the university.

In 1955, her master's in education in hand and the doctorate on her mind, she thought of a better way to fund her next degree: she'd open a new 1–6 grade school in the barrio. Yes, she was planning on marrying Tío Angel, and she hoped to become a mother soon, but she'd find a way to get that doctorate—and a master's in mathematics after that. She'd finish her education and bring the rest of the barrio right along with her.

Tía set up her school in a house that Don Manuel had helped

build and later purchased. When Tía and Tío got married, they built a second floor to create an apartment. Tía set her school fee at an affordable three dollars a month per student, or less if they were siblings. She enlisted my mother to teach first, second, and third grades, and Abuela to teach students to read and write. Over a seven-year period, the trio educated more than two hundred children.

Tía's revolutionary record was equally impressive. She'd stayed away from the anti-Batista rebels in the '50s, but, after the revolution triumphed in 1959, she marveled at how the new regime was transforming society, almost overnight. She admired the discipline of the young revolutionaries, their commitment to higher goals, their vision for a better Cuba. Soon she was front and center at every meeting of our block's *comité*, the new neighborhood associations that ensured revolutionary discipline on every block. She was an early member of the prestigious Cuban Women's Federation and joined the student revolutionary groups that sprouted up everywhere in the new Cuba. Tío, who'd been a boarder at Ceiba del Agua Military Academy since being orphaned at the age of nine, joined Tía in a complete embrace of the new society. He was so well trusted as a militia leader that he was allowed to take his Walther P38 gun home after completing his weekly militia duty, a rare privilege after the revolution when private gun ownership became illegal.

My mother, who'd been the only active revolutionary in the family during the Batista years, lagged behind Tía and Tío in supporting the new regime. She worried when Fidel took full control of the government, even though he promised to keep Cuba "greener than the palm tree." And her concerns were soon proven justified: when Cuba nationalized US businesses without compensation, the United States imposed an economic embargo, and by the end of 1961 Fidel had declared himself a Marxist Leninist.

Mami watched in disbelief as the government took over or shut down all newspapers and broadcast networks and the regime began to rule by edict. New laws popped up overnight. Lifelong neighbors denounced each other as anti-revolutionaries in front of the new *comités*—often with disastrous results for the accused. Families rushed to get out of the country. When Radio Bemba said that the new government would be sending children to indoctrination camps, some parents began sending their children to the United States, where the Catholic Church was finding homes for them until Cuba stabilized or their parents got out. This secret resettlement program of "lost children" became known as the Pedro Pan Flights and eventually whisked fourteen thousand Cubanitos out of the country.

The changes obliterated the last remnants of Mami's revolutionary dreams. This was just another dictatorship, she realized, not the restored democracy the revolution had promised. "I'd been lied to," Mami used to say. "But even worse, I'd let myself be lied to." When she tried to vent to Tía about the searing betrayal she felt, the world's unraveling, the sense of desperation and powerlessness—Tía doubled down. "Your aunt," Mami told me once, frustration still in her voice, "with all those brains of hers, had her eyes nice and shut about where we were heading—about the *paquetazo* of lies we were being fed."

Tío Manolo had been right to worry. Goods began to disappear from shelves soon after the revolution as the disorder in the country and the new agrarian reform laws disrupted the economy. Fidel's frequent, hours-long speeches angered Mami and Tío Manolo, who compared Fidel's flailing arms and oratory style to Mussolini and Hitler. Mami worried more about the disappearing civil rights, the growing repression, the denunciations, the end of the rule of law. The regime began seizing not only foreign but also Cuban-owned businesses and replaced her dreamed-of 1940 constitution with new laws, including the Ley Fundamental, which allowed the government to take any action necessary against anti-revolutionary elements. "I felt like I was suffocating," Mami said one day, describing how fast everything had changed.

Tía Silvia's "forward march" approach to the regime stunned my mother. They argued often, always closing the shutters and lowering their voices first. With the new *comités* on every block, the regime had eyes and ears everywhere. Tía actively supported our block's *comité*, hunting for volunteers for marches, farmwork, and street cleanups. Mami and Papi concocted excuses and began to avoid her whenever she was in roundup mode.

Tía first heard the rumors about one of her former students while she was standing in a food line—another change that came with the revolution—at our designated bodega on Ulacia. Radio Bemba was crackling with whispers that her beloved Barbarito and his father had been arrested.

Tía tried to stay calm. Barbarito had to be in his mid-teens now, old enough to land in one of the abysmal prisons that were being packed with the regime's opponents. Barbarito's family owned a tiny patch of land just past the river where they raised vegetables, chickens, and a few cows and goats. They were honest, hardworking people.

After she picked up her rations, Tía went directly to Barbarito's house. His mother told her that her husband and son had killed one of their own calves for the family's consumption and to pay off debts. But the new laws forbade profiting from private property in any way. Someone had denounced them. When the police arrived, father and son each tried to take sole responsibility for killing the calf. The guards said they didn't care who was responsible. They were taking them both to jail.

Tía and Mami differed on almost everything, but they shared a devotion to their students. They wanted to help Barbarito. Doing so was dangerous, however. Associating with anyone accused of anti-revolutionary behavior drew negative attention that could—and likely would—be used against you.

Given Barbarito's age, they hoped for his release. Then word arrived in the barrio. After a brief hearing, the father and son had received one-year sentences. Tía and Mami were furious. "The government takes their land, but they still have to pay taxes on it," Tía said. "Then, when they tried to use what they owned to pay their debts, they land in jail?" They fed off each other's anger. In no time, they found themselves on the Ruta 10 bus to visit Barbarito in jail. For once, Tía and Mami saw the regime in the same light. And neither of them would ever forget that moment of unity.

"That boy was so brave," Tía said, recalling the visit years later. "Even in that filthy place. He tried to calm us! He wanted us to tell his mother they were fine." After Tía visited Barbarito in prison, his mother would come by during severe shortages with a tomato, an orange, whatever she could spare for her son's teacher.

Mami's last doubts about the course the revolution had taken vanished after a group of soldiers paid a surprise visit to Tía's school. She was in the middle of a lesson when the soldiers knocked on the open door. Everyone sat still as the heroic visitors roamed around the room, making small talk with the kids, smiling.

"*Compañera*—would you permit us to give your students a lesson today?" one of the men asked Mami. Abuela and Mami looked at each other.

"Of course, comrade, go ahead," Mami said as she and Abuela stepped aside.

"Who likes ice cream?" the soldier asked the kids.

The class erupted in cheers and whoops. Some of the kids stood up.

"Sit down, now, listen . . ." the rebel leader said. "I want you to lower your heads on your desks and pray to God for ice cream."

The kids looked around, confused.

"Go on," he said, "lower your heads on the tables, cover your eyes, really think about God, and pray hard for that ice cream!"

The students lowered their heads on their folded arms, covering their eyes.

After a minute, the soldier called out, "Open your eyes!"

The students, their faces lit up with expectation, looked up and found nothing but their books in front of them.

"Oh, that's too bad," the soldier said. "Should we try again? Good. This time pray to Fidel for ice cream. Go on, cover your eyes, no peeking."

As the kids covered their faces with their arms, the other revolutionaries, who'd left the room a few minutes before, streamed in carrying ice cream cups. They quickly placed them on the tables in front of the students.

"Open your eyes!"

The kids roared with happiness and tore open the cups. Total joy.

Mami focused on keeping her mouth closed, mostly in response to Abuela's pleading eyes. She wondered if she was dreaming. For this regime, exploiting children was as easy as eating ice cream. This was why the new government had been stressing education, putting so many of the country's resources behind the new educational initiatives. Schools were the vehicle to shape young minds to fit the new system, its prescribed new values, its required beliefs. She felt a burning disgust—toward the regime but also toward herself. She'd done nothing to stop the manipulation of her students and couldn't open their eyes to why what had just happened was so wrong. Nothing but trouble would follow such a lesson.

Tía's barrio school didn't last long in the new world that was rising up in Cuba. One of the new government inspectors brought Mami the bad news not long after the ice cream party. He was a decent man, a former teacher. They had quickly developed a respectful friendship, which he honored that day by tipping her off: "They'll be shutting down all private schools very soon," he told her.

Mami had worried about this moment ever since the regime had gradually begun to confiscate Cuban-owned property. She wanted to at least be able to hold on to the lower floor of her grandfather's two-story house. She and my father were close to getting married and dreamed of having children and their own place. Following a common custom, Abuela would move in with the newlyweds. Mami needed the space.

"Will we lose the house?" she asked.

"Definitely."

"What if I moved in some furniture—to show I was living here, not just teaching?"

He smiled. "You'd have a chance." She saw in his eyes that he'd back her up.

Later that night, Tía, Tío, Mami, and Papi pushed a bed, dresser, and an armoire down the street from Don Manuel's house to the house on Castillo. Over the next few days, they furnished the sink area with a little table, an alcohol-fired stove, dishes, a few pots and pans.

Tía had always believed her school would be spared from any government takeover. It was small, served a needy area, and was barely generating enough income to pay the teachers.

Mami wasn't convinced. "We'll be next," she'd told her more than once.

Tía had reassured her, reminding her there was logic and justice behind nationalizing foreign-owned properties, banks, etc., in a socialist system. These were necessary changes for Cuba to achieve its new goals. It would be pointless to take over a school like theirs.

But now they were about to lose the school and the chance to keep the ground floor of Don Manuel's house.

Mami summed up how they'd arrived at this moment: "We were wrong, Silvia. When it was the Americans' companies, we said fine. When it was the rich Cubans' sugar mills, we said okay. Then it was the pharmacists, and the *bodegueros*, and the kiosks, and we said *now, wait just a minute*. Well, now it's our turn to lose what we had."

6

Rudolph

Nashua, December 1967

Mami knew we needed more money for food—and that the Thom McAn shoe factory was going to solve our problem. She picked up a Saturday shift on one of their lines soon after she started working full-time at the rubber boot factory. Suddenly, she was more relaxed when we walked down the cookie aisle at Alexander's—even allowed us to put a box of Vienna Fingers in the cart now and then. I didn't understand the connection between the cookies and my mother's sore hands until much later in my life, but once I did I could never look at those cookies without thinking of my mother's gnarled fingers.

After each of those Thom McAn shifts, Mami would sit at the kitchen with her hands submerged in a bowl of ice water. The heavy material, the nail guns, the gluing, the pressing left throbbing reminders on her fingers and palms long after she left the assembly line. Papi kept her company while we watched TV and Abuela finished washing the dishes.

Tía walked into the kitchen one Saturday night, looked at the bowl of ice, and shuddered. "Consuelo, how can you stand that?"

"*You* try running that pneumatic tack machine all day," Mami said. She envied Tía's cushy job in quality control. "You'd be right next to me."

Papi stood up, chuckling. "The poor bastards who end up in your shoes are out there like this." He walked across the kitchen on tiptoes, hunched over, moaning, "*Ay, ay, ayyy.*"

Mami didn't smile. Her mind was elsewhere. She was thinking about a song she'd heard over and over that Christmas season. She called us away from our favorite program, *Star Trek*—which we called *los Orejones*, the Big-Eared Ones.

"Tell me about this Rudolph song," she said.

We were hearing "Rudolf the Red-Nosed Reindeer" everywhere we went that December. I was learning it at school.

Angelito, already good at English, filled Mami in on the lyrics.

She was quiet for a moment, thinking. "So, if I understand this correctly, this little deer is different, and everyone is mean to him, but then he gets Santa Klos out of a jam, and—just like that—everybody is his friend."

We looked at each other, confused that she saw a problem with the message, which encapsulated life on the playground for all of us.

Mami was still thinking about the lyrics as she dried her hands and took a puff of her cigarette. "*Caballeros*—I think this country is going to be all about performance."

I thought Mami was talking in riddles that night, but as the years passed and I decoded our new world, I began to understand what she had tried to tell us that night. Independence, skill, talent—what one could *do*—mattered more, or at least in a different way, to Americans than to Cubans. I would crash into that cultural difference many times in my new world, and each collision would force a reckoning of values, the choice of a path. Often, as I shook myself off and looked at the road ahead, I'd hear Mami's voice preparing us for the journey.

I didn't want to go anywhere on those icy school day mornings, warm under the blankets, finally enjoying a sound sleep now that the sky had lightened and we were safe from the risk of fire. But just as I fell into that deep sleep, Abuela would begin harassing me to get out of bed.

I woke up every day half-dressed and pleading. "*Cinco minutos más. Por favor, Abuela . . .*"

She didn't have time to negotiate, so she dressed me while I was still asleep. I'd wake with her standing over me, stretching itchy wool socks over my legs and securing them in place with elastics just under my knees. She didn't want to expose my Cuban skin to the frigid cold. The elastics held up my socks but cut off my circulation; she knew this, but it was a risk she was willing to take. I waddled away from the bed, sleep-deprived and groggy but fully dressed: long johns, undershirt, blouse, sweater, and pants under my skirt.

While we ate, Abuela attacked our static-filled hair with a wet comb. To us, electrified hair was just another wonderful northern phenomenon, but Abuela battled it every morning on four moving fronts. After she tamed our hair she moved on to outerwear, demanding we grip our sweater sleeves in our fists as she wrestled on our mittens, scarves, hats, and, finally, coats. Abuela saw the cold as a lethal enemy. She sent her most vulnerable assets into battle every morning properly armed, gently kissed, a silent prayer floating behind them.

At school, I battled English, which Americans seemed to speak without opening their mouths. Most of the kids were kind or ignored me, but a few teased me. Mary Paradise, a tall girl with a powerful stride, pinched her nose when I walked by her, especially if we were by the coat hooks, where my coat, suffused with the fried cooking smells from our previous night's dinner, offended her. To be honest, we did reek of olive oil, onions, garlic, and green peppers—the sofrito that is the base of most Cuban dishes. I counted on Cathy, my first American friend, and a hyper-friendly classmate named Bernice to keep Mary in her corner. But Cathy was often absent, and no one paid much attention to the bouncy Bernice.

One afternoon, several classes gathered in the main hall to rehearse "Rudolph"—again—for the Christmas concert. Mary, the biggest American girl I'd ever seen, stood next to me, too close and pushy, as usual. I still didn't know the lyrics to the song, so I watched the other kids' lips and mimicked along. I could feel Mary watching me when we finished singing.

"You don't know the words! You're a fakahhh!" Mary jabbed her finger toward my face.

I pulled back, my heart dropping. The kids formed a circle around us. I didn't understand exactly what Mary Paradise was saying, but her message was clear and landed on me like a slap. I looked around for an ally. Somewhere I heard Bernice's voice, twanging.

Out of nowhere, I remembered *Star Trek* and Captain Kirk, so handsome that even a six-year-old girl listened to what he said. In a recent episode, he'd said something about "paradise" and "outer space." I glued those words together, looked into Mary's laughing face, and let it rip.

"Shut up, jyu paradise from outer espace!" I yelled.

The kids all gasped at the same time. Mary's mouth gaped. Suddenly, I had the advantage because no one—including me—knew what the hell I was talking about, but it sounded right, mighty, and a little goofy. The kids started laughing. Someone patted my back. Bernice crashed into me in celebration.

I won something that day. I'd grasped for something and found it. I was small and dark, smelled funny, and wore Salvation Army clothes, but for that one moment I'd found my "brave" and stood my ground. The kid from Cuber was using her thinking cap.

The lessons I'd been absorbing were congealing in my mind.

Rudolph's triumph, Captain Kirk's language, my mother's *ponte guapa* mantra, and even that story I'd been reading about a small train chugging up a big mountain carried the same message: stand up, get tough, keep going.

On that day, at least, I was the little immigrant that could.

7

Mean Man

Nashua, February 1968–June 1969

That first winter, the *viejos* showed us how to keep moving up the mountain, through the confusion and the doubt, to get to the other side. In the early mornings we saw them gathering strength from each other in the cold kitchen as they got ready for their factory shifts. We watched Abuela crawl her way through her grief. And we saw the tropical *viejos* confront the icy demands of the North after every snowstorm. They armed themselves with their bittersweet café, wrapped themselves in wool, and trudged out to the driveway in their heavy boots. Even Abuela pitched in during those marathon shoveling sessions, slipping and swearing just like the others, until the driveway was scraped clean of snow.

After conquering the driveway and sidewalk, the *viejos* turned to the backyard. They wanted us to have a place to play outside, so they shoveled out part of the yard, often getting all the way to the crusty green grass—until, gradually, they noticed that, in the other yards, the Americanitos played *on top* of the snow just fine.

Another lesson learned, another inch forward. Push the doubts away, keep going.

The rush of those days—Papi's multiple shifts at the factory, confusing lessons at school for us, unyielding sadness and work for Abuela—slowed only when we sat down to eat together. Every night after dinner, with the dishes cleaned and the floor swept, the moms finally relaxed. Tía read her Spanish–English dictionary in the kitchen, savoring it like a bon-bon. Mami sat on the sofa, her hair in curlers, smoking, watching the six o'clock news reports about the rising turmoil in her new country, the riots, the war in Vietnam, a serial killer in the Northwest.

I was Abuela's relaxation most nights. She pulled me onto her lap, and we sat on the chair at the foot of the stairs as she "read" from English books but spoke in Spanish. I remember a book about Cinderella, full of blue and silver drawings. Abuela invented the words and the sounds, the clomps of the horses' hoofbeats over cobblestones, the clink of the glass slipper when it fell. She worked so hard to distract me, I realize now, while the TV in the corner of the living room blared away news that no one wanted to know. I'd memorized the images by then: helicopters dropping from the sky, soldiers bleeding on stretchers, flames devouring jungles. And the sounds—of machine guns firing, reporters yelling, the dull *whup, whup, whup* of those blades.

I can almost feel her hands on my head, turning me away from the TV. But who could resist the mayhem on the screen?

"*¡Mira que tú eres chismosa!*" Abuela would say, guiding her nosy granddaughter's gaze back to the book.

We listened as the trustworthy Mr. Cronkite told us the good, the bad, and the ugly. We faced him in a semicircle in front of the TV, some of us standing, some sitting or leaning on the few pieces of furniture we pulled up close to the set. We watched, open-mouthed, as hippies smoked pot, Black Americans fought for their rights, jets shot napalm, and anti-war protests turned violent.

Mami and Tía exchanged looks: *What the hell have we done?* Their adopted country was in free fall. Often, the protestors shouted what to their ears sounded like communist chants. Would they need to bail out of this place too?

Mami sat on the couch, her legs crossed, smoking. "Look what *libertad* turned out to be."

Tía shook her head. "No. It's not the same. Those kids on the street, insulting the president, marching against war, taking over university buildings—it's tolerated, unless things get violent. As long as they let mobs form, marchers protest, and the press stays free, we're okay."

Mami wasn't so sure. "I'm just glad the Canadian border is right there," she said, pointing out the window. "From now on, we should keep the Studebaker's tank full."

As that first winter grew colder, the country's—and Mami's—temperature spiked. The Tet Offensive in February dominated the news. Protests increased, in numbers and intensity, and Mami worried out loud more often. I pretended not to hear, but I tuned in to anyone's worries, not just my own. I still remembered what I'd learned at my Cuban school: imperialist American soldiers killed women and children in Vietnam. But weren't the Americans on our side now? Was it good or bad that the Americans were getting shot and their helicopters were exploding?

I kept quiet, night after night, listening to the *viejos'* spoken and unspoken worries. These were some of the worst days for them, early 1968—no sign that Tío would ever leave Cuba, the reality of losing everything settling in, homesickness growing instead of fading, Abuela's depression pressing down on her and touching all of us.

I had so many questions but stifled them. I felt ashamed to be afraid, embarrassed to admit fear at a time when being brave was so important.

One night, my fear won out. I hoped no one else heard the weakness in my voice as I asked: "How far away is Vietnam?"

That moment stuck with my mother. She had been so busy surviving day to day—putting one foot in front of the other, caring for our physical needs—that she hadn't considered the possibility that our minds might be suffering. We played, after all, we laughed, we fought, we were silly. But in my question Mami heard something that threw those assumptions into doubt. She remembered my questions about Vietnam when we were in Cuba, how angry she'd been that teachers were breeding fear in first graders' minds.

Now their tampering had reached all the way to Nashua.

"It's so very, very far away, Anita," she said, "that it's on the other side of the world! Too far to worry about."

The familiar anger flared up again at all of the injustices she'd had to witness without speaking out. She wasn't sure she'd picked the best country for us and feared we might be in for more political turmoil and chaos, but at least her kids weren't being fed terrifying propaganda in school, we were all free to leave for Canada if we had to, and we could live our lives without politics demanding more and more of our spirits each day.

While Mami cycled through those thoughts, Tía hunted for evidence she could use to shield me from the Vietnam War. She scampered from the room to look for books, maps, anything to prove just how far away we were from danger. She pulled me to the kitchen table.

I remember the map she drew as she talked. It showed a robust, squarish United States, a vast stretch for the Pacific, a tiny circle for Asia. Tía wanted lots of distance between the war and us. Some might call her map propagandistic in its own way, but that night it bred calm, dispelled fear, restored the sense of safety that children need to live, to sleep, to thrive—what she wished for all children.

During those nights, Mami thought a lot about the hippies on TV and in Nashua's parks. She was about their age, but her values were more like their parents'. Free love and commune living looked fine, as long as children weren't dragged into the mess. But she abhorred the idea of drugs. The casual attitude about marijuana, especially, scared her. She knew many heavy lifetime users in Cuba whose lives had shriveled away. Would her kids grow up to be like these young Americans?

Each night, as she lay awake in bed with waves of doubt about this new culture enveloping her, she thought herself back to calmness: *This culture will never be mine,* she told herself, *but maybe my children will feel it as theirs. They'll study and build careers and live their lives in it. As long as they can take the good and leave the bad, as long as they hold on to our values and this country stays free, it will have all been worth the effort.*

By late spring, Mami was beginning to see signs of hope. English was making more sense to everyone—even to Papi, who wrestled the most with the language. We kids interpreted for the adults whenever they got stuck, feeling proud. And Abuela felt drier, less fragile.

Papi had found a used shortwave radio in his ever-widening rambles around Nashua. Now Abuela could listen to Spanish at night from the lips of non-relatives. After dinner, she'd press her ear against the speaker and fidget with the coat hanger she'd attached to the radio's broken antenna. Crackling static eventually produced the distant sounds of the *Voz de America,* her favorite Spanish news program. I sat at her feet on the floor, watching as she bent over her radio, one hand fidgeting with the antenna, feeding on her language and getting stronger. Nearby, around the kitchen table, the *viejos* practiced the rubber boot factory vocabulary they were picking up—Boston accent and all—like "guedas" (waders) and "conbeyah" (conveyer).

That summer brought us two great joys, one behind the other, although the first started off with a scare. One early morning we padded to the top of the stairs and heard Tía crying in the kitchen.

Tío was on the phone from Spain. He'd made it out of Cuba, thanks to crucial help from distant Spanish relatives. Everyone started hugging and crying. Tío was coming home to us.

Tía gradually pieced together the information she gathered from Tío and our barrio friends' letters. He'd made it out just in time. The afternoon he left for the airport, agents from the Ministry of the Interior had arrived in Juanelo looking for him. "We're going to offer him a job," the men told our neighbors, who covered for Tío, saying, truthfully, "Oh, he left for Spain." They didn't mention he'd left just that afternoon. Everyone knew the Ministry of the Interior showed up only to take you away.

The second great happiness that summer came bounding into the house one afternoon when the Cernudas brought us a chunky-pawed German shepherd puppy. From the beginning, Blackie padded around the house like he belonged there. His head was too big, his muzzle too black. One ear flopped. He was perfect. We buried our noses in his fur and loved him almost violently. We fought over him, dragged him into our beds, hugged him so hard he had to nibble us so we'd release him. He smelled like popcorn.

Abuela and Blackie took to each other like two lost souls reuniting in a new life. He shed like crazy, so Abuela groomed him lovingly each night—a therapy session for both of them.

After school started that fall, a single gray cloud appeared in our sky. A cranky neighbor had been unfriendly from the start. He seemed to enjoy shouting at us kids when we made too much noise. Now we had Blackie and a new crop of classmates tumbling in the mounds of dry leaves all around the yard, and all the commotion—Blackie's barks mixed with the shrieks of kids playing—incensed Mean Man. He yelled at us constantly.

I can still see him on the other side of the fence, stomping mad.

Almost every day, the *viejos* had to go out and try to reason with him in their clunky English, but that only made the pale ogre madder.

"Stay away from his fence," Papi warned us once as Mami pulled him back toward the house. It seemed like Papi was trying to convince *himself* to stay away from the neighbor. My father was working two shifts at two different factories. He was almost as irritable as Mean Man.

One cold afternoon, the mean neighbor shouted so loudly at us that Abuela came outside to investigate. Abuela looked puny next to that potbellied guy, her face gaunt, the dark circles under her eyes heavy. She'd lost so much weight that her green housecoat floated over her body when she walked. He kept on yelling, and it wasn't long before we saw Abuela turn away from the fence and walk, head down, back into the house.

That afternoon, Mean Man transformed from an annoyance into an enemy for us kids. Alberto devised a ring-and-run plan to get back at him. We planned carefully—all the hows and whens, the escape route, and the alibis we'd use if we got caught. Alberto knew his way around a caper.

We ran back to the house after the ringing and running, the neighbor in hot pursuit. At the door, he shouted and jabbed a finger in Papi's face. Tía and Mami had to step between the men until they calmed down.

Later, there was some loose spanking, hard scolding, and a lot of lecturing at close range—the worst punishment of all. We deserved it, but the man had shouted right into Abuela's skinny face and nothing had happened to him. Mami tried to make us feel sorry for him. "Think of how unhappy and *amargado* he must be," she told us, "to act like that toward a dog and kids. What a miserable way to live. Pretend he's not there."

We tried, and we failed. Maybe we wanted to fail, so we could avenge Abuela in some way. After the ring-and-run, the man seemed to come out even when we weren't making noise. I can still see him hovering near the fence, pacing. We may have deliberately provoked that man after that night, the way kids do, barely aware of making a choice but celebrating the victory just the same.

We didn't understand that by fighting back we were fueling a threat that would one day cost us dearly.

Even with the angry neighbor glaring at us from his side of the fence, the promise of warmer days cheered the *viejos*. They'd made it through another winter, this time better equipped to handle the snow, at peace with the steam radiators, and no longer afraid to inhale below-zero air.

The growing confidence of the family made it easier for Mami to share the secret she'd kept for weeks. She walked into the living room one night while Alberto, Angelito, and I were watching TV. We ignored her at first, but when I heard her say *bebé* I listened right up. I bounced on the couch as she made one of my dreams come true. I was going to have a baby brother or sister to hold, to feed, to dress. Even my cousins started to cheer.

"What names do you like for the baby?" Mami asked.

Visions of my favorite cartoon character popped into my head. "Pebbles."

Mami squinted. "I think that means little rocks."

"No, it doesn't. Please, please, name her Pebbles." I saw a perfect baby girl with a bone in her hair, heard her cooing.

"Maybe," Mami lied.

Later, Tía, ever the scholar, looked up the word in her worn-out Spanish–English dictionary and put an end to the name "Pebbles."

Tía and Abuela reacted coolly to Mami's news at first. My mother had expected their disapproval, so she'd kept her secret for weeks.

She needed time to process the situation herself. Even with three adults working full-time, money was extremely tight. Papi earned the most at $1.75 an hour, plus time and a half when he got overtime. The Cernudas had by this point started building houses, as they had in Cuba, and Tía, Papi, and my mother dreamed of making a down payment on one of the Cernudas' duplexes. Every time Tía and Tío spoke on the phone, they talked about the duplex. A new baby would complicate everything.

Abuela and Tía sat stone-faced when Mami delivered the news. Finally, one of them said, "Consuelo, how did this happen?"

"I think you know exactly how this happened," she snapped. "And besides, I brought Anita and Sergito into the light in far worse conditions than this."

8

Love and Mortar Shells

Havana, 1961

My father had ended his baseball career that January, when he'd wrapped up his last season in the Mexican leagues. Back in Juanelo, he noticed my mother's new carefree mood now that her beloved revolution was in power. He began stopping by Don Manuel's porch after dinner to chat with Vicenta, Mami's grandmother—a clever move that won him the old woman's support and drew my mother outside each night. The game was back on.

My parents had ties stretching back to childhood, like many of the barrio's couples, even though Papi was nine years older than Mami. As a boy, he'd walk down Ulacia, throwing a baseball in the air on his way to the sandlot for a game. He'd pass Vicenta as she sat on the porch, rocking my mother on her lap. The old woman and Cuca's mischievous son bantered about baseball, boxing—Vicenta never missed boxing radio broadcasts—and life in general. "Take care of that cute *bebita*, Vicenta," Papi would say. "Maybe I'll marry her one day."

Their dates took place on Saturday nights at Don Manuel's house, with multiple generations eyeing my father as he held my mother's hand on the couch. One night during a sudden power outage, he stole a kiss in the dark. My great-grandfather coughed loudly when the lights came back on and revealed my parents' embrace. Don Manuel's Galician accent broke the family's shocked silence: "I think it's time for you to go home, Sergio."

The soundtrack to my parents' honeymoon in April 1961 included gunfire and exploding mortar rounds. It coincided with the Bay of Pigs Invasion, when, on April 17, fifteen hundred US-trained-and-supplied Cuban exiles landed on the island's southern coast, in the area of Playa Girón.

The invasion—Brigada 2506 to many Cubans—was doomed almost from the beginning. The Kennedy administration decided to drastically cut back on the air support it had promised the exile fighters and, in another last-minute change, switched to a landing site near the Zapata wetlands, the same place where Mami had met Fidel in early 1959. The wetlands around Playa Girón proved an unwise choice; they were thick with mangroves, nearly impenetrable, and Castro knew the area well—it was one of his favorite fishing spots.

Besides fighting the invasion force on the coast, the regime rounded up suspected enemies throughout the island to suppress a possible uprising. Officials arrived at the *comités* asking for a list of troublemakers, *gusanos*—anyone who could be with the enemy.

The president of our *comité*, Juana, refused to give them any names. Tía joined other regime supporters on Juana's porch that morning and never forgot how Juana defended her neighbors.

The officials kept bringing up a man named Miguel, a police officer, and Berta, a pharmacist. After a half hour of back-and-forth, Juana had had enough.

"*Compañeros*, the people you're talking about help me whenever I ask for volunteers. Berta can't always help. She has a bad leg. She lives over there"—Juana pointed down the street—"and that's where she stays, quiet, respectful. I don't know who denounced them, but it wasn't anyone from this *comité*, and we know best. You won't be taking anyone from here today."

Meanwhile, my parents were bouncing along the highway with my father's tío Juan and his wife, Nena, in their '58 Buick Special, on their way to Los Jazmines, a resort in the tobacco-growing region to the west of Havana called Viñales. Throughout the long drive, they heard scattered gunfire and the whistle of mortar rounds sailing into the hills around them, presumably from government forces fighting insurgents. They never thought about turning back. Instead, Tío Juan used the *doble fuerza* of his new Byui and sped through the worst of it.

My father worried that his frayed nerves would prevent him from performing that night. Evidently, he managed. I was born a short nine months later.

The level of repression and forced politicization increased after the failed invasion. Firing squads remained active, a constant reminder of the cost of refusing to join the new society. And Russians were popping up everywhere. No one was surprised when members of the DTI, one of Castro's special police units, arrived with bad news for the residents of the Reparto Eléctrico, a development near Juanelo. Their homes would be given to Russian advisors and technicians, who were arriving in droves to help the revolution advance.

Throughout most of her pregnancy, Mami trudged all over Havana giving literacy lessons door-to-door, at fresh-air markets, and in factories. The revolution's literacy campaign required all teachers to participate. The government shuttered most schools to allow for the transfer of teaching talent. The *comités* handed the teachers the lists of names and addresses and they, like Mami and Abuela, set off— every day, all day, for many months—to places like the Havana fruit market and a private school the regime had nationalized in the Cerro neighborhood. I consider myself a member of that literacy brigade, having been ported along until I arrived on Día de los Reyes—Three King's Day—1962.

The Spanish term for giving birth, *dar a luz*, means "bring into the light." And bringing a new baby into the light gave my family joy during a dark time. Many neighbors were leaving Juanelo for the United States, mostly Miami. Food, clothing, household goods—especially electrical appliances—had all but disappeared from shelves. A few months before I was born, the government, acting on its announcement that religion was incompatible with communism, had expelled hundreds of priests and nuns from the country. And a few months after I was born, the regime introduced the Libreta de Abastecimiento. *La libreta*—as Cubans call the ration book—is still used by each family today.

"Russian condoms and communist bras," Mami said once, remembering that era. "Those kinds of changes reminded us every day that we were in a new Cuba." When her last pair of underwear had more holes than fabric, Mami raided Papi's drawer and started wearing his. When their old fridge broke, they replaced it with the only alternative, an even older one they found in Abuela Cuca's shed. This Frigidaire was missing its handles and the doors were rusted and dented. They got written permission from the *comité* to transport it to their house, where they painted it a bright yellow—the only paint they could find—and named it El Canario. To open the Canary's door, you had to stick a screwdriver where the handles had been and hope for the best.

In his constant, seemingly unending televised speeches, Fidel blamed the United States for all of Cuba's problems. My parents had little patience for his ominous predictions by that point. When the mounting repression and growing scarcity threatened to overwhelm them, they reassured themselves with a belief that many other Cubans clung to by then: "The Americans won't let this happen so close to their shores." They needed to stay positive so they could focus every ounce of energy, every minute of free time, on solving the new problems of daily life: foraging for food, connecting to Radio Bemba, trading on the black market, and acting sufficiently revolutionary to avoid denunciations. Meanwhile, instead of addressing the severe shortages, the rolling blackouts, and the breakdown of the supply chain, the government mobilized new militias and pointed to the enemy. With thirty-five hundred miles of coastline, Fidel wanted the country ready for a full-fledged American invasion.

9

Tía's Revelation

Santa Maria del Mar, Cuba, 1966

For the first time, our annual vacation brought us nothing but problems. Those couple of weeks at the beach together had been a family tradition since long before the revolution, and was one of the few respites still possible for us since Castro had taken power. Even though my parents had lost their jobs and couldn't help with costs anymore, Tía and Tío planned to rent a beachside cottage in El Megano, to the east of Havana. But when Tía arrived at the rental office, the woman she'd always rented from said the cottages weren't available.

"Those are for the government now," the woman told her, and she offered Tía a rental in Santa Maria del Mar—twenty minutes from the center of Havana, and about a block or so from the beach—instead.

When the ten of us arrived (cousin Cecilia had also come along), we saw that the house didn't have air conditioners or fans. The handles on most of the glass window shutters were rusted and broken. There were no screens on the windows. And there was no refrigerator. The excitement we'd felt earlier in the day, as everyone talked about long days on the beach, vanished.

Tía and Mami sent Tío and Papi back to Juanelo to get all the mosquito nets they could find—and to retrieve El Canario. "And don't forget the screwdriver," Mami said.

Tío and Papi took longer than expected. It turned out that as they were loading El Canario in the back of a borrowed truck, Juana, our *comité* president, had come out to investigate. They'd had to prove they weren't planning on selling the fridge before she would give them a written statement permitting them to transport El Canario to the beach.

That night we hauled the mattresses off the beds and out onto the front porch, rigged up the nets, lit the mosquito-repellent coils, and prepared to sleep packed head to foot on the tiled floor as the August heat—a wet, sticky burden that lasted all night—smothered us. As my cousins giggled next to me, I stared up at the mosquito nets from my corner of the porch. The veils draped around the mattresses, all of us sleeping together—the whole scene felt magical.

The smoking mosquito coils filled the air with a medicinal smell that didn't stop the mosquitos from drilling into us. *ZZzzzing.* Silence. Then, *WHAP*, followed by a thrilling cascade of whispered adult swears. Soon we were all scratching. Mami and Tía started applying the dreaded Mercurochrome to the bites, its sting leaving us shrieking and wailing.

Somewhere in the distance we heard gunfire.

"Another miserable bastard trying to escape on a launch," someone said.

The next morning, Yuyo, Cecilia's father, showed up to check on her. He'd worked at a dry cleaners most of his life but was now a big fish in the government-purchasing pond. He'd loved our family ever since Don Manuel took in Yuyo's large family after their house burned down.

A lifelong communist, Yuyo's career prospects had improved

dramatically after Castro came to power. He'd left his new house and his dry-cleaning job in El Cerro and moved into a mansion in the Alturas del Vedado—the former home of the teacher of Batista's children—with closets full of evening gowns, fine paintings on the walls, and a grand piano.

Tía and Abuela marveled at all that opulence each time they came back from visiting Yuyo. Everyone knew Batista's government had been corrupt to the core, but for a teacher to have lived like that baffled my aunt and my grandmother. And now here was cousin Yuyo, an uneducated former dry-cleaning clerk, living in all that finery just because he had connections in the Communist Party. Even years later, as they described what they'd seen in that fancy house, it was always hard to determine which injustice offended them more, the one under Batista or the one under Fidel.

That next morning at the cottage, Yuyo walked in and found us all scratching and sleep-deprived. "No, no, no," he said. "This won't do." And with the absolute confidence that only someone with real clout can muster, he promised to solve our problems.

No one believed him.

He returned later that day brimming with good news. "Tomorrow, you'll be moving to a big house with plenty of room, air-conditioning, and lots of windows—right over that way." He pointed across the street toward the beach.

Everyone clapped and cheered and patted Yuyo's back, astonished that he'd come through.

The house was everything Yuyo had promised: enormous, directly on the beach, two stories full of bedrooms and bathrooms and multiple garages, a working AC—and functioning windows with screens!

We didn't learn until later that we had two noteworthy neighbors. On our left, in an even bigger mansion, was Raul Castro,

Fidel's brother, and his family. On our right was Armando Hart, the Minister of Education, and his family.

Given all the room, Yuyo, our hero, wondered if we would allow his family to join us. Of course, everyone agreed that he, his wife, and his other daughters should share in our good fortune. "Except," Tía warned him, "we've only got one *botellón de agua*. It was the only large bottle of water I could find, and it was more than twenty-five dollars."

"*No hay problema*," Yuyo said.

This time everyone believed him.

Yuyo arrived bearing family members and many gifts, including two huge *botellones de agua*. He loaded up the house's three refrigerators with meat, chicken, coffee, milk, Italian wine, Dutch beer, British cognac, and olives, and passed around cigarettes in metal cases—all items that had been scarce for years, that no one could even find in stores let alone afford. Everyone was thrilled . . . but where in the hell was Yuyo finding this stuff?

Tía watched as Angel, his eyes closed, enraptured, speared the imported Spanish olives out of the jar and popped them in his mouth. He'd begged her for olives many times; they had been a favorite treat before the revolution.

"It hurt to see him so happy," she told me once. "Such a simple thing, to provide a treat for your child. Why could Yuyo have olives any time he wanted but not Angel?" She remembered Tío Manolo's observation about hunger—that there are many kinds, not just the hunger of a completely empty stomach. Here she felt a hunger to provide something that was possible to find, but only if you had the connections and the power.

A few hours later, out in the surf, Tía and Mami wore ratty shorts over their old bathing suits to cover the frayed and torn bottoms. New bathing suits were beyond luxury items. You couldn't find them even on the black market. When Yuyo's wife and daughters came out in new Jantzen bathing suits, Mami and Tía flashed a look at each other. *Where are these people finding these things? And how can they afford them?*

That night, freshly showered, Yuyo's wife and daughters smelled of violets and talcum powder. They wore brand-new lacy blouses and gorgeous sandals. Tía and Mami tried not to stare at Yuyo's immaculate tennis shoes and crisp clothes. When Tía and Mami were alone, they ticked through all the signs of Yuyo's wealth. But Tía marveled more at the *access* he had to these things. "Every shelf and rack in Havana is bare—has been bare for years—but he can get his hands on all of this . . ."

Tía saw signs of Yuyo's buying power every day of that trip. She'd been worrying that Sergito, about two and a half years old, would choke on the worn-out, cracked *tete* he refused to give up. It wasn't even a real binky, just a nipple from a baby bottle. Tía scolded Mami for taking the risk, but Mami said the *tete* helped calm him when he was hungry, which was all the time. What else was she supposed to use?

One day, Yuyo walked in as they argued, again, about the worn-out *tete*. He looked over at Sergito. "I think I can get another *tete* for that baby."

Yuyo solved our *tete* problem quite easily—by pilfering several brand-new ones from the stash of nursery items he'd recently procured for Vilma Espín, Raul Castro's wife. She was either expecting or had recently had a child; no one remembers exactly, but everyone remembers Sergito's new *tete*.

Tía eyed the Hernandez sisters' Jantzen-covered bottoms, Sergito chomping on his new binky, Angel savoring his longed-for olives, and she thought things through, logically, as she always did.

Mami knew Tía was simmering, but until they were alone on the porch one night, watching the black, glossy waves rolling into shore, she didn't realize that Tía had reached the conclusion she had been praying for.

"Consuelo, this revolution isn't for everyone." Tía was quiet for a while. "I thought it was a decent, honest thing. I was wrong."

Mami remembers the cigarettes that Yuyo gave her that summer, the shiny case they came in. But Yuyo's most important gift was ensuring that Tía would be in Mami's future.

If Tía needed another example of the intractable problems of our revolutionary society, she got it when she and Tío returned to the barrio at the end of the vacation. El Canario was hard to miss in the open-bed truck they'd borrowed from a friend. As they inched along the broken streets to avoid further damaging the already heavily dented Canario, the president of another block's *comité* stopped them and asked for authorization to transport an appliance.

Tía showed her the note signed by our block's *comité* president.

The woman shook her head. "That's permission to take it *from* your home, not to return it." She raised her voice and pounded her hand on the side of the truck as she flung threats and accusations at Tía and Tío.

Tía let her finish. Then, unfazed, she looked at her and said, "You know, you're not even our *comité* president. Juana is. So you can take this up with her."

She gestured for Tío to keep driving, and he did.

La Universidad de la Habana, Cuba

Even prior to our vacation, Tía had been dodging requests to join the university's militia, citing her job and children and pointing to her excellent revolutionary record. But now she was sitting in a meeting room, facing the student junta that would conduct her *depuración*. The young revolutionaries had the power to conduct this "cleansing" and expel her from the University of Havana, where she'd earned her PhD in education and was finishing her master's in mathematics.

Tía paid little attention to the junta leaders as they ranted about her responsibilities as a revolutionary, the debt she owed the country—the many sacrifices they'd each made for Fidel and Cuba—and waited for her chance to speak. She would point to her full-time work on one of the most important missions of the revolution: training the country's new teachers, the Makarenkas, in Tarará—an hourlong bus ride on the Ruta 62 from Juanelo. She would describe how she was an active member of La Cruz Roja Cubana and La Federación de las Mujeres Cubanas, and the main recruiter of volunteers for our neighborhood *comité*. All of that on top of mothering two young children and finishing her master's degree. Maybe this list would finally satisfy these smug *sabelotodos*. The more she worked through her arguments, the angrier she became.

I imagine Tía sitting in that room, fuming at having to defend herself in front of the young students, the images of our vacation at Santa Maria del Mar that summer still fresh in her mind. The vacation had been a turning point, the moment when she'd stopped thinking of the revolution as a "fair and decent thing." How lucky we'd been to have had Yuyo's help, to have landed in a mansion next to a beach neighbor like Vilma Espín, Raul Castro's wife. She was the president of La Federación de las Mujeres Cubanas, the prestigious group Tía belonged to, the one she would cite in a few minutes—if these junta members ever stopped their moralizing and scolding.

When Tía finally got the floor, however, the junta was unmoved by her reasoning, so she changed course. "You may not know, but my husband is an active leader of his work militia. He attends weekly drills, sometimes they're overnight, and he trains all the new recruits . . ."

The blank faces told her she was losing them.

"My boys are very young, they need—"

"We know all of that and none of it matters," one of the students said. "You simply can't be a student here unless you join our militia. Besides, we offer childcare, so the children are no excuse."

Their cold expressions, the way they gloated over the power they had, infuriated Tía. She must have shown her anger on her face. She always did. That left eyebrow rising, that sideways look of disgust, and then the piercing look up at the opponent.

"I didn't have my children to have them cared for by other people," Tía said, and then she turned around and walked out.

She was expelled from the university that same day. Her dream of a master's in mathematics shattered around her—but to her surprise, she didn't care very much. She saw new goals and a new future forming.

To reach that new place, she would have to argue with Tío, who had vowed not to leave the old aunt who had raised him after he was orphaned.

Tía and Tío fought, they debated, they weighed the intangible treasures in their lives—love, duty, children, elders, home, family—and finally, they landed on a heartrending compromise: Tío would stay in Cuba, for now, but he would give permission for the boys to leave the country with Tía. They knew that reuniting would be a years-long process—at best. But Tía wanted to get the boys out soon, before they reached military age—a number that had dropped already—and the government wouldn't allow them to leave.

The only benefit of Tío staying in Cuba was that they'd still have an income while Tía waited for her *permiso*. But with a *gusana* wife, Tío's job would be in constant jeopardy. They were sure that Mami and Papi would get their *permiso* before Tía. At least Tía wouldn't be alone with the boys in a foreign place, a thought that tormented Tío.

Within weeks, Tía had the paperwork in order and filed. In the meantime, she'd devised a plan for getting her PhD diploma out of the country.

"Silvia," Mami said, "if they catch you with that diploma at the airport, they'll send you back here like a rocket. If you're lucky. You could end up in a cell somewhere."

Radio Bemba said *gusanos* could be turned away for any reason at the Camarioca airport. New rules popped up at the whim of the guards, but one was hammered into every *gusano*'s head: nothing of value could be taken out of the country. Tía's diploma fell decidedly in that category.

Mami was rushing through reasons why Tía should abort the plan, but Tía cut her off mid-plea with, "I need it if I'm ever going to teach again."

Mami looked at her in utter amazement.

Tía was the picture of calm certainty. "Tolín's wife is finishing the bra today."

"And what if she denounces you?"

"I trust her. Ofelia's decent, loyal. You know that. You're just trying to stop me."

"Of course I am! I don't want you dumped back in Juanelo."

But Tía had decided. "It's parchment. I can't fold it up and hide it that way. Ofelia cut it into three strips. She's a great seamstress. She said she'd finish today."

Tía's optimism baffled my mother. There was no guarantee that Tío would make it out of Cuba. He loved Tía and the boys with everything he had, but he was torn by competing loyalties. How many nights had Mami held her medal of la Virgen while praying in bed for one more miracle—help him change his mind, apply for that *permiso*? The thought of Angelito and Alberto growing up without a father—and such a wonderful one—terrified her.

She looked at her sister, still imperturbable, serene.

"I trust Ofelia completely," Tía said.

"Silvia, Silvia . . . *Esto es pura locura.*"

Tía's *permiso* arrived within a few weeks, an unheard-of turnaround. No one ever understood how this happened. "Things always turned out right for your aunt," Mami used to say, a touch of jealousy in her voice. "That might have been the luckiest break she ever got."

The moto clunked into the barrio midmorning on June 29, 1967. Tío was at work and the boys were at school, hoping Tía would produce Coca-Cola and cake for their father's thirty-seventh birthday dinner. Juana, the *comité* president, wasn't home, so Gloria, another neighbor and the mother of one of Angel's friends, took her place. Tía was waiting at the door when she and the guard came up the stairs.

"You're a teacher?" the guard asked as he walked by her. He sat down before Tía had a chance to offer him a seat.

"Yes—primary, secondary, university."

"*Increíble.* Look who we left our children to. A *gusana* in charge of educating our kids—"

"Just a moment, *compañero*," Gloria said. "This woman is respected here. She taught my kids and many others in the barrio to read and write—taught them everything, from kindergarten through the sixth grade. She's an excellent teacher." Gloria was just a stand-in for our *comité* president, but, luckily for Tía, she was just as noble as Juana. Always fair, direct, calm.

The guard scoffed but kept his harassment to a minimum after that.

The *viejos'* plan had unraveled. Tía and my cousins wouldn't be joining *us* in the United States; they'd be going first, on their own, dependent on a distant cousin who lived near New York City. Guilt and worry pounded Tío.

Everyone was still in shock when Tía told Mami she couldn't say goodbye to Don Manuel. She couldn't face him.

"Oh, no. No, no. You have to," Mami said. "You're not leaving me with that."

But that's exactly how things turned out. The night that Tía and the boys left, Mami found Don Manuel on his porch and told him the news.

The old man blinked behind his thick glasses and looked up at the dimming sky.

"*Chica*," he said. "They never said goodbye."

Tía sat between Angel and Alberto on a bench in the waiting area of the Camarioca airport. They leaned against her shoulders, somehow asleep. She stroked their arms as the names were called over the PA. The wires of her paneled bra, into which Ofelia had sewn the strips of her diploma, scraped her skin raw. Every stab from the wires reminded her she'd have her diploma in the United States. She and her sons would be on that plane in the morning, and Tío—she was certain—would one day come to his senses and find a way to join them.

When the guards called her for interviews, she leaned the boys against each other and told them she'd be back. They whimpered but behaved so well it made her want to cry, just to see the effort they were making.

She tried to match their grace by faking a serenity she could barely conjure. *Think logically*, she told herself as she walked toward the guards, fearing they would search her clothes for the diplomas they knew she'd earned. They had all her records, knew her history as well as she did. *If they'd suspected anything they would have searched me by now. Even if they do, they'll never think to search the lining of a bra.*

Tía knew logic could only get her so far. She'd been lucky. Her *permiso* had arrived faster than anyone else's. Too fast, maybe. But Mami's *permiso* had to be coming soon. Three years she'd waited.

That night, for the first time, Tía realized how Mami must have suffered when it looked like she would stay behind. Rebuilding new lives in a foreign world would require all hands on deck: her mother, her sister, their husbands—all pulling in the same direction. Together. They needed to be together.

10

Poisoned

Amherst Street, Spring 1969

I can still see Tía Silvia's framed diploma hanging on the wall of the old farmhouse on Amherst Street. Three long strips of parchment were taped together under the clear glass. A delicate black script, severed here and there, swirled across each section.

I loved Tía's diploma story so much that we turned it into a game. I'd pass by the diploma and ask, "Why is that paper torn up like that?" She'd smile and, when she wasn't too busy, sit down with me for another round.

"I wanted to be a teacher in America," she'd begin, "just like I was in Cuba. But the soldiers didn't let *gusanos* take jewelry, or money, or important documents. I didn't have jewels. My diploma was my jewel! It proved I was a teacher!"

I loved the idea of my brave aunt taking a risk so she'd have what she needed to live in liberty. That's how she described where we were. *Libertad.*

Tía taught all the time—student or no student, school or no school. She couldn't help it. Almost every weeknight, she called us to the kitchen table to work on our lessons. I didn't have homework, so she created assignments for me as Angelito and Alberto whizzed through theirs. And when she wasn't teaching, she was learning. Tía knew how Juanelo got its name, which is the kind of question I've asked all my life. She told me the barrio was named after "Juan" Castillo. Juanelo. Ah.

He named the streets, she continued, after his daughters: Serafina, Rita, Guadalupe.

What about my favorite street, Blume Ramos? Tía knew. It was the name of a German laboratory that had once occupied most of the block.

We'd made it to Liberty, and Tía was teaching us—but she was working in factories, not schools. In New York, she'd worked in a powder puff factory feeding the *moticas* into a machine that pinned looped labels into the puffs' centers. In Nashua, at Hampshire Manufacturing, she worked the seven-to-three shift in the rubber raft department. Papi worked nearby in the boot department and Mami on an assembly line using hot glue and loud machines. Mami made a lifelong friend, Terri Pelletier, on the line. (Terri talked almost as much as a Cuban and she taught Mami to drive and to speak English with a strong Boston accent and a French-Canadian twist. Most Sundays, Terri would walk into the house, all smiles, and call out, "Connie, you bettah remembah what I taught you last Sundee!") But Tía was too shy to form quick friendships. She learned English not by making American friends but by studying the dictionary at night, and she spoke it only when she knew her sentence's grammar and pronunciation and was sure her words would convey exactly what she intended.

Like Terri, most of the factory workers welcomed the *viejos* from the first day. They taught them how to salt icy porch steps—not pour hot water on them, as Abuela had been doing—monitor the water supply for the steam radiators, drive to the best spots in the White

Mountains, and roast a hot dog to perfection on the outdoor grill at Greeley Park. The Cubans working the assembly lines were too few, probably too white, and definitely too friendly to pose a threat to anybody. The mostly French-Canadian workers wanted to know about Cuba and why anyone would leave the tropics for New England in December.

Tía stepped in to teach them all things Cuban. "Do you have ice cream in Cuba?" someone asked her one day. She described patiently, through Espejo, a bilingual Mexican coworker who translated for all the new Cuban arrivals, the range of flavors and number of shops she'd grown up with. "They think Cubans swing from trees," Tía told us that night, laughing.

Espejo became a friend. He also revived Tía's teaching career. He was a slightly built, energetic man with sparkly eyes and a beaming smile. He usually brought us small toys, candy, and old Spanish magazines or newspapers from his most recent trip home to Mexico. Abuela fell on those Spanish magazines as if her life depended on it. Maybe it did. But it was Espejo's bright outlook that truly lifted Abuela whenever he visited.

Espejo's American wife had deep roots in Nashua. They seemed to know everyone. When Espejo heard that the superintendent of schools was searching for a new high school Spanish teacher after the sudden departure of the last one, he remembered the framed diploma on our wall and Tía's impressive credentials. He put in a good word with the superintendent and arranged an interview for her.

Tía was horrified. "How could I teach high school students? I can barely get by at the grocery store!"

Espejo would hear none of it. Abuela, Mami, and Papi agreed. If the superintendent was willing, why not meet him?

"Since when have you been afraid of anything, Silvia?" Mami asked.

Everyone was feeling a new hopefulness that fall. Mami's

coworkers had just thrown her a baby shower and the entire house smelled of baby-to-be. Tío was due to leave Spain and would be joining us any day. And with Papi's shift at a different factory on weekends and the prospect of four incomes, the *viejos'* dream of buying a duplex in the Cernudas' new development seemed within reach. Faced with a wall of positive thinking that afternoon, Tía finally agreed to the interview.

At the meeting, Espejo eagerly told the superintendent about Tía's accomplishments and her enthusiasm. Tía insisted Espejo convey her serious lack of English too. But the kind superintendent seemed unfazed by the English problem and impressed with Tía.

"Let us worry about your English," he said. "Tell me more about your teaching experience."

As Tía told him about her doctorate in pedagogy and how she'd taught chemistry and physics, had been working on a master's in math, and had created and run her own small school, she felt tears fill her eyes. How she'd loved those years of teaching children in Juanelo—and teaching in general.

The superintendent reached cross the desk and handed Tía a Kleenex. "We'll help you," he said. "I know that with a little time, you'll be able to handle those classes. Fill out the paperwork. You're very qualified. But I'll need some kind of proof—anything—of your credentials."

Tía beamed. This man understood how much help she needed, yet he was still willing to support her. She'd have a chance to teach again. She felt strong, capable. She put together her sentence with a new confidence.

"I haff proof, bot ees in pieces."

We were finding kind Americans almost every day in this old mill town. At school I had Cathy, my interpreter, lifeguard, and unwavering ally. It would be decades before I would fully understand the vital role she had played in my new American life. When we met, I was small, foreign, and voiceless, but this solid, pint-sized friend laid a foundation under my feet. She taught me where to step, how to stay upright, how to giggle again. I had a wing-girl.

The problem was Cathy's frequent absences, which rattled me with their unpredictability and the instability that they proved existed in this life too.

One morning at recess, I spun around in the schoolyard looking for Cathy. She was hard to miss. Loud, bossy, a bit feared, she knew how to get one of the red balls, even from the boys, or elbow us into someone else's game. That cracked asphalt–covered courtyard claimed at least one knee every recess. Someone was always bent over wailing, hand over a shredded knee, with Cathy nearby, shouting in her gravelly voice for help. Cathy was the Great Stabilizer in and outside of the classroom.

Earlier that morning, my teacher had spoken to me slowly. "Cathy is at a new school. She couldn't say goodbye."

I'd understood her words but couldn't accept their meaning. Now I believed my teacher. I pushed down the urge to cry. Bernice, the girl I couldn't seem to shake, was probably there that day, sticking next to me, trying to be helpful. But I needed Cathy like I needed air.

Angelito would know what happened. He and Cathy's older brother were friends. I'd just have to make it through the rest of the school day, then I'd ask him.

I ran to Angelito and Alberto at our meeting spot after school.

"She was sent to live with another family," Angelito said.

I felt like I'd been punched. "But she has a mother! And brothers and sisters!"

Angelito shrugged and started walking. "Her mom just couldn't take care of all of the kids," he said. "She knew Cathy would be better off with the other family."

None of it made sense. Angelito kept walking as I threw panic and questions at him. I kept stepping in his way, and he kept walking around me. I cried as I argued with him, as if he could fix any of this.

For a long time, I sensed Cathy's absence like an echo—a painful, empty sound. Her sudden loss proved that the world could tip over in an instant, even in this place that was supposed to be safe. Nothing stayed where you put it—not even people, not even Cathy the Great Stabilizer.

I craved sameness. Our daily routines delivered it. My favorite chore was the weekly visit to Haggerty's that Alberto and I took to pick up whatever Tía or Mami said we needed. We felt like big shots walking down Amherst Street, Blackie pulling at his leash, tail a-wagging.

That cool afternoon, we tied Blackie to a parking meter in front of the store and went inside. Haggerty's smelled like warm sawdust and fresh flowers. With no adults looking over our shoulders, Alberto and I roamed through the little store, running our hands over everything, sniffing the air of that mysterious place. The bell on the door tinkled as customers came and went. Sunlight spilled through the huge window at the front of the store. We were at the counter to pay, feeling proud of ourselves, when someone burst through the door, slamming it open, rattling the bell, and letting in a howling moan that shook our bodies.

The adults ran outside. Alberto and I stood very still, listening, until we realized what was making that moan. Alberto sprinted ahead of me and out the front door. Blackie lay on his side, writhing in pain, his tan paws scratching at the concrete as if he were trying to run away. The poor creature's shrieks destroyed us. We crumpled over him, trying to cradle him. Foam from his mouth spewed over our hands and on the sidewalk. His eyes rolled around in their sockets, wild.

The adults around us finally went into action. Someone gently guided us back inside the store. Alberto and I cried uncontrollably as he tried to remember and then say our phone number. Time warped as we listened to our dog's agony on the other side of the window. We clung to each other and waited. Neither of us remembers much after that, only the kindness of the people in the store, how some of them were crying, too, and that we lost Blackie that day.

My parents and Tía tried to comfort all of us, even as they struggled to understand how a healthy young dog could die suddenly in such agony. Abuela cried right along with us. She had lost her constant companion, a dependably joyful spirit that had rounded the edges of her depression. When she could, she told us stories about Blackie playing in a green heaven full of chickens to chase, hamburger to eat, a place where he could bark all he wanted, not a mean man in sight. Mami talked to us about life, how everything that lives must die, that it hurt but we would feel better after a while. Tía hugged and kissed us, calling us *mi cielo* and *mi vida*, sniffling, a Kleenex tucked under the wrist of her sweater's sleeve.

In the days that followed, the *viejos* spoke quietly with each other, trying to keep their suspicions to themselves. They didn't want to believe that hatred of us could lead someone to harm Blackie. They kept that possibility far from our ears. Maybe keeping it from us made it easier to hide the ugliness from themselves. They reminded each other that most Americans had welcomed us with warm helpfulness and respectful curiosity. They let doubt buffer their pain and the anger that hid behind it.

Thanks to the *viejos*' choice, I grieved without the burden of hate. My grief was simpler: a heaviness in my heart, the stone of loss. Unlike a country or language or home, this loss was tangible. When I reached for Blackie, there was nothing there. I remember playing in a corner of the living room and finding a tuft of his fur. I held it in my hand for a long time, trying to touch him again.

Without Blackie to groom, Abuela's hands lay still on her lap each night. She had lost more than the rest of us: her first American friend, protector, and companion. Like all the *viejos*, her grief was complicated by the suspicion that hatred had taken Blackie away—and that it was just over that chain-link fence.

The images and sounds of that day at Haggerty's took a long time to fade. Even now they hurt. Years passed before we learned the truth behind Blackie's death. Through a circuitous route, Angelito learned that the mean neighbor had bragged about poisoning a "spic family's mutt." Angelito held on to that awful discovery for a while, wanting to shield us from the pain that rushed back the moment he put the pieces together.

Blackie had brought us so much joy during such a bleak time that he healed something in all of us. That great dog rescued us, but we couldn't save him.

11

Bernice

Amherst Street, Late Spring 1969

A few weeks later, the front yard was covered with the matted yellow grass of late April. Islands of gritty snow stuck out here and there, but the ground was swallowing them up a little more each day. I would be a third grader in the fall. I understood almost everything the Skipper and Gilligan were saying to each other. We were nursing a baby blue jay that had fallen from its nest. Abuela and Papi took turns feeding it droppersful of milk and soggy bread.

Papi had become the bird rescuer on the block. He'd bred homing pigeons in Cuba, so he knew his way around a beak—a fact that made us proud.

The fledgling had grown strong enough to fly out of its box and poop on the couch. Abuela ran after the bird as it bobbled through the air, trying to catch it before it dropped its payload.

The bird also had a friend. A fat gray cat had shown up on our doorstep one day, enjoyed the leftover rice and beans Abuela had fed it, and never left. We'd named him Tuffy. Sometimes the baby blue jay hitched a ride on Tuffy's head as he walked around the living room.

So many reasons for hope, yet I felt a sadness everywhere in our house. It was more than Abuela's tears, more than the inexplicable bouts of back pain that Tía and Mami suffered. Hanging over everything, even the happy moments, was an absence. Something was missing. Not just Tío.

An emblem of that absence sat open and half-filled on our kitchen counter. *El paquete para Cuba* contained the carefully selected items that Tía, Abuela, and Mami wanted to send to friends and family in Juanelo. The package was filled with powdered milk packets, toothpaste, deodorant, pretty underwear, vitamins—maybe a pair of shoes. Papi argued with the mothers; money was tight, he said, we shouldn't be splurging on gifts. But the women banded together. If your family was still in Cuba, they said, you'd be doing the same thing. (Abuela Cuca and the rest of Papi's family had made it to Spain, just like Tío, and were hoping to join us soon.)

The women occasionally wired money to their family, which Papi saw as bolstering Castro's government. Their arguments often escalated into a loud back-and-forth and hurt feelings. Mami stepped over to Papi's side when Tía and Abuela generated too much heat on the subject. They were thinking of the ailing Don Manuel—the medicine and supplies he needed—as well as the subtle, dignified requests for help from some of their barrio friends. Sometimes, these arguments ended with Papi storming off to the bedroom or out to the yard, Mami close behind him. Once he was gone, Tía and Abuela would settle down, whispering to each other about why they were right.

Something else added to the emptiness I sensed. Once a month, Tía, Mami, and Abuela organized a call to Cuba. This took days to arrange, through various operators here and in Cuba. The mothers compared lists and notes about who would say what so they wouldn't waste time repeating stories or themes. They carried the lists around with them, adding or scratching off topics, preparing to talk with Don Manuel, Tío Manolo, and Tina. Tina and Tío Manolo's son, Alfredo, had married recently and lived in El Vedado now, but he often came back to the barrio for the calls.

In the days before the call, the house filled with a strange mixture of excitement and despair. Everyone was on edge, watching the phone, afraid to leave the room. The mothers checked their notes, folded them up again. Waited. When the call came, the ringing sounded sharper, louder, than usual, and the mothers pounced on the receiver. They gobbled up the voices they ached for, knowing they would lose them again in minutes.

The mothers held the phone between them so they could all hear, their heads touching. The connection was always garbled and full of echoes and static. "*¡No te oigo!*" they'd shout when they couldn't hear the person on the other end. Sometimes the call dropped completely, and they'd agonize about the cost of trying again.

Afterward, they'd recount what each had heard, trying to make sense of the words they'd snatched through the static. Then, just as when they finished reading a new letter from Cuba, they'd float away to deal with their headaches and backaches.

I trailed after them, like the mournfulness that filled the house.

I spent hours in our yard, the air crisp but free from the bite of winter, studying ants as they transferred their eggs, running from one tunnel to another, grasping the translucent beads in their mandibles. This is what I was doing one afternoon as I waited for my cousins to finish their lunch before walking back to school together—crouching low on the ground behind the bushes, watching the ants.

The troubling news I'd heard at school must have been churning in my mind that afternoon. A boy had yelled out that Bernice had cooties. If she touched you, you'd get them too. Bernice was always jumping and bumping into people—a bruise waiting to land. Her hair and arms had grown even stringier over the winter. She'd glommed on to me from the beginning, and ever since Cathy left, Bernice had smothered me with an unrelenting kindness I couldn't appreciate.

I watched the ants. In the past I'd helped them, but recently our relationship had changed. I didn't clear their paths anymore. Instead, I built barriers of packed dirt and rocks. I stole their eggs. Sometimes I crushed them. Just like things got crushed in the world. Cathy, Blackie, the boy who died in the fire. Abuela. Me.

These should have been minutes of tranquil nature study in my new world, followed by another ordinary afternoon at school. Instead, they turned into a memory that I buried deep inside its own tunnel until one day, late in my adulthood, it rose up to demand my grown-up reckoning.

I heard her before I saw her. Bernice spiraled down the sidewalk in that pokey, disorganized body of hers, all scabby elbows and knees. I held my breath and watched her from behind the bushes. Something unfamiliar built up in me as I watched her, a coiled hard thing.

I leapt at Bernice in airborne fury. I knocked her to the ground and sat on her chest. She thrashed for air under me. I scratched her face, felt the scoop of her flesh lodge under my fingernail. A triangular gouge on her cheek leaked blood.

I stood up, panting. Bernice knelt in front of me, wailing, her mouth wide open. I could see the ugly pink tongue pulsing. *Why?* she asked without speaking.

I stumbled away from her. Bernice crawled back toward the sidewalk and ran back toward her house.

I wiped the tears from my face and turned toward school. I wasn't going to wait for my cousins that day. I walked fast down Amherst Street to the crosswalk. Kids started to gather at the corner. I could hear the first bell ringing.

Bernice's mother appeared in the doorway of my classroom that afternoon holding her daughter's hand. Mrs. Drew called me over, a new expression on her face. I looked at the floor as she spoke.

My memory clouds up after that. I see the mother and the teacher talking, Bernice mad but whimpering. I hear myself denying everything, shaking my head. *No. I didn't do it.*

The women talked for a while and then Bernice's mom left. I think my teacher convinced Bernice's mother that she would handle things from there. At some point, I was sent back to my desk. I felt ashamed, not about what I'd done—I think I convinced myself I hadn't done anything wrong—but that I'd been called to answer for it. I couldn't feel guilt then. I was too selfish for such a generous emotion.

My teacher and Bernice's righteous mother gave me a gift that afternoon: the chance to apologize. Instead of accepting it, I dug into my anger and stayed there.

Anger dominated me completely that day. I'd been filling up with it. But anger at what, exactly? When I think back on those days, I feel the prevailing wind of sadness, steady and constant. Occasional happy moments float by, but sadness grows until it turns to tension and then a fury.

I aimed all of that at the most innocent creature around. Bernice, I am so sorry.

12

Impossible Choices

Amherst Street, Fall 1969

Mami never stopped praying for Tío even after he made it to Spain. Until she had him in front of her, she'd pray just as much as when he'd been in Cuba, tormented by duty and love. Mami believed in miracles. A handful of them over the years had transformed her from a hardline atheist into a fervently spiritual being.

One of those miracles took place on a beach in Cuba.

She'd brought us early on a weekday morning to El Megano. "The ocean was a big silver platter. So still . . ." she said, remembering. "And the beach was completely empty."

The image I have of that day is of Sergito's outstretched fingertips rising above the water—the only part of him I could see by then. I was next to him, working hard to keep my chin lifted and my mouth out of the water as I reached for him. I clung to the tips of his fingers and moved my feet to feel the sandy bottom, but it kept falling away from me. My mother looked up from her blanket on the sand in front of us, where she'd been leafing through a magazine. I saw her stand and fall. Stand and fall. Stand and fall.

Two men suddenly appeared, ran into the water, and pulled us out. They laid Sergito's floppy body on the sand and began pressing on his back. Sergito vomited his own little ocean into the sand.

Mami was still shaking and crying as she changed us in the cabana. She picked up Sergito and something glittered on the floor, in the precise place where his feet had been. A gold chain. As she picked it up, a medallion of la Virgen Milagrosa fell through the chain. Mami broke down, praying her thanks to the Something that had saved Sergito that day.

From that day forward, she chose la Virgen as the guide to that Power. Tío's just-in-time exit from Cuba had proven to her that la Virgen still listened to her prayers. And his impending arrival to New Hampshire from Spain was yet more evidence.

As the day of Tío's arrival approached, the house thrummed with a new energy. Angelito and Alberto could not stand still. They wrestled, they fought, they laughed at everything—which made me laugh too. Papi scolded us and called us los Tres Chiflados. The entire household could have come from one of those Three Stooges episodes, especially on the actual day of his arrival. We kept bumping into each other, dropping things. Abuela yelled at us for running in the kitchen near the stove. I was a jittery mess.

In his absence, Tío had become part movie star, part hero, part super dad. Tall, slender, serious, and quiet, he had always presented more like an Englishman than a Cuban—so much so that Papi had actually nicknamed him "El Inglés," though the moniker hadn't stuck. (Tío was one of the only Cubans I've ever known who was impervious to a nickname.)

I was nervous about seeing him again. His celebrity status rattled me. What would he be like now?

I felt sick to my stomach all day as we waited for Papi to come back from Boston's Logan Airport with Tía and Tío. Why wasn't I happy? It suddenly hit me. I was *afraid* of Tío, and that confused me—which scared me right back to the place where I'd started.

I hid behind Abuela as Papi, Tía, and Tío clomped up the porch steps. Everything was about to change, the air told of it. I wanted Tío back, but I didn't want anything to be different. I understood our days without Tío, their patterns and rhythms. Change meant something would be lost—I'd learned that well, and feared it.

We saw shadows in the doorway and inched toward our new future. Tío walked through the door and we threw ourselves at him, kissing his hands, wrapping ourselves around his legs, tripping over the suitcase he dropped on the floor—a clamorous household full of joy and confidence that was completely unprepared for a loss waiting just around the corner.

I had visited the duplex a few times while it was being built—a big yellow box with two doors leading to each family's house, located in a neighborhood on the other side of town. Mami tried to rally our excitement about moving, but none of us wanted to start again at a new school. Things at Amherst Street School had finally started to click for all of us.

What worried me the most was the new bedroom arrangement. Mami didn't want me to sleep with Abuela anymore. Sergito and I would share a room instead. But what good would Sergito be in a fire? If I slept with Abuela and a fire started, I'd be the first thing she'd grab. But I didn't want to tell Mami why I needed to sleep with Abuela; as always, I wanted to be brave. I still carried two secrets to bed with me every night: the electric voices and the fire I was sure would consume us one night as we slept.

To distract myself from my fears, I focused on my new baby sister—named Diane, to my dismay, instead of the Pebbles I'd dreamed of—and on not squeezing her too hard, which proved almost impossible. I couldn't control myself when that baby bubble was in my arms.

The urge to squeeze her didn't matter much. With so many adults in line ahead of me, I never seemed to get to hold her. All the fuss about the baby had turned out to be for nothing. Yes, she smelled like powder and squirmed deliciously in my arms, but there was always a *viejo* right over me, supervising. I grumped about this and almost everything around that time, and Angelito made fun of me. I'd gotten chubby, thanks to Abuela's calorie-packed purees. He called me Tanker. I howled at the name and pummeled him whenever he used it.

Only Tío could make Angelito stop bugging me. The tranquil way he talked to him stole the air right out of Angelito's bluster. Tío was the new superstar in the house, especially with Papi working all the time. He took us swimming at Silver Lake, fixed our toys, bought us gum whenever we asked. He sat with us sometimes when we watched TV, a serene island in a sea of noise.

One night, we were sprawled across the living room watching a program, Tío nearby eating something out of a box. Someone suddenly jumped up and pointed at the box. "*¡Eso es para los gatos!*"

We freaked, but Tío barely reacted. He looked down at the white cat on the Friskie's box, finished chewing the crunchy treat, and swallowed. "They're good," he said.

We were rolling on the floor laughing when the rest of the adults ran in. Tía pulled the box away from a reluctant Tío.

"I've been eating it for a while," he said.

Tía scanned the box and shook her head. "He'll be fine, it's just cat food. But really, Angel, ask somebody before you eat anything again."

We passed the box around and smelled inside to see if we'd missed something. No, we decided. It was gross.

I monitored Tío out of the corner of my eye when we started watching TV again. He seemed unaware, but then, without taking his eyes off the TV, he said, "Meoww . . ."

We felt almost complete now that Tío had joined us. And the *viejos'* dream of moving into the duplex was at their fingertips. A clean, happy excitement filled the house.

But just as we began packing up Amherst Street, everything changed.

We woke up late one night to the sound of Abuela's cries trailing in the air, breaking it with pain. We ran downstairs and saw Mami and Tía passing the phone around, trying to speak with Tío Manolo on the other end of the line. We were sent away to our rooms, where we listened to Abuela's wailings, wondering.

I learned the details about that night over the years from the *viejos*. Each remembered different parts of Abuela's anguish, but the result was the same. Abuela's heart had disintegrated from just a few words. Don Manuel had died in Cuba.

Tío Manolo had hoped to catch Tía or Mami first, but Abuela must have answered, because the others remember the crash of the phone hitting the floor, and then Abuela slashing the air with her arms, yelling at God. She didn't believe in God anymore! She'd prayed and prayed. Where was God? Nowhere!

They all knew instantly, even before they picked up the phone. It had to be Don Manuel.

He'd died quietly in his bed, Tío Manolo said. He and Tina had cared for him as best they could, given the shortages of everything in Cuba. He'd been comfortable, always, he said. As Tío Manolo wept into the phone, Mami and Tía understood the layers of his grief. He'd pushed Abuela to leave, promised he'd care for their father. But in every photo of Abuela that we sent him, he saw her heartbreak. The fragile light he'd noticed in recent photos would go out now and the dullness in her eyes would return, reminding him that he owned a part of her pain.

In the days that followed, Abuela seemed lost, as if she couldn't find her own body. She had gone deep inside herself. She sighed constantly, including when she sat at the table doing nothing, just looking out into the yard. Mami thought Abuela had cried herself out that first year in the United States, but now Abuela's tears spilled out of her eyes without her even noticing. Mami watched for signs of the black depression that had swallowed her mother whole the year before. But Abuela had a baby to tend to all day, and that new life helped her find her way back to us.

After Don Manuel's death, I stuck to Abuela more than ever. I sat next to her while we watched TV programs that she couldn't understand. I drew her pictures of stone houses with gardens and arched gates. She loved my maps of our barrio. Sometimes she redirected a street or corrected the name I'd written over a neighbor's house. I shadowed her even when she played solitaire. If I saw her sweeping the kitchen floor after dinner, I knew it was almost time. I'd stand next to her while she sat at the table, layering the worn cards in neat columns. Her soft sighs and the ruffle of the old cards lulled me.

Mami and Tía let the dream of reuniting with their own *viejos* slip away. Abuela's grief sucked the hope right out of them. The anguish she'd felt during that first year had proven well-founded after all. Her father had been ill, and frail, and she had not been there to give him the love and care she ached to give him. She'd traded her love for him for her duty to her daughters.

Mami and Tía remembered their grandfather's kindnesses and tried to keep their mourning to themselves. Abuela's pain left little room for theirs. The memories of Don Manuel trickled out at odd times, like when one of us hummed while we did our homework and one of them would say, "*Tu bisabuelo tarareaba asi cuando se concentraba en algo.*" It was good to know we were like him and that it made the mothers smile.

Abuela's grief taught my mother something she never forgot: guilt complicates a death. Abuela felt, and would always feel, the burden of an unfulfilled duty when she thought of her father. The cost of her choice would be compounded over time, each time she thought of him. Mami and Tía had asked everything of Abuela, and she'd given it to them. Her role at home—even when she was mired in depression—had allowed the *viejos* to throw themselves at their jobs, earn overtime, save pennies, and reach their dream of owning a home.

Now the pride of owning their own home was tainted with a worry. Would the life they were building here offer some kind of happiness for Abuela, who'd chosen her daughters over her father and brother and culture? Would they ever be able to create something like what they'd lost?

13

Mami Joins the Revolution

Havana, 1957–1958

My mother walked toward the busy *calzada* that night, away from her house on Ulacia, with the clueless confidence of a seventeen-year-old. She was tired of watching the revolution from the sidelines, reading about young rebels who were tortured or killed. The dream of restoring democracy in Cuba and ending Batista's dictatorship never left her mind. She wanted in. She'd heard of women joining the rebels in the Escambray Mountains, in the center of the island, where the real fighting was taking place. She was ready.

To start, she needed information from one of the nosiest people in the barrio.

Secundino owned a small bar up the street from Don Manuel's house and a kiosk on the *calzada* selling newspapers, books, bus tickets. Mami approached when she saw no other customers around.

"*Buenas.*"

"*Buenas*, Consuelito." Secundino smiled. He had the long face and sharp nose of a Spaniard.

Mami let the conversation meander for a while before asking, "So, just out of curiosity, how much is the fare to Santa Clara?"

The long-nosed Spaniard snorted. He was too old and too wise for this game. "Who do you know there, Consuelito?"

Mami told a tale too long to work on the old man.

"So, round trip?" he asked, playing along.

"No, just one way—for now."

Secundino's smile faded. "You don't know anyone there, but I know why you want to go," he said. "There's another way you can help. But you'll have to be very careful. You hear me? *Muchísimo cuidado*, Consuelo."

Without knowing it, Mami had run straight into the leader of a small cell of students who were working for the rebels. Secundino convinced her that she'd help the revolution more in Havana than in the mountains, which were swarming with Batista's soldiers at that point. The rebels needed medicine, medical supplies, and money. He wanted her to sell bonds—certificates to raise money—that would one day be worth double their current price.

Mami hadn't heard about the bonds, but she knew people who supported the rebels. Within days, she delivered her first hundred pesos to Secundino.

She approached a doctor who seemed sympathetic to the revolution about the medical supplies. Dr. Roche quickly signed on, and from then on regularly handed her bags filled with antibiotics, syringes, bandages, and first aid supplies. He ended each transaction like Secundino—"*Anda con cuidado*."

It took two buses and more than an hour to get to Dr. Roche, but he always delivered. The ride back was never easy. She was loaded down with supplies—sometimes two large bags—but it was the fear of being stopped by the police that really weighed on Mami.

The Ruta 12 bus was jammed with passengers when Mami got on near the harbor. She stood near the front, shifting her weight from one aching foot to the other, her heavy purse tucked into the crook of her arm. Blue smoke from the diesel engine streamed into the hot bus. She found a seat, leaned her head against the rattling window, and closed her eyes. Secundino would be pleased: $150 in bonds sold, and a good stash of antibiotics and new syringes collected. All tucked in her purse or in her tote. She needed to warn him about the number of policemen in the city. They were everywhere. Avoiding them the last few hours had added more work to an already long day.

When the driver announced her stop on the *calzada,* she was already at the door. Two policemen stood on the sidewalk just in front of the bus. She glanced at them as she got off and her foot turned on the last step, pitching her forward onto the sidewalk, kneecaps-first. Her purse flung open in front of her, a pile of loose bills, bond notes, and vials naked to the world. She swept at the mess with her arms and stuffed everything back in her purse and tote as quickly as possible, but the policemen were yelling as she stood up. They wanted her purse and the bag.

Her heart hammering in her chest, Mami looked behind the officers and saw Manso, a family friend and high-ranking officer, walking quickly toward them.

Manso jostled past the officers. "You two step aside," he growled. "I know all about this one. I'm handling this myself!" He yanked Mami by the arm and she limped along, stumbling every few steps. She'd never seen him like this. He was almost running as he pulled her down a side street. They never looked back.

Manso turned down one alley after another, still yanking her by the arm, red-faced. Mami panted, terrified. She'd known Manso all her life, but would he arrest her? No one in her family knew about her work for the revolution, not even Tía. If anything happened to her, her family could honestly deny any involvement. If Manso told them what had just happened, that would all end.

"What's in here?" Manso demanded, pulling the purse from her arm. When he saw its contents, he shook his head. "¡Coño, Consuelo! Do you know what they'll do to you for this? Don't think because you're a woman they'll be lenient. The opposite." He leaned toward her, his face inches from hers. "Do you *understand*? . . . Of course. You think you do, but you kids have your heads in the clouds."

Manso lectured her for what felt like hours, changing location from time to time, describing the violence that awaited her if she continued on this path. As he monologued, Mami began to recover from the shock of her fall and near arrest. She wanted to get everything she'd collected to Secundino; what she was afraid of wasn't all that Manso was warning her about, but the possibility that he might take all the cash and supplies she'd worked so hard to gather.

She wasn't sure if she was telling him the truth when she promised she'd stop all of this—that she just wanted to make this last delivery.

Manso's face told her everything. He was sure she'd be back at it, even if she wasn't. Still, he let her go and never told her family.

Mami stopped working for Secundino but stayed actively involved with the movement through her contacts in the DRE, a militant student revolutionary group, and a Catholic student group as well. On March 13, 1957, just before the DRE's failed attack on the presidential palace, a cell member came to the barrio looking for her—they wanted her to join them for the attack. Her cousin Alfredo, who had also been trying to help the rebels, said he'd go in her place. As Alfredo and his group approached the palace, they met two young men they knew from their high school. "Turn away," one of the men told them. "It's a complete disaster. It's all over." More than twenty of the young attackers were killed by Batista's men, either at the scene or during the search for conspirators.

Manso had been right. Even after the palace debacle, Mami remained committed. She let some time pass, then resumed working for Secundino.

She'd stopped dating my father by then. Better to keep him safe and completely unaware about her work. "I lost her trajectory completely," Papi said of that time. "She vanished."

Mami never stopped looking for him, though. One night, there he was at la Virgen del Camino Park rotary near Juanelo. Four main avenues feed into the rotary near the park, making it a convenient spot for meeting friends. Mami knew it well; she'd roller-skated there almost every day as a kid. She saw Papi with a couple of friends, walking away from the fountain. The urge to run over to them almost overwhelmed her. She looked up at the statue of la Virgen del Camino, the patron saint of travelers. She'd begun to respect the Virgin after praying for and then witnessing a miracle: the sudden cure of Don Manuel during a grave illness. She tossed a few coins into the fountain.

Decades later, she still remembered her prayer that day: a future with my father, once this was all over.

Mami dedicated herself to teaching at Tía's school during the day, finishing her baccalaureate degree at the institute in Havana at night, and working for Secundino and El 13 de Marzo movement—the DRE's new name, in honor of those killed in the palace attack. Still, she found a little room each day for dreaming about reuniting with my father. She knew she would marry him.

One afternoon, she walked into Don Manuel's house with overflowing shopping bags.

"What's all that?" Abuela asked.

"Towels and sheets for when I marry Sergio."

"Did he propose?"

"Not yet."

Abuela's mouth dropped open as Mami passed by her and into the bedroom, where she placed the items in the armoire and closed it shut.

14

Are We Americans _Now?_

Hunt Street, Early 1970s

Mami led us through our side of the new yellow duplex. 23D Hunt Street smelled of polyurethane and fresh paint, just like 23C, Tía's side. I clapped my way through the rooms, listening to the echoes bouncing off the naked walls. Abuela carried Diana—we'd Cubanized "Diane" early on to _Dee-ahna_—up the glossy wooden stairs and worried about the baby stumbling down one day. Above us, a pendant lamp threw white diamond shadows over the stairway walls.

Mami pointed out the pink bidet in the upstairs bath, the avocado appliances in the kitchen, but what she was thinking about was the long path to this moment—the twists that had taken all of us from Juanelo to Nashua—and all the hope she had for our new lives. We were on our way; she could dream about the future again.

When my American friends came over, they would always show the same expression when they saw soupy black beans over white rice—a kind of panicked horror that asked, _Can I get out of this?_ Mary Lou's face showed all of that as we sat down to our first Christmas Eve feast in the basement of our new house. Cuban Noche Buena menus vary, but they always feature _lechón_ and rice and black beans. Mary

Lou wanted to bolt, but there were too many people packed into that tiny basement for a clean escape.

Besides our family of ten and a group of local Cuban friends, a handful of Americanitos—all sharing Mary Lou's expression—sat in folding chairs around our Ping-Pong table and several other tables lined up in rows. Mami and Tía had decorated the basement with plastic poinsettias, snow-tipped mini Christmas trees, and lots of fat Santas, and covered the tables with red-and-green paper tablecloths, plates, plastic cups, and even tinsel. The buffet table sagged under the weight of twenty-five pounds of Cuban roast pork, fried plantains, and garlicky yuca. Abuela had been cooking for days, and it showed—on the table and on her face.

My mother's dream of creating a lasting home with my father had taken almost ten years, a scramble to freedom, and who-knows-how-many factory shifts to achieve. That first Christmas Eve on Hunt Street, she pushed back worries about Abuela and the future in order to enjoy the hard-won bounty in front of her. The *viejos* all felt the same thing that night: pride, love, and gratitude.

Not me. I carried a guilty embarrassment that night, even as Mary Lou and the other smiling Americanitos dug into their black-and-white, garlic-saturated food with the gusto of the newly converted. I was used to guilty feelings by then. I wanted to blend into the new neighborhood and school, where I had started third grade, but everything about us screamed, *We are not from here, we are not like you, and we really like stinky food.*

We were the darkest people around—even in December, when we turned olive green with that hint of brown that promises to toast up nicely by mid-June. We did everything in a great, big, massive crowd of loud foreignness. With us, it was never just a family of four quiet people—Mom, Dad, Kid 1, Kid 2—who took turns speaking and knew how to make a proper "th" sound. We confused everyone. One house, sort of, but two families, sort of. Three mothers and two fathers, two dogs, at least one bird, a shortwave radio spouting Spanish, TVs fighting to be heard, an *abuela* in constant battle with swarms of kids who refused to stop running around her while she tended the rattling pressure cooker on the stove, which she swore was always about to explode. We'd found the only other Latinos in New Hampshire, and they tended to stop in for six-hour-long visits. Relatives arrived in caravans from New Jersey and sometimes Florida with boxes of *pastelitos* and *tamales*, stacks of Spanish newspapers and Cuban records.

Almost every American who called the house asked the same question: "Are you guys having a party?"

We'd look around to make sure, but it was always the same answer: "Nope. Just four Cubans talking."

At some point that Noche Buena, after all the *viejos* had downed a rum and Coke or two—none of them normally drank more than an occasional beer—they started singing "Jingle Bells" in very loud Spanish: "*Cascabel, cascabel, lindo cascabel.*" Mary Lou giggled, but I sank into my folding chair. Someone ran upstairs and brought down the record player and Cuban albums, the covers already worn thin. Beny Moré's nasally tenor reverberated off the concrete walls as people moved the tables and chairs back. The middle of the room filled with dancers, in pairs and alone, all swishing hips and pumping arms to a rhythm from another planet. My mortification knew no bounds.

I tolerated Cubanosity inside the house just fine, most days. But with Americanos witnessing the displays of another place and time, I felt naked. I pulled Mary Lou out of the basement and took her upstairs—where she, once again, asked to see "the Cuban toilet" in the bathroom. "Bidet," I reminded her, but Mary Lou preferred her term for the strange contraption.

When I first complained to my mother about the bidet—that people thought it was weird, kept asking about it—she swatted away my concern. "Tell them Cuban ladies like to have clean bottoms," she said. "Europeans use them too." But I refused to get into that kind of detail with my friends. I had enough trouble reminding them it wasn't a toilet.

"Don't ever pee in that," I said to Mary Lou once again.

"You really wash your bum in it?"

"Not me," I said. "Just old ladies."

She wanted to see how high the bidet shot water up in the air. Over our heads, it turned out. We left the bathroom floor so wet I went in search of a mop. When I pulled out *el palo de trapear* from the closet, Mary Lou cracked up.

"Where'd you get that?"

I looked at the *palo de trapear* as if for the first time. A four-foot-long wooden pole doweled into a smaller one, forming a skinny "T." A ratty towel draped over the top of the "T" turned it into something no American had ever seen: a Cuban mop. I remembered how Abuela had gushed with happiness when our cousins brought this one up on their last visit.

"New Jersey," I mumbled, swishing the mop over the mess we'd made.

Crammed all together, our daily routines entangled, we kids were growing up like we would have in Cuba—as *primos hermanos*, cousin brothers. My cousins and Sergio, Diana, and I spent every day together, constantly arguing, laughing, competing, and, often, pounding the crap out of each other. We ran between the two houses, coming and going through the basement or through the two side-by-side front doors. People and dogs collided with each other on the tiny porch, bumping their way to either 23C or 23D Hunt Street, in search of the best chips, Fantas, or TV shows. Alberto and Angelito's friends came one way, Sergio's and my friends the other.

"Is it okay to just take these Cokes?" my friend Colleen asked one day as we looted Tía's refrigerator.

"Yeah—they're ours too," I said, without understanding her confusion.

When dinnertime rolled around, if we didn't like what was on one table we showed up at the other and pulled up a chair. The lines between one family and the other blurred entirely for me—for all of us. One distant day I'd realize we had been the last in our family to grow up as *primos hermanos*, and I'd see even more magic in my Hunt Street memories.

With so many kids at the house, Papi formed baseball teams with a snap of his fingers. On his days off, he drove some of us to the field at Fairgrounds Junior High while the rest biked behind his car, a trail of hooting kids carrying bats and gloves. He drilled *rolies* at us, taught us to put our bodies squarely in front of the ball, keep our knees loose, scoop, and throw in one fluid movement. Other boys showed up to watch. Papi always waved them into the games, assigned them positions, and pointed out, in his horrific English, what they needed to do: "Ju gotta estand like dees, see de knee? De arm up here. No down. Dat bad. When boll comeh swing nice, like dees."

I cringed when the kids laughed behind his back or mimicked him. I fought conflicting urges: punch the jerks or hide in shame. But I saw that, even when the boys laughed at his English, they listened to Papi and practiced the techniques he taught them.

I was good at baseball. Papi complimented me often, laughed at how hard I tried to keep up with the boys. But Papi's dark summer skin, his tight black curls, his exaggerated Cubanness, and his bizarre English threatened my attempt to pass as an American girl. I realize now the impossibility of the goal I set for myself and for our family back then: to stand out and to blend in at the same time.

It seemed that sometimes Papi turned up the accent and the volume whenever I was near, and especially if there were new boys around. I think he wanted to teach me how to take it, how to put myself squarely in front of the thing that scared me, keep my knees loose and easy, scoop it up, and throw it away. But back then, all I could do was to crouch low and attempt to hide my embarrassment.

Mami buffered my father's ultra-Cubanness—she was younger and spoke better English—but she was working nonstop. That left Tía in charge more than ever of our after-school lives. We had all reached a bratty rebelliousness at the same time, and we gave her and poor Abuela plenty of reasons to screech and scold. We were almost always in trouble: Alberto for shooting his BB gun at inappropriate targets, my brother and I for brawling at all hours, Angelito for not cleaning his room or mouthing off to Tía.

I was at Tía's kitchen table one afternoon when Angelito gave Tía a nasty answer. Angelito sat at one end of the table and Tía at the other. The rest of us were at our forced labor stations, doing homework. Tía's electric coffee pot was about an arm's length from her on the counter. Before Angelito could finish backtalking—and Tía never tolerated a *mala contesta*—she flung the metal coffee pot at him. He ducked just in time to avoid injury from her ferocious Cubanosity. The rest of us gazed around the table, open-mouthed. Tía finished her cookie as Angelito stomped upstairs, shouting about his mother's insanity.

Angelito showed up in our living room later that night, his pillow and some blankets tucked under his arm. "I'm staying here tonight. My mother's crazy."

Papi laughed and put his arm around his shoulders. "We need to work on your reflexes in case this keeps up." Angelito cracked a smile and sat on the couch.

As I watched Angelito settle in for the night, I felt lucky. Abuela hit us with her slipper and Papi spanked us now and then, but at least we didn't have to worry about airborne stuff.

The afternoon of the flying *cafetera*, I probably checked to make sure the windows were closed. I needed to camouflage our differences from The Others. Full frontal Cubanness was too excruciatingly intimate to be shared with Americans—and the big picture windows in both living rooms revealed far too many Cuban shenanigans to passersby.

In winter, I closed the curtains, even in the daytime, using the excuse of improved heating efficiency—I had the OPEC gas crisis to back me up.

Summer was harder. Mami flung open every window, letting the smells and clamor of Cuban living pour out onto the street. She sang and mamboed at full throttle in the living room, Pérez Prado's grunts echoing from the speakers. I snuck around her, shutting the windows as she closed her eyes to some memory while she danced.

Those afternoons tore at me. I loved seeing her happy, finally home from work, carefree. But the trumpets, the congas, the rattle of the *güiros*—those sounds wrecked the new identity I was creating.

Mami would open the windows I had closed, still dancing, singing. One day, she turned to me, her eyes two black dots, glinting. When she fixed her gaze on you like this it felt like she'd cracked open your skull and peered inside. Did she know my embarrassment about Papi too?

"Don't tell me you're ashamed of your heritage."

It was more of a dare than a question. I let the thing hang in the air, where it had been floating long before Mami asked her question. We both knew the answer. And that I would never admit it.

15

How to Handle Blockheads

Hunt Street, Early 1970s

Mami left for her first day of work as a cashier at CVS full of pride. She returned limping in spirit. The whole family had celebrated when she got the non-factory job—and the 20 percent discounts it offered at the sparkling new store full of Snickers and bubble bath. When Mami saw the want ad, she'd polished up her English and applied. The store, tiny but on our busy Main Street, showed promise, Mami said. There were just two or three employees. And she'd liked the manager—a tall, redheaded woman who laughed as hard as she worked—immediately.

I listened from the living room as Mami talked to Tía and Papi. Her face looked all wrong—mad at first, then her voice changed, and the hurt seeping out of her scared me. Tía and Papi huddled with her at the table.

A man had come into the store while Mami was at the register ringing up customers, the line a few people deep—a mob to a new cashier in a small store. The man started grumbling loudly before he reached the register, but his anger quickly escalated into shouts.

"My wife applied for this job. And they gave it to you, a spic. A fucking spic!"

As he railed Mami stood motionless, her hand on the register, her face burning. A couple of shoppers stepped in front of him, trying to calm him. The manager, at the other register, yelled at him to leave or she'd call the police.

When Mami finally shook herself free of her humiliation, she thanked her manager and the customers—who seemed almost as rattled as she was—but her voice trembled. They told her the man was crazy, to just ignore him. But it wasn't so easy to shake off. She'd never seen that kind of hatred from an American before.

And she would never forget the depth of the embarrassment she felt that day.

I only heard parts of her story that night, but I remember Tía and Papi getting louder as they talked. Papi wanted to look for him downtown, wait near the store, and then jump him. Tío Andrés, Papi's brother, would help him.

Tía lowered the heat quickly. "Don't be an idiot! Let *him* be the idiot." Then she turned to Mami. "Consuelo, that's the type of American who thinks Cubans swing through the jungle on ropes. Remember the guy at the factory who asked if we had ice cream in Cuba? Don't waste your time on *seborucos*. Be proud of what you accomplished. Focus on that."

Tía knew how to handle blockheads and use blinders. She could block out anything that interfered with her goals. That skill had its price, but it sure came in handy sometimes. All the *viejos* used it to get through tough times, run-ins with racists, setbacks of all kinds— most of which they glossed over with the typical barrio bluster. "There are no victims here: *¡Ánimo y Adelante!*"

Mami followed Tía's advice. In just a few years she moved into management, at one point managing the largest CVS in New England. I spent hours after school in the back office of those stores, listening to her count in fast Spanish at the end of the night, watching her tear into boxes on inventory days. Usually she put me to work re-counting money, cleaning, or fixing endcaps by pulling merchandise to the front of the shelves.

The dozens of high school girls she hired over the years loved her, and I loved them. They hung around in the back office after their shifts ended, eager to receive Mami's lectures on everything from personal hygiene to unfaithful boyfriends ("—Domp them!").

One night, one of the young women bragged about how much her boyfriend preferred her to his ex. As she listed the ex-girlfriend's flaws, Mami looked up from her paperwork.

"Have you considered what he'll say about you when you break up? Because chances are you will, you know. A boy who talks about his ex-girlfriend will talk about you too."

"Domp heem!" someone cheered, and everyone laughed, although maybe not the new girlfriend.

Teachers teach. Mami just couldn't help it.

Theft was always a problem in the store. The long row of mirrors on the store side was actually a two-way mirror that looked out into the store. During breaks, Mami pointed out suspicious shoppers—the ones who were looking around too much, kneeling on the floor, resting hands on hips, crossing arms. She kept a pile of sliced-open product boxes to show new employees shoplifters' handiwork.

CVS sent plainclothes investigators regularly through the stores to catch shoplifters and dishonest employees. Mami came home one night worried about Cindy, a quiet, hard worker. Two investigators had accused her of stealing—something about her not ringing in items correctly and pocketing the investigator's cash.

Mami sat in during the questioning, which turned heated as the two men tried to get Cindy to admit she'd stolen the money. Cindy denied stealing and they berated her, threatening her with calling the police. Cindy became hysterical and they agreed to end the meeting, but afterward they demanded that Mami fire Cindy.

Mami refused.

"That girl did not steal," she said. "Even before hearing what she had to say, I knew she didn't steal from us."

"We have the tape!" one of the men said.

"Then someone on your end made a mistake."

"You keep this up, you'll lose *your* job too."

"Well, then, you can fire me too," Mami shot back, "but I need more proof before I fire that girl."

Days passed. Calls came in from headquarters in Woonsocket, Rhode Island, demanding that Mami fire Cindy. At home, the *viejos* worried that Mami was risking too much. She earned more than my father, even with his two shifts. That fact kept the problem at the store front and center at both 23D and 23C Hunt Street.

Woonsocket's call a few days later ended the standoff. There had been a mistake after all. The two inspectors were heading north to apologize in person to both Cindy and Mami.

Almost forty years later, Diane, one of Mami's favorite's, remembered what she said as the CVS sisterhood celebrated Cindy's return:

"Paper can lie. The soul does not."

Mami stood by Cindy for many reasons. One, I see now, was the Juanelo ethos of standing tough with your people and of protecting the young, the old, the vulnerable. That barrio ethos was helping the *viejos* make progress at the factories and the store. We kids were finding our places too: Angel and Alberto as science and math whizzes, Sergito as a gifted athlete, four-year-old Diana as a preternatural Cher impersonator, and me, well, I was playing flute in a town-wide band, reading everything in sight, and dreaming of playing baseball with the boys out on the street. We could advance, even take risks. The rest of the clan had our backs.

The lessons Mami had learned from the revolution also helped her stand up for Cindy. Mami never forgot the denunciations and the *actos de repudio* she'd witnessed in Cuba. Reputations and lives were ruined during these acts of repudiation. It was mob rule, justice unserved. That wouldn't happen to Cindy, or anyone in Mami's vicinity, if Mami could help it.

And yet Cuba's fingers kept reaching for us even as we walked deeper into our American lives. We again felt the push and pull of our transformation when we were becoming US citizens—something Tía ensured would happen as soon as legally possible by filing all the paperwork for both families early on.

Exactly five years and twenty days after our family's arrival, the eight of us sat in a Manchester, New Hampshire, courtroom awaiting the official stamp of Americanness. Sergito, seven years old and irritable in his suit and tie, felt the pull of Cuba enough to bellow, "*¡Yo no soy Americano! ¡Soy Cubano!*"

As the rest of us cowered in embarrassment, Tía grabbed Sergito by the ear and reminded him who was in charge. The court officials ignored the irate Cubanito in the back row, and we became American citizens that day. But Cuba was in the room.

It was a reminder that, while we might be climbing pine trees in the woods across the street—unless Abuela caught us—building snow forts at the end of the driveway, making honor roll, and landing better jobs in factories and stores, Cuba was just below the surface of our skin. The half-filled *paquete para Cuba* sitting on the counter; the latest letter from Neri, or Tina, or Nena—already velvety from so many readings—left on the table for the next person to read a story that would resurrect one of Juanelo's saints, thieves, or locos—all reminders of who we were, where we came from, how to make ourselves brave.

16

Saving Manso

Juanelo, New Year's Day 1959

Batista had fled, the rebels had won, Cuba's democratic future would be restored—and Mami was dreading talking to Tío Manolo. She didn't want to hear her uncle's predictions that the revolution would turn communist.

She had successfully avoided him the night before, a night that had been full of triumph and camaraderie, the happiest night of her life—but that morning, she met up with him at the breakfast table.

Still foggy from the celebrations, she kissed him and sat down. "Maybe this will help," she said, reaching for one of his cigarettes.

Tío Manolo laughed and brushed her hand away. "*Al contrario.* Smoking makes hangovers worse." He leaned toward her. "You smell like rum. Better shower before Fina finds you."

"Mima won't care. Even she understood that her daughter needed a celebration last night. She said she wouldn't worry."

"She was a wreck listening to those gunshots all night."

"They were happy shots. Just a people celebrating."

Mami braced for one of his warnings about the rebels being too young, too inexperienced, and too leftist. But Tío Manolo just smiled.

She was grateful. He was going to let her enjoy the glorious morning despite her hangover and his predictions.

She told her uncle about the joy and patriotism she'd seen everywhere the previous night, the decency of the men and women all around Juanelo, how everyone had shared drinks and cod fritters on the *calzada* all night. The main road of the barrio was glowing, she told him. With hope.

That afternoon, Mami felt that hopefulness begin to slip away from her. News of chaos in the city and the sound of gunfire in the barrio had everyone in Don Manuel's house flinching. Gangs were hunting for the Batistianos who'd harassed, jailed, or abused them. Scores needed settling, and there was no law enforcement to control the violence that was erupting.

As the family sat in the living room to watch the news, a group of neighbors barged through Don Manuel's front door, shouting. "Consuelo! A mob! At Manso's house! ¡Corre!"

Mami and Tío Manolo understood immediately, and they ran out the door with the other neighbors. Manso, the Batista police officer who had saved Mami not so long ago, was well-liked and respected in the barrio, but police and military personnel—all those associated with Batista—were in danger now. In some cases, gangs were shooting them on the spot.

Manso's house was packed with young men who were pacing and buzzing with energy. He was sitting, quite calmly, in his front room, surrounded by men who were shouting at each other and at Manso. Mami knew a couple of them from the barrio, but most were outsiders. Several carried revolvers. One had a long length of rope wrapped around his arm.

Mami was trembling. Images of the day at the bus stop flashed through her mind: Dr. Roche's syringes falling out of her tote, vials and pesos scattered on the sidewalk, Manso appearing just in time.

"I outrank everyone here," she said loudly, "and if you doubt it, you can ask anyone in El 13 de Marzo." She stood on one side of Manso; Tío Manolo stood on the other. Mami couldn't stop her knees from shaking. "This man got me out of a tremendous problem when I was working for the revolution. He probably saved my life. He's an extremely decent human being and he's never abused or killed anyone, so put those ropes and the guns away and get going."

She waved them toward the door. They didn't budge.

The men argued with Mami and shouted at each other, gesturing wildly, full of bravado and threats. Mami and Tío Manolo struggled to stay calm as Manso, in his blue uniform, sat mute and stared straight ahead.

More neighbors arrived and spoke up in Manso's defense. The gang's voices started to lower back into normal range. Gradually, Mami and Tío Manolo were able to herd the young men toward the door. They stood with the other neighbors on Manso's porch and watched as the last of them disappeared down the street.

"Of course I was terrified," Mami said, years later, when I asked her about the day of Manso's near-hanging. "But it was just the right thing to do." There was a hint of anger in her voice.

She didn't like to talk much about the dark days in Cuba—I usually heard about them from one of the other *viejos* first. More than any of them, Mami faced forward. Her Cuba stories centered on her mischief-filled childhood—"swimming" in the spray of fire hydrants, racing on homemade stilts, pilfering eggs from a neighbor's coop, escaping from Abuela's over-protectiveness. She thought of the revolution as an accident the whole country had been in together. She wasn't interested in rubbernecking at the scene. But if I asked for insights, the "whys" and not the "whats," her impressions and lessons flowed.

As she searched for those, I realized the anger in her voice stemmed from the times that she—and other Cubans—had not done the "right thing." She and her neighbors had watched as good people were denounced in front of *comités* or at work or harassed on the street—and done nothing. "Imagine if we'd all found our valor then," she said.

I ticked off a list of the times she or one of our other family members had stood up.

She shook her head. "It was never enough."

But I knew she'd used her voice and what power she still had to right many of the wrongs she'd seen after the revolution. Mami's power came from her fearlessness and her sense of moral duty.

Papi had a different kind of power; you could see it in the way he walked through Juanelo, the way people looked at him, the former *pelotero* who'd played professionally in three countries, a charmer who rescued injured birds but had earned every man's respect for his fierce loyalty and hard punches, which he used freely whenever someone threatened him, his family, or his pride.

That physical power propelled us forward in the United States. Papi endured sixteen-hour days of factory work for years, found odd jobs on his few days off, provided the food and clothes and shelter we needed. But that macho physicality also slammed into a wall in the States, where the rules of male honor and respectability left little room for barrio-style fighting. Papi was playing in a different game now, and he kept forgetting that the rules had changed.

17

Papi, a Forklift, and the Hulk

Hunt Street, Early 1970s

The wear and tear of working double shifts at two different plants was showing on Papi's face. Sometimes I saw him pulling into the driveway in his brown Plymouth Duster (a sporty two-door with great pickup that Mami had opposed—until she took it for a spin). I would kneel on the couch in front of the picture window that overlooked the driveway, knocking on the glass. I remember the exhaustion on his face, a heaviness that pulled at me through the picture window, through the windshield, even as he smiled and waved back at me.

His second shift started at the chemical plant at four. He showered at the boot factory, changed into the other uniform, drove home to eat the special dinners Abuela cooked for him, headed back to work, returned after midnight to sleep for six hours, then started the cycle again at seven.

More than fatigue, Papi struggled with loneliness, though none of us knew how much back then. He made friends easily, even with his inside-out English. But he missed us. "Hard work doesn't kill you," he said once, describing those days. "But a bitterness grows inside when you see other families with their kids—walking together, playing."

Mami wanted him to quit one of his jobs, but he refused. He loved earning money, providing. They argued, but he always swung back to the money, the money. She let it go but kept an eye on him, worrying about him driving home late after sixteen hours of work, his lack of patience with us when he was home, his brooding.

One night, we got a call from the chemical plant. At first Mami didn't understand what Papi's supervisor was saying—or even that he was talking about Papi. He kept calling Papi "Sam," the nickname they'd given him at work.

Finally, Mami understood: Papi had been in an accident. He was in the hospital.

She and Tío rushed to Memorial Hospital and found Papi in a room in the ER. He'd slipped on the ice-covered roof of the train he'd been unloading, fallen off. His forehead was stitched up by then, but he was badly shaken up and confused.

A nurse walked in and asked if he was dizzy.

"I no Dizzy," he said. "I Sam."

This got everyone, including Papi—once Mami explained things—laughing pretty hard. But everyone understood how serious the accident was and could have been.

Papi stayed in the hospital overnight, but no amount of lecturing from the doctors, Tía, or Mami could convince him to slow down. Even Tío, who chose his battles wisely, took Papi aside, man to man, hoping to persuade him.

"Isn't messing with cyanide on those trains enough?" Tío demanded, coming as close to shouting as Papi had ever seen him get. Tío sighed, recovered his Englishman vibe. "Just give up the other shift. Pick up a part-time now and then."

Papi shook his head. "It's not every day—the cyanide."

"¡Coño! I don't care if it's once a year! Give up a shift!"

Papi respected his quiet brother-in-law, usually listened whenever he offered advice. Not this time. Papi's identity in this country, where he stuck out and didn't speak the language, was anchored to his ability to provide for his family. He couldn't weaken that crucial source of pride. He *could* handle the pressure.

Seeing Papi like that—banged up, stitches all over his face—shook up the solid sense of the world I'd enjoyed since our move to Hunt Street. Both the metal voices and the fire fears had faded away, gradually, as if they couldn't find me anymore. But around the time of Papi's accident, thoughts of the new house going up in flames roared back.

I knew this fear was stupid, but it won most nights, especially if I heard rain or sleet clinking against the windows. No one would understand, I thought, so I stayed up late, first waiting for Mami to go to sleep and then turning on my lamp and reading until deep in the night, when I was too sleepy to worry about fire.

On the nights the worries proved more powerful than my sleepiness, I tiptoed down the hall and into Abuela's bed—and like all good *abuelas*, she scooted over and let me in. She woke me at 5:00 a.m. those mornings, knowing Mami had insisted I sleep in my own bed, whispering, "Anita, your mother's about to get up. Go back to your room."

After he recovered from his accident, Papi returned to his grueling two-shift days. He was in no shape to handle the problems with a few of the guys at the chemical plant who treated him roughly, laughed at his English, poked fun at him in other ways. One in particular, a six-foot-four, two-hundred-plus-pound hulk, took every opportunity to belittle him in front of the others. Papi made things worse one day by tinkering with his forklift instead of waiting for the Hulk, a crack mechanic in charge of engine repairs.

Papi was reaching deep inside the engine, trying to retrieve a spark plug he'd dropped between the distributor and the oil tank, when the Hulk arrived.

"Get the hell away from there!" the man yelled. "Are you a mechanic?"

"I sorry. Try to fix. I make mistake."

"They should send all you people back where you came from."

Papi tried reasoning with him. "Why you disrespect me? I talk respect to you. I make error. Everybody make error. I sorry."

The Hulk just got angrier. He swore up a storm and walked back to the shop to get the tools he'd need to retrieve the spark plug.

Papi avoided him as much as possible after that. He took the Hulk's and a few of the other guys' abuse and mostly ignored it. His buddies stepped in sometimes or helped him laugh it off. But about a year and a half later, after making many repair calls to the Hulk and getting no response, Papi reluctantly asked the Hulk's supervisor for help.

Papi was working near the train tracks when he saw the Hulk swaggering toward him.

The man was huffing. "Whaddya want? You screw up your 'fuck lift' again?"

"I no know what wrong but need to fix becos—"

"I gotta tell you," the Hulk said, "you people make me sick to my stomach." His face showed a disgust Papi couldn't ignore.

"If you sick, why u no throw big fahrt?" Papi said.

The Hulk exploded, arms flailing, practically spitting into Papi's face. He mentioned family for the first time and let loose a flurry of "motherfuckers."

The mention of "mother" in a fight between Cubans—and Latinos in general—is the gravest insult. All bets were off.

Papi, five foot ten and maybe 185 pounds, charged at the Hulk, somehow lifting him by the belt and throwing him backward to the ground. As he scrambled back on his feet, Papi punched him in the face. The fistfight lasted a minute or two before Papi realized he was losing badly. He ran back to the train tracks and picked up some of the rocks between the railroad ties. The Hulk ran toward him. He was no more than twenty feet away when Papi threw three missiles in a row, missing the man's head by inches.

Papi watched the Hulk turn and run away. He sank to his knees, panting. He said a silent prayer of thanks for missing the Hulk's head. He was sure he could have killed him.

"The union's gonna back you," the union steward, Roger Delray, told Papi. "I don't know what's going to happen. But don't say a word at that meeting. You keep quiet or they'll toss you out. Let me do the talking."

Papi stayed mute during the meeting with management. The Hulk spoke plenty and mostly truthfully, from what Papi understood.

"I insulted him first," the Hulk said. "I was mad at him from before—for wasting my time, giving me extra work that other time," he said, describing the spark plug incident. "And I insulted his family."

One manager wanted to fire Papi. The other, Gerry McNulty, who'd always been kind to him, argued for a twenty-one-day suspension and won. The Hulk went away unpunished.

We saw a lot of Papi after that, but the house was filled with a dark mood. Papi looked so different during those days of punishment. I realize now what I saw in his face: a man overwhelmed by guilt and confusion.

I tried to figure out what had happened, but no one really explained anything. I knew he'd been in a fight at work. Mami gave me only a murky explanation that she finished with, "We should pray for your father. We should thank God that he didn't get hurt or lose his job."

She'd been furious with him at first.

"This isn't the barrio!" she'd shouted. "People don't solve problems with fists here!"

"You expect me to just sit there like a *come bola* while some son of a bitch insults you, our kids—all of us?"

"That's precisely what I expect!"

"None of you know what it's like." Papi scowled. "I can get another job. I can't buy honor."

"You could have killed him and ended up in jail. The guy could have—well, he still may sue us."

Papi regretted his actions but also believed he'd behaved as a man, defending the honor of his family. He'd always been a fist-first kind of man, not just in the barrio but also as a Triple-A ballplayer in the Jim Crow South. There, too, the barrio ethos of standing with your own and defending the underdog had drawn him into fights. The macho rulebook had worked for him all his life. Why was it failing him now?

I kept after the adults, asking questions and getting shushed—"*Eso no es tu asunto.*" I may have heard the word *racista* for the first time, a word that sounded ugly, though I wasn't sure why. I only knew Papi was in trouble at work and at home.

The *viejos* all stood by him—aside from the occasional sideways judgment that slipped out of Tía and Abuela. But their support couldn't lift the weight Papi carried. It showed in the way he held his head when he walked, the new tone in his voice. It hurt to look at him now.

As Papi's suspension came to an end, Roger recommended that he ask for the day shift. "That way," Roger said, "you won't have to be around those assholes." This meant Papi would have to give up the job at the boot factory and earn a lower hourly rate at the chemical plant, but Papi saw the wisdom of Roger's recommendation.

The plant refused to give Papi the day shift at first, but Roger pushed for him and he got it. Papi's friends at the plant stood solidly behind him throughout, and he never forgot the brotherhood that pulled him through those storms.

Forty-six years later, two of those men, John and Kenny, remain Papi's close friends. They gather together for beers at Christmas and trips to Fenway when Papi's beloved Yankees are in town.

Decades later, when Papi finally told me the details about the fight, he was still full of gratitude for the men who'd helped him back then. His throat tightened, his voice pitched higher, when he said, "I'm so grateful I missed that man's head. *De verdad que eso fue una bendición.*"

It was *a blessing*, I thought, as he fell silent.

He came back to the Hulk at the end of our conversation. "He could be a decent man," he said, "at least he was on the day of the meeting. He told the truth."

As Papi admired him, I admired my father for sharing that moment of grace with me.

The canaries were Mami's idea. She knew Papi needed something, especially during the baseball offseason, to keep busy. He worked only one shift at the chemical plant now, and even though he also put in some overtime and worked as a handyman and plumber on weekends, it was still too much downtime for Papi.

She wanted to encourage the nurturer in him. He loved birds. Canaries were selling for fifty dollars or more at the pet shops. Maybe he could make money breeding them. That would fuel Papi's main source of pride: providing for us.

What began as a couple of yellow canaries in a cage soon turned into a massive flock that took up a whole room in the basement. Papi built a floor-to-ceiling aviary and closed it off, still leaving plenty of room for Sergio's bed and the TV and sofa we kept down there. My brother said he dreamed about birds almost every night. The house sounded like a jungle, with trilling canary song rising and falling all day long.

Every day after school, I ran downstairs to watch Papi care for his birds. I leafed through the notes in his journal, a rumpled, dirty notebook tied by a string to the side of one of the cages. A chewed-up pencil hung from another string. His uneven handwriting meandered over the lines but recorded faithfully the lineage of each bird. He circled ones that fought, starred the ones that were good parents.

One day I found him holding a dead bird in his huge, calloused hands—the hands of a barrio tough guy, hands that provided for us but had recently almost cost him his job. The bird looked tiny in his palm. He stroked its downy feathers with the tip of his finger. I thought he might cry.

I asked him what had happened.

"I don't know. He was fine, just a baby. Look." His voice softened to a whisper. "Most of his feathers were in."

The pain on his face tore at me. "It's okay, Papi."

He didn't speak for a few moments. "Don't you see?" he said. "They're such innocent creatures." He stroked the creamy feathers with a tenderness I'd never seen in him. "They count on me for everything."

18

The Problem with Russian Condoms

Juanelo, 1961

Papi barely recognized post-revolutionary Cuba when he came back from playing in the Mexican leagues. There was the new vocabulary, for one: *Milicianos, cooperativas, denunciaciones*. The *federación* of this and the *comité* of that. Politics was the center of life now, with everyone asking which side you were on and demanding proof.

One thing that hadn't changed in Juanelo, however, was the need for factory workers. Papi's American baseball scout, Joe Cambria, knew a manager at the cannery. When Cambria, known as Papa Joe to all the Latino players, failed to convince Papi to return to the minors, he put in a good word for him. So Papi joined the barrio men who worked at Continental Can Company of America, which packaged canned goods in Cuba—lobster, ham, chorizo, condensed milk, tomatoes—for export to Latin America. They paid their workers well, gave them free cafeteria meals, and offered good benefits, including paid vacations and sick days. When the revolution expropriated all private property, all of that ended. But before the American factory directors left Cuba, they gave each worker $1,200, preferring to leave their cash in workers' hands rather than turn it over to the rebels.

There were new revolutionary bosses at the factory now, guys who didn't know much about factories, let alone canneries. Some carried guns, which troubled the old-timers; they'd never experienced armed management before. Like the rest of post-revolutionary Cuba, the cannery was arming itself against counter-revolution and sabotage. Armed guard duty was new and, basically, mandatory. My father refused to "volunteer" for those shifts despite the hounding and threats. Because of this he became a vulnerable target, like workers who were religious or who refused to attend political meetings or demonstrations.

None of these men frustrated the communist bosses more than Chíviri, Don Manuel's crusty, provocative front-door neighbor.

Chíviri defied the new bosses at every turn. He had quit soon after the communist management took over, but he was a tremendous mechanic, so they'd sent a couple of managers to his house and talked him into going back.

Come back he did, but Chíviri never stopped muttering under his breath when the new bosses passed him, saying just loud enough for the old-timers to hear, "One of these days I'm going to hang a communist son of bitch from one of these beams." He sabotaged the lines repeatedly, throwing in screwdrivers or hammers to jam them. The machines spat out cans at rates of up to twelve hundred cans a minute, so those sudden stops threw the entire plant into disarray. Somehow, Chíviri never got caught.

One day, while Papi was driving his forklift around the plant, Chíviri waved him to a stop. Chíviri made small talk, joking about a lover he had at the plant—a pretty, well-liked woman with a limp. Then, suddenly, his tone changed. He showed my father a metal pipe. He wanted Papi to throw it into one of the machines.

Papi didn't want to look weak in front of one of the toughest men in the barrio, but he had to stay neutral to keep his job. He'd be married soon.

"Breaking that machine isn't going to topple the revolution, Chíviri," he said. "It'll just land me in jail. Are you going crazy, *viejo*?"

Chíviri spat out his answer. "No. I'm not. But you—you're a coward and a *pendejo*."

Under the new management, suspicions and rumors spread fast—and often. When supplies or parts went missing or machines broke, the finger-pointing began. *Gusanos* and anyone with a lackluster revolutionary record were the first targets. One worker, a man known as El Reglón, was arrested after he was caught sabotaging one of the lines. Papi had warned him to be careful, but El Reglón had told my father not to worry—he had a *santo* who protected him.

El Reglón was quickly tried and executed, as was another worker at the plant: Casimiro, a mechanic who often worked three shifts at a time. My father never knew the details about Casimiro, but both men served as bleak reminders of what could happen if you went against the system.

One afternoon, the word spread that management had accused Luis Piedra of stealing some of the *goma laca*—shellac—pellets that were used to make can linings. Piedra had turned to mud during the interrogation, the workers said, vomited, cried, shit himself. As he was led away, people said he called out, "You sons of bitches are worse than Batista!"

Papi moved away from anyone who talked about the incident. He felt lucky they hadn't come after him.

The following day, Papi walked into the plant at 6:30 a.m., as usual. His boss, a meaty guy named Leobaldo, stopped him near the entrance. "*Compañero*, take a seat. Management wants to talk with you."

Papi tried to stay calm: *I haven't done anything wrong. I've stayed away from trouble . . .*

He knew the missing fifty-pound bags of *goma laca* would be the topic of conversation, wherever he was going.

Fifteen minutes later, Papi was sitting across a table from one of the top managers at the cannery, a guy named Maceo, who everyone suspected of being a member of G2, Castro's secret police. He always carried a pistol.

"What were you doing last Wednesday at six thirty a.m.?" Maceo hitched his foot up on a chair and leaned toward my father.

"I don't remember that exact date, but I start my shift at six thirty," Papi said.

"You had the keys to the room with the *goma laca*."

"Absolutely not. I never have those keys. Only Leobaldo has those keys. I go *near* that room at that time. That's where I wait for them to bring me my forklift. Sometimes I help feed the lead sheets into the cutter while I wait, so I prob—"

"I'm not interested in those details," Maceo said, raising his voice. He started firing so many questions at my father that he couldn't answer properly. "We know you're involved!" Maceo shouted at one point—and in one fluid movement he was on Papi's side of the table, pushing him against the wall.

"I don't know anything!" Papi said. "I swear it on my mother's name."

The manager tried to laugh, but he was seething. "You have to come up with something better than that."

"You don't have to treat me this way," Papi said. "I'm innocent."

That just earned him another push.

Papi felt lightheaded, nauseated. He fought the humiliating urge to cry.

"You're a fucking *gusano*," Maceo said. "And none of you are innocent."

The interrogation lasted thirty excruciating minutes, with Maceo yelling, pushing chairs, and threatening Papi with either arrest and a long sentence or a firing squad. At one point, Papi started to wipe his face. He was crying. He watched through blurred vision in disbelief as Maceo swung around the desk again, this time waving his pistol at him. He felt the cold metal press against his temple.

Maceo spoke slowly: "I'm going to blow your brains all over this table if you don't confess."

Papi muttered, "How can I confess to something I didn't do?" He felt his bladder begin to release and knew he'd lost control.

In the end, Maceo let my father go with this warning: "You can go, but you're going to end up in a jail for many, many years. The wheel of history will catch up with all of you *pendejos*."

The investigation into the missing *goma laca* lasted several months and resulted in two arrests: Leobaldo and another supervisor, Maldaleno. The armed managers and police showed up at the men's homes after getting a confession from a carpenter who'd bought one of the bags of *goma laca*.

Leobaldo returned to the *fábrica* about six months later—unrecognizable, skinny, shaky. The men teased him about his tiny ass, thinking they'd get a smile out of him. But Leobaldo wasn't in the mood for jokes. He focused on his new job filling large crates with cans and loading trucks—hard and fast work, nothing like his old job as a supervisor.

None of the men wanted to be in the back of that truck at 5:00 a.m., bouncing up and down, smashing their asses on the metal floor each time the six-wheeler hit a bump on the Carretera Central. They'd left Juanelo before dawn for a day of cutting sugar cane. They tied open the back doors of the windowless truck to catch the wind. Even at this hour, the humidity bore down on them.

The *fábrica* was out of raw materials again. Supply lines often dried up completely in the post-revolutionary economy. With production at a standstill, management at the plant had, once again, "volunteered" this handpicked group of unlucky workers for a day in the cane fields wielding machetes in the blazing heat, fighting off the rats and snakes that slid out from under the infinite wall of sugar cane they faced.

The men returned from those days sunburned, covered in bites and cuts, hungry, and so weak their knees bent at the wrong time when they tried to walk. They felt lucky to come back with fingers intact and limbs uninjured. They knew nothing about cutting cane. They often cut the stalks lower than the required three inches, which meant the new growth would sprout weak and wilted. All the scolding and reprimands of the supervisors meant little to the factory workers. They just wanted to save their ankles and survive under the fierce sun.

Papi cursed Maceo to a pulp on those mornings and even worse on the ride home. Ever since the *goma laca* incident, Maceo had bullied Papi every chance he got. And when Papi wasn't cursing Maceo as he cut cane, he was worrying about my mother. She was eight months pregnant and walking all over Havana—she'd been volunteered, too, as part of Castro's literacy campaign. She liked teaching factory workers and working with adult students in rural areas, but she complained about the propaganda, the infamous *"F" is for Fidel* and the politics behind every lesson. She'd barely gained any weight during her pregnancy. She waited in long food lines and brought home almost nothing. Somehow, she and Abuela Fina pulled meals out of thin air. Any leftovers ended up on a plate for Blanquita, the highly fertile mutt who wouldn't leave their front porch. "She's ours now," Mami told Papi one night as she scraped food off her plate for the dog.

My father felt a grinding bitterness toward the regime, its ideology, its politics, its never-ending demands. The revolution had taken his present and, now, his future—his unborn child's future. He swung the machete rhythmically at the cane, the tarantulas racing around his feet, but all he could think of was my pregnant mother and a future he feared. The only condoms he could find were Russian, full of holes and so useless he knew he'd have another mouth to feed in no time.

19

Let Your Body Turn to Water

Nashua, Early 1970s

Papi had painted my room a neon green and then, realizing this wouldn't help my sleep problems, a soft peach. The *viejos* were always giving me advice about how to fall asleep, how to relax when I got into bed so I wouldn't end up in Abuela's and get a tongue-lashing from Mami in the morning for violating her rule that I sleep in my own bed. I was too old now for this nonsense, she said.

I still kept the reason for my sleeplessness to myself. But by this point, the end of fourth grade, my paranoia about a house fire had me by the neck.

On the nights she caught me in Abuela's room or en route, Mami's whispered scoldings scared me and made sleep even more difficult. Meanwhile, the blue hours ticked by on the table clock. I woke up in the dark many nights convinced I heard flames licking the walls. The pinging of our heaters, the roar of the boiler starting up, and the typical night sounds of five people sleeping in close quarters gave me ample reason to sit up and worry. Some nights I was so convinced I smelled smoke that I felt my way downstairs in the dark, my heart pounding, to make sure we were okay. I moved through my school days in a sleepy fog, my eyes gritty, begging to close.

During one of the forced sit-downs with Mami about my sleep problems, I finally caved. I told her everything, even mentioning Barbara's house.

"Who's Barbara?"

I reminded her about the fire and the newspaper report, how the family thought it was raining, that Barbara's brother had died. Mami hugged me, listed all the reasons why we were safe. She used logic. I used my own, describing how the rain could trick us into thinking we were safe if a fire started. "Where would we live if we lost this house?" I asked her. She listed the obvious alternatives—Abuela Cuca's, Tío Andrés's, the Cernudas'—but quickly realized that none of her explanations mattered to me.

Mami saw more than just fear of fire in me, so she decided to get me help. She scheduled an appointment with a child psychiatrist, a profession I later learned she barely trusted, like so many Cubans—at least of her generation. With my knack for eavesdropping, I quickly picked up on the disdain the *viejos* had toward this strange kind of doctor. *Siquiatra.* The word itself sounded sick. I felt a deep shame and fought Mami long and hard about going. Meanwhile, she was fighting her own battle: let her daughter slog through each night or break with our culture's *siquiatra* taboo?

I argued even as we walked into that dark office where the round-faced psychiatrist, barely taller than me, sat across from us at his massive desk and asked me a perplexing question: "Do you like to draw?"

I fell like a lover on the crisp white paper he passed me, pencil in hand, sketching like my life depended on it. Drawing was my thing. When I sketched, I lost myself and any worries that circled above me.

Dr. Roundface talked as I drew, asking questions that I readily answered—so he'd leave me to draw in peace. At some point, he asked me to draw the perfect girl, or the girl I'd most want to be friends with.

Easy. I drew a girl in a pretty dress, behind her a house with an arched door.

"Tell me what she looks like. What color is her hair, her eyes?"

I pointed the pencil at her blonde hair, told him about her blue eyes. We chuckled as I dotted freckles on her face. This pleased Dr. Roundface, and he set me free to draw in the waiting room while he talked with Mami.

I went back for a few more drawing sessions and things started to fall into place. Mami cut back on the café in our after-dinner café-con-leche ritual. She taught me deep breathing and relaxation techniques lying down next to me in my bed. We turned our muscles into water, as she described it, starting from our toes and moving up through the tops of our heads. Lying in bed next to her and playing this game felt like a present. She smelled like the CVS soap aisle and Revlon's Charlie perfume, a whisper of menthol cigarettes in the distance.

We practiced the relaxing games often, and, gradually, I learned to fall asleep by myself, without Abuela next to me. My fear of fire went up in smoke.

I could never have known then what I understand so clearly today: The possibility of being hurt, of others dying in a fire, terrified me. But it was the fear of losing our home again, of the separation of the family, that tormented me those nights. If I listened for the rain, if I kept the curtains away from the radiators, if I looked for the light from the red flames, I might be able to save our house. The *viejos* weren't paying attention to the danger. This was on me.

Stay awake. Be ready. Save our home. Worlds disappear at night.

The night of the moto hadn't ended at all.

20

Play Bol!

Hunt Street, August 1973

I was crushing on Carlton Fisk, the Red Sox catcher Papi hated. Thurman Munson was Papi's guy, a scruffy, short blockhead of a catcher loved by all Yankees fans. Papi revered the Yankees even though the rest of 23D and 23C Hunt Street rooted for Boston. Papi bristled whenever I complimented the cute, clean-cut Fisk, and especially when I gagged over the tobacco juice–spitting Munson.

Of the four baseball-playing kids in the family, I was the only one with enough patience to watch an entire televised ball game. Papi never took his eye off the TV during the games, and he often predicted where the ball would be hit, who'd strike out, who'd get a piece of a pitcher's "nokleh boll."

"Look at Felipe Alou," Papi said, pointing at the elegant Yankee player who'd made it to first base. "I told you I played with him, right?"

This kind of revelation made those interminable games with Papi worthwhile. Besides his nearly magical ability to see the future, he usually rolled what was happening on the field into a story about his days as a pro player or of his childhood—sneaking out of school to play baseball, stealing mangoes from a rich American's farm, all kinds of urchin lore. And he always laced in stories about his days playing Triple-A baseball in the Jim Crow South.

I listened for discrepancies but rarely caught any, especially in stories about brawls or standing with his Black teammates, whether Latino or American, against the racism they faced in the South.

Papi met Felipe Alou in the late '50s when their teams faced each other in the farm leagues in Louisiana. Alou, one of the first Black Latinos in the minors, played for Lake Charles. Papi pitched for the Thibodaux Senators. He was on the mound one day when Alou stepped into the on-deck circle to warm up. The crowd suddenly came alive—shouting, throwing fruit, trash, who knows what. Papi stopped, looked around, and realized that Lake Charles fans were shouting at Alou, who kept swinging his bat as he ducked to avoid the flying fruit.

"He was on their team!" Papi said, still dumbfounded that fans would turn on their own player. "They threw their hate at him any way they could."

In typical fashion, Papi remembered statistics lost to all but his memory by now.

"Felipe was batting around .350, six home runs in twenty games. He had an elegance, a dignity. Those people couldn't take it."

Papi could barely focus on home plate with all the yelling and the debris flying down off the stands. Alou's manager finally came out and walked him back to the dugout.

"That's when I stopped pitching," Papi said. "I just walked off the mound."

Papi's manager threw a fit, told him to get back on the mound. Papi refused. He barely understood the manager's angry English, but he caught this: "If you're so insulted, play for someone else."

Papi didn't have to think about it. "Okay," he said. "I play some-place else."

The Senators sent Papi to Texas and then to Gainesville. One day, warming up in the outfield with another Latino player before a game, he saw Felipe again. All these years later, Papi still remembered Alou's warmth and humor, how he talked about his days throwing the javelin for his track team in Santo Domingo.

"I was happy for him—that he was playing for Cocoa Beach. At least he got to stay with the Giants. And look at him now. A Yankee."

Every time I saw or heard of Alou or any of Papi's ballplayer brothers, I thought of the Louisiana story. Alou played in the majors for a total of seventeen years for the Giants, Braves, and Yankees, led the National League in hits and runs several times, and ended his career as manager of the Expos and the Giants. Papi and I followed his career with admiration and Latino pride. Underneath it all was the quiet glow of justice.

Papi was firing grounders at us in the infield, slamming the ball just far enough between the bases to make us run hard for them. We were at the Fairgrounds field—my cousins, Sergito, and I, and whatever stray kids had joined us that day.

A group of new boys clung to the backstop fence watching Papi's easy swings at the plate. I started to show off, calling for more grounders. Papi ignored me. Maybe he had noticed that I was starting to see these older American boys as more than just competition. Papi waved the new boys onto the field, and soon enough, they stood with him on the mound.

Pitchers. Papi attracted them like flies. They'd heard he'd pitched for teams in three countries during his career and liked to give lessons. They wanted in. I winced at Papi's whacky English, the way he pronounced "slideh" and "hon ron," but the new boys hung on his every mangled word. Like the other boys, they'd soon stop mimicking his English. Instead, they'd copy the way he bent his fingers so the ball looked like it was hovering in front of his hand, the perfect position for launching an erratic "nockleh" ball over the plate. The boys flexed and unflexed their fingers as Papi bumped along in English, correcting and guiding them.

I saw Papi through their eyes that day, and I saw him as he really was. A bighearted jock using every skill and talent he had to make his way in a foreign land. Papi crashed into unseen obstacles all the time. He was old-world in a new world that was changing by the second. He was different. But he was absolutely fine with that. There was something downright charming in that kind of confidence.

It took those boys' relishing not just Papi's skills but also his difference for me to see him more clearly. I let my embarrassment slide away and made a little room for some Papi pride.

21

When the Rule Falls on You

Hunt Street, Spring 1975

In a tiny house with one full bathroom and five people, private bathroom time felt like a birthday party. Cubans seemed to view the need for privacy with concern, even suspicion, including time spent in the bathroom. After a quick rap on the door, the mothers walked in and out of the kids' bathroom sessions with absolute aplomb. Things changed when we got into our teens, but, even then, if Diana or I forgot to lock the door, Abuela and Mami would knock once and walk right on in.

Mami sometimes asked us to sit in the bathroom while she showered if she had something private she wanted to talk about. Where else could we be alone in that house? Even after she told me about periods during one of those sessions and I watched that awful fifth-grade filmstrip about reproduction, the rust-colored spots I found on my underwear one day stumped me. I ignored them. But since Abuela did all the laundry in the house and always checked our underwear for signs of disease, improper hygiene, or sexual malfeasance, she caught the new development right away.

"*A Anita le bajó la regla,*" she announced to Mami, Tía, and me as we sat at our kitchen table.

"Why didn't you tell me?" Mami asked.

"I thought it was supposed to be red and bloody."

As Mami explained the varieties of menstrual experiences, I thought about the Spanish phrase for getting your period. "The rule has fallen on you" captured exactly how I felt at that moment. A new burden to bear, along with the stretch marks on my hips, the hair popping up in weird places, and the sparkling interest in boys.

But I didn't feel shame—except for not understanding the significance of those spots. Abuela's semipublic announcement fell right into place with the lack of privacy I knew so well. The mothers knew everything about everyone.

That next weekend, waiting for Papi to drive us to the baseball field, I sat in front of the TV tossing a baseball into my glove. Tía was crocheting something beige on the couch. Papi came up from the basement carrying the equipment bag and walked past me.

When I got up to follow him, he turned around, somber—or was he sad?

"You're a *señorita* now. You can't play with us anymore."

The words landed like punches on my chest. Baseball was joy, time with Papi. He said I was good. What did menstruation have to do with any of that? Was this ban forever? Then, to my eternal embarrassment, the realization that Papi knew about my period. Who else knew?

"No, no, no!" I said. "I'm not a *señorita* right *now*." I would take up the breach of trust with Mami later; she had to be behind this. Right now, I had to find a way into Papi's car and onto that field.

Papi shook his head. "You can't play with the boys anymore."

He stepped onto the porch and the door clicked shut behind him. I stood in the middle of the living room, mouth open, watching through the picture window as he and the boys got into his car and pulled away.

"You'll find new things to do," Tía said from the couch. Her needle bobbed happily in and out of loops of yarn in a steady rhythm.

"What are you talking about?" I'd forgotten she was there. "What am I supposed to do on weekends if I can't play baseball?"

"*Señoritas* do their chores in the morning, shower in the afternoon, and then wait for visitors."

I stared at Tía. She looked up from her gold needle and the creamy yarn. Her face conveyed the meaning of all of this better than her— or my father's—insane words: *That's life. Deal with it.*

"I am *not* going to sit and wait for visitors, today or *any* day!"

Abuela ran into the living room. "*¿Qué pasó?*"

"We're in the United States of America now!" I said, shaking. "Visitors! Wait for visitors? Who does that?"

Tía raised an eyebrow at me. "*Respeta para que te respeten.*" It was one of her favorite Spanish aphorisms: Respect so you will be respected.

The Spanish words I was grasping for caught in my throat. English wanted to flow, but Tía had a strict rule for all of us kids. Speak English to each other, Spanish to the adults. No mixed-language sentences. "Otherwise, you'll be an adult but speak Spanish like a toddler." I stomped my foot often at moments like this one, waiting for my Spanish to kick in so I could argue with one of the *viejos*.

Tía kept crocheting. "You will have to change your ways now, just like every other *señorita*. You shouldn't have been out playing with the boys all that time anyway. I told your mother . . ."

A torrent of incomprehensible English-Spanish shot out of me. Was Tía the mastermind behind all of this? She and Papi had thought this up—the two most Cuban of the *viejos*, the traditionalists. Why couldn't they see that I was American? Their Cuban thinking was stealing a game I loved, trapping me inside the house, wrapping itself around my neck, suffocating me.

I argued with the air around me. Tía was impervious. Abuela stroked my arm. My eyes stung, but I blinked back my tears. I was not going to cry in front of Tía.

Tía put her needle and yarn in her bag, stood up, and walked calmly by me and back to 23C.

The next load of Cubanness landed on me soon after the baseball ban. Our two old aunts, Carmelina and Juanita, had come from New Jersey for the weekend. Carmelina barely reached five feet. Neckless but good-humored, she chuckled at everything. Her much taller older sister, Juanita, laughed easily too. Juanita spoke in a monotone soprano that floated pleasantly above the usual din. The sisters sat, walked, ate, and slept together. They reminded me of the fairy aunts in Disney's *Sleeping Beauty*, although everything Carmelina said in her raspy voice sounded ominous.

We were in the living room when she looked down at my hips.

"Too wide, too fast," she said, shaking her head. She turned to my mother. "You have to do something, or her figure will be ruined."

Juanita drew closer to me, put her hands on my waist, and squatted to get a better view of the impending disaster. I'd never seen the old *tías* so worried. I looked at my mother for help.

"Maybe," Juanita said, "you should put her in a girdle. Even at night."

As the aunts gurgled away about how to contain my exploding hips, Mami winked at me. "A girdle," she said. "Something to think about, right, Ana?"

Another betrayal, I thought, as Mami laughed about the scene later. I had always loved these cute old ladies. They were so formal and always *vestidas de luto*. At their age, people died all the time, so they were always in mourning clothes. I liked hanging around them when they visited; their constant cooing about Cuba, the latest dress they were sewing, their funny neighbors in New Jersey, reminded me of two black doves clucking softly.

Now the cute *tías* weren't so cute anymore. They were piling on more of the Cuban weirdness that kept pushing me down.

"They meant well," Mami said. "They're old, old, old. Don't pay any attention to them." She drifted away toward her chores. "You'll be glad you've got those hips if you have kids," she said from somewhere down the hall.

I was not comforted by this. The old *tías'* assessment of my hips felt like a violation, and Mami's casual acceptance made it worse. These Cubans seemed to think a girl's growing body was everybody's business. American families kept things like that private, and I admired that. But the *viejos* measured me by and with Cuban values, whether it was my un*señorita*-like behavior, changing body, or need for privacy. They were blind to my hunger for the American system of measurement, where progress was measured in opportunities created and freedoms gained.

Just when I thought I'd seen the last of my baseball days, a loophole opened up. I had gone to one of Sergito's Little League games, watching what I wanted to be doing, and after the game, Coach Desmond waved us over.

His wife was coaching their daughter on a girls' softball team, he told us, and they needed more players. Was I interested?

The thought of playing on a team—with real uniforms—almost made up for the baseball ban. My parents liked the Desmonds, a rowdy Irish clan full of kid baseball players. Their approval of the softball league made it easier for Mami to soften up my father on the subject. And Title IX, signed around that time, helped my proud immigrant family see that they were on the right side of the new American law.

For the next few years, I played in the league with girls from all over the city. I loved feeling like any other American girl out on the field.

My parents came to my games when they could—but they attended far more of my brother's games. At first, I created excuses for them. Then, after noticing how many of my American teammates' parents and siblings came to our games, I made some noise. My parents came more often after that.

I knew they loved me deeply, but there was no mistaking it: the male-centric Cuban thinking that dominated at home reached all the way out to the softball field too.

Just like the need for privacy, the desire for independence could spark the *viejos'* suspicion. Someone who needed independence would distance herself from home and family and had the potential for being, well, *egoísta.*

Tía, Mami, Abuela, Papi, and even Tío scolded me sometimes with their accusation of *"Tu eres muy independiente."* But wasn't being independent good? At school, at play, on TV, in literature, Americans revered independence. I needed more control over my life if I was going to make myself American.

I stumbled on a solution. Money. Earning it would buy me more freedom *and* the *viejos'* respect and pride.

I started cleaning the cars of our Cuban visitors. (I never told them what to pay me, but they saw me out in the driveway for hours with the vacuum cleaner and Windex, paper towels flying, and they inevitably paid me anywhere from five to ten dollars—a fortune. Maybe they felt guilty after seeing me hold my nose and gag when I cleaned out their ashtrays.) I babysat, even on school nights. I took on an afternoon newspaper route for the *Nashua Telegraph.* Some of the old customers hired me to clean their houses on Saturdays.

With my earnings, I began buying my own clothes, paying my way at the movies, purchasing my own books—all without asking for permission or help. I ate up the *viejos'* compliments and approval.

I set my sights on a lime-green Schwinn ten-speed. That $160 dream fueled me through all the Wednesdays when the added weight of the circulars sank me into snowbanks.

Within a few years, there she was. A glorious, neon-green machine. I kept her locked up tight against our chain-link fence with an expensive combination lock. Papi took her out for a spin when I first brought her home and came back smiling. He shook his head as he handed her back to me. "*Tremenda bicicleta.*"

Damn right. I let his pride flow over me.

I had won back something from the Cuban junta on Hunt Street. Mami understood my push for freedom and worked on the *viejos'* conservative views. She was nine or so years younger than the others, but it was her spirit that helped me with my breakaway. She'd always needed her own space, room to think and act for herself. She had broken rules during the revolution and then broken with the revolution itself. Unlike the other *viejos*, she waded right into our new culture, absorbing the reverence that Americans have for independence and the individual. And Mami believed in standing up for what was right. She saw that I needed to stretch beyond Hunt Street's walls and would find a way to do that eventually. By nudging the *viejos* away from their old views, she created a crack I could slip through now and then.

I flew down Hunt Street on my lime-green Schwinn—savoring the American girl independence I longed for and that felt, in those glorious moments, within reach. Womanhood may have cost me baseball with the boys and confirmed the pro-boy bias in our Cuban home, but in America, womanhood was linked to a rising sense of power.

I intended to hang on to that version of the beast from now on.

22

Throw Away Your Communist Bras

Hunt Street, Late 1970s

"Fidel is going to turn Yimmy Carter into a girl," Papi said.

Tía looked up, her eyebrow perched high above that left eye. She stopped sorting through the suitcase on the kitchen table. "He can turn him into a goat, for all I care, as long as I get to meet my new niece and nephew."

"He's giving Fidel new funding and power. Doesn't matter that Fidel is all over Ethiopia helping the communists."

"Not my problem. I'm not going back to Cuba to support Fidel, just my family," Tía said.

Carter's Cuba-friendly policies included lifting restrictions on Cuban Americans who wanted to travel to the island to visit family, allowing them to return legally for the first time since the embargo was imposed in 1962. This had opened up a new battlefield on Hunt Street. The mothers had all saved for what would be their first trip back, but only Tía and Abuela would go. To save money, everyone said, but the real reason was to lessen the tension between Mami and Papi.

Mami walked the fine line of supporting Tía and Abuela while avoiding angering Papi. The three women presented a powerful opposition to his running commentary about how their return to the island would allow Castro to continue to ruin Cubans' lives. They knew the hardships Cubans faced far better than Papi. In every letter and call from Alfredo, Mami and Tía's *primo hermano* in Havana, or their Juanelo friends, they heard about the never-ending food lines, the overt and hidden costs of opposing the government, the constant fear of being denounced or jailed for failing to meet revolutionary standards. Tía detested Fidel, but reconnecting with Alfredo and his family and bringing them gifts and money to ease their daily problems was worth the compromise. So Mami worked hard to both lower Papi's volume and to dampen Tía and Abuela's excitement.

Every night, the same scene played out in the living room: The women poked through the suitcase full of presents for friends and family—the shoes, razors, vitamins, Denture Grip, Carnation Instant Milk packets, piles of colorful, lacy underwear. The calculus of what went in the suitcase was the same as for the packages they sent to the island: the item's utility minus its weight and cost, balanced by the level of need of the recipient.

One night, Abuela pulled a pair of heavy men's shoes out of the suitcase. "Imagine all the stuff we could fit in here if Alfredo didn't have such huge feet."

Papi watched everything from his chair, radiating disapproval. An electric tension snaked through those nights, fluctuating but never dying out.

The day they left for Cuba, we drove to Logan in a disturbingly quiet car. I sat between Abuela and Tía in the back seat. Abuela kept folding and unfolding her lacy handkerchief as we traveled down Route 128. Mami and Papi sat in the front, Papi driving.

The silence in that car was loaded. Papi was aiding what he saw as treasonous behavior, but his sense of duty to the women demanded he support them somehow. Maybe he was making up for all his criticism with this gesture of support.

The women, meanwhile, were dreaming of family and friends, especially those who had died: Don Manuel, Tío Manolo—just two years after Don Manuel—and a few of the older women in the barrio. All the moments they'd missed in their lives—the birthdays, the good and the bad days. This was their shot at redemption.

When we said goodbye at the curb, love rose above all the sore feelings. Papi hugged Tía and Abuela, who spilled a tear or two, and the nerves and tension finally faded as we pulled away from each other.

The ten days without Tía and Abuela passed quickly, with work, school, and sports keeping the eight of us as busy as ever. But for Mami, the extra cooking and cleaning and tending of pets and humans felt like months.

No one was happier to have Tía and Abuela back home, telling us about their time in Cuba, than she was.

"Even a Kleenex!" Tía said.

We were in her living room, sitting on the couch, on the floor, leaning against each other, listening to Tía's and Abuela's stories about their trip back home.

"I was about to wipe my nose when Alfredo took the Kleenex out of my hand—you know how he admires anything American; remember how he dreamed of going to MIT?"

The *viejos* nodded, though that was news to me.

"Alfredo looks at the Kleenex and laughs. '*Estos Americanos . . . inventan soluciones hasta para soplarse la nariz.*'"

The exhaustion from the trip still showed on Tía's and Abuela's faces, but their eyes lit up as they talked. They brought back new stories about old friends, as well as the longed-for photo albums we'd left behind (kept safe all that time by our neighbor Neri). We were unusually quiet, on the edge of our seats—even Papi—peering into a world that had almost been ours.

Tía described Alfredo's reaction when she gave him the huge bottle of aspirin she'd packed. He took the bottle and told the family, "These are American, better than ours, so halve the dosage. Plus, they'll last longer."

"*Ay, y Adrián.*" Tía smiled, remembering Alfredo's little boy. "That little *pícaro* broke my heart the night before we left. He begged me to take him back with us. Said he could fit in our suitcase."

Abuela passed around the Spanish gold coin she'd snuck out of the country, boasting, "Papá would have been proud." Don Manuel and Vicenta had given her the old gold coin as a wedding present. "I wasn't leaving it behind this time."

Grinning, she mimed how she'd fooled the Cuban airport guards who searched passengers for valuables before boarding. She'd held her handkerchief in one hand, clutched the medallion in the other. She'd waved the empty handkerchief at the guard as he searched her, then coughed and transferred the coin into the handkerchief hand, holding up the other empty one for all to see.

We laughed at the idea of old Abuela tricking the Cuban authorities. We passed the photos around, studying the faces of our new cousins and old friends. I didn't remember most of them, but seeing the houses—all those familiar porches—proved the world I'd left behind ten years earlier still existed. It had just grown up without us.

23

If Only the Americans Would Bomb Havana

Juanelo, October 1962

The new *apagones* kept the people in our barrio close to home after dinner. But as soon as the power came back on, kids wandered farther down the street, people went for walks, TVs and radios crackled back to life.

Every night that fall, after the power returned, our clan on Castillo—Tía, Tío, the boys, Abuela, Papi, and Mami, carrying a ten-month-old me—walked over to Don Manuel's on Ulacia. Tina, Manolo, and the squinting Don Manuel waited for us in the living room, where the four generations of our family gathered in front of the TV or radio, the adults hoping for good news but finding only uncertainty and dread.

A year and a half had passed since the Bay of Pigs, but the government's warnings of a full-on American invasion were increasing rather than dying down. By October, the already crackling tension in Juanelo had risen to dangerous levels. Pro- and anti-government families kept farther and farther away from each other, bringing out the worst of both sides as they fed on their own suspicions and fears.

Strange noises in the middle of the night—a *chirrín, chirrín, chirrín* of heavy machinery moving in the distance—added to the pressure building up in the barrio.

One evening, my parents brought Angelito, Alberto, and me to Don Manuel's without Tía, Tío, and Abuela. They were about to turn on the TV when the roar of a jet shook the house like it was made of paper. Carrying me close, Mami ran with the boys to the kitchen and crouched with us under the table while Papi raced up the stairs to the roof terrace. He caught sight of two American Phantom fighter jets flying so low that he could make out the number 104 on the body of one of the jets.

A third jet thundered over the barrio, and the rooftop felt like it would collapse under him.

As the glowing jet engines faded in the distance, Papi heard shouting down below. He leaned over the rooftop, took one look at the chaos below, and froze.

Miguelito, a soldier for the new regime and a hardline revolutionary, stood in the middle of the street, in front of his house, shouting, waving a revolver in the air, and spinning around. Whatever he was aiming at refused to stay still. Then Papi saw Chíviri, ever ready to confront a communist, appear within a few feet of Miguelito.

Papi rushed down the stairs and reached the sidewalk at the same time as Mami, who'd left us under the table with Angelito in charge.

Miguelito's eyes bulged as he screamed at Chíviri, "You were signaling the jets with your porch light! I saw you! Traitor! I'm going to kill you!"

Chíviri stopped circling Miguelito and began walking toward him. "You done now, son of a bitch?" He pointed at the gun. "You took that piece of shit out, now use it!" Chíviri kept walking and talking, until Miguelito's revolver was digging into his chest. "*¡Habre el gatillo, coño!* Pull the fucking trigger!"

Chíviri's wife wailed from their porch as neighbors on the

sidewalks pleaded with the men. Papi raised his hand to quiet them as he drew closer to Miguelito, certain the gun wobbling in his hand would go off at any moment.

As Papi approached Miguelito, Mami tried to reason with Chíviri, who'd always had a soft spot for her. She kept her voice low and calm until Chíviri finally turned away from Miguelito. As he did, he seemed stunned to see others around him, as if he'd forgotten there was anything else in the world other than the gun-wielding communist in front of him. He used the nickname he'd given Mami when he finally responded to her pleas. "Pepa, back in that house! Now!"

Mami backtracked but kept talking to him, from the sidewalk now, her knees shaking. She reminded him of his family, his good name, his children. Neighbors watched from their porches. After a while, the men's shouting subsided and each retreated back to his house, promising to finish the other off in due time.

The jets made another pass over Juanelo later that night. Inside Don Manuel's, everyone held their breath as the house shook and the windows rattled, wondering if Chíviri and Miguelito would go at it again. They were sure Chíviri would end up dead in the next round. But the men stayed in their homes, and Juanelo stayed quiet.

Days later, Fidel appeared on TV, blasting Nikita Khrushchev and the Soviet Union for leaving Cuba defenseless and unarmed. Only then did my parents, like most of the country, begin to understand that Cuba had been at the center of an international nuclear crisis. The Russians they'd encountered on buses, on the street, and at work had been providing more than logistical support to a fellow communist state. They'd been lining up their nuclear missiles along the northern coast of the island, just ninety miles south of Key West.

Papi remembered the dairy farmers he'd met at the bus terminal the week before. They'd been right after all. They *had* seen tanks in the middle of the night on their trips to Havana to deliver their milk. And Papi realized that the *chirrín, chirrín* that had been waking him up at night was the sound of the tanks' continuous tracks clinking over the wheels of the machines.

The resentment my parents felt toward the Russians sharpened. All they had to do was present their Russian IDs at the best-stocked kiosks or shops to get whatever they wanted. In the beautiful Sevillano neighborhood, where many houses had pools, the owners had been evicted and their homes given to Russians. "All to secure communism in our hemisphere," Papi said. "Even if it means we'll all be incinerated."

After the Missile Crisis, the tremendous tension that had been building crept into almost every Cuban's soul. People eyed each other with even greater suspicion. *Gusanos* stayed in their homes to avoid confrontations and denunciations. Revolutionary neighbors watched them, and if they had scores to settle, they watched even more closely. *Gusano* men disappeared for weeks, picked up by plainclothes police with pistols who loaded them into trucks and forced them to work in the fields. The mothers, wives, and sisters cried to their neighbors and begged for help. But people were afraid to be sympathetic to *gusanos*.

For provocateurs like Chíviri and zealots like Miguel, who had already been on a collision course, the Missile Crisis revved them up and drove them toward each other, dared them to ignite.

Soon after the flyovers, my mother stood by my crib as I napped. She heard rumbling in the distance and wondered for a moment if the United States was bombing Havana. *Good. Let them*, she thought. *Better to destroy the country than to live like this.* The fervor of her wish surprised her even more than the wish itself. She meant it. She preferred dying to this life. She looked down at me, her sleeping infant, thought about the future, and landed back on the same wish: *Better it all ends than to go on like this.*

When Mami told Tía about her wish, Tía scolded her. "Really? Your baby, your husband—us? This will get better. It's still early. We're trying to change a *country*."

Mami barely heard her. She was used to Tía and Tío's passionate excuses for the revolution's abuses—or "necessary tactics," as they described them. She had used the same excuses herself for a while. Maybe Tía and Tío would come around to her way of thinking. All the risks she'd taken for this cause, all the decent, brave rebels who'd died, all the victims of the regime—this was the prize? The answer was in front of her. *I was so stupid.*

Mami began thinking seriously about leaving the country—"abandoning it," as the regime called it. But to leave behind Don Manuel, Tía and Tío, her nephews—everything and everyone she knew? She'd seen her future so clearly in Juanelo, with family around the corner, lifelong neighbors and friends nearby, teaching the barrio kids in her little school. All of that would be lost.

But wasn't it lost already?

My husband will come around, she thought. And she'd convince Abuela too. Maybe once her family had gone, Tía and Tío would join them. Whether or not they did, she had to be willing to never see her home or family again. Getting out of Cuba would be difficult, maybe impossible. Getting back in to visit family, with the United States and Cuba battling through the Cold War, was unimaginable.

A mournful sadness settled over her. She was ready to pay that price.

In 1964, my parents tuned in to Radio Bemba for the "how-tos" of getting out of Cuba. That kind of information never made the country's official newspaper, *Granma*, named after the boat that Fidel and his rebels used on their trip from Mexico to Cuba when they joined the other rebel groups fighting Batista. *Granma* printed mostly triumphalist news and never acknowledged the real problems in Cuba's new society, let alone reported on the few remaining ways for *gusanos* get out of the country. The regime was trying to stop the flow of the tens of thousands who'd left or were trying to leave Cuba, not clear a path by providing useful information for the *gusano* hordes. So Radio Bemba, as always after the revolution, provided the best answers to my parents' questions.

Sifting through the rumors, the offhand comments, the firsthand accounts, they sketched out a plan. Somewhere in the Interior Ministry's building in El Laguito, an office existed for processing applications for the *permiso*. They'd have to find the office, file their application, and, immediately afterward, resign from their jobs and obtain dated letters from superiors confirming that fact. They'd be able to keep the family's ration book but would have to figure out how to pay for their rations—and everything else.

In the United States, when the *permiso* stories came up, Mami and Papi would argue about their actual *permiso* number—which *gusanos* compared to calculate where they were in the line to get out of Cuba.

Papi said it was 88,675—"I had that number imprinted on my brain for three years. How could I forget it?" Mami said it was 89,075. Whatever it was, I saw it as a symbol of the unknowns they faced. Would they actually make it out of Cuba? How would they survive in the States without Tía and Tío, their families, the barrio friends they'd known all their lives?

More than anything, Mami worried about leaving Tía and Tío and the boys behind. Why couldn't they see that tearing away from Cuba was the only way to repair their lives?

Tía, Tío, Mami, on wedding day, Havana, Cuba

Tía and barrio school students, Juanelo, Cuba

Papi, front row, 2nd from left, Gainesville G-Men, Gainesville, Florida

Mami and Papi's wedding day, Juanelo, Cuba

Ana at 1st grade desk, Juanelo

Last family photo, Juanelo

Blackie, Alberto, Angelito, Ana, Sergito, Amherst St., Nashua, NH

Cousin wrestling match, Ana, Alberto, Sergito, Angelito, Amherst St.

Basement Noche Buena, Hunt St., Nashua, NH

New Jersey Cuban cousins visit Hunt St.

Papi and Ana, Nashua High School graduation, Nashua

Mami, Mary, Irela, Ana, front yard, 23 D Hunt St

Ana, Andy, Baby Natalia, Needham, MA

CubaClan, Lexington, MA

Abuela and her 11 great-grandchildren, 23 D Hunt St.

Noche Buena, four generations, Merrimack, NH

24

Cuban Chains, American Dreams

Nashua, Late 1970s

The strain between Papi and Tía and Abuela had eased after the women returned from their trip. The Hunt Street détente was delicate. If the conversation lingered too long on Cuba, communism, or the women's experiences in Cuba, we braced for Papi's call of, "Traitors!" But mostly they all were managing not to engage on the topic.

Shaky or not, everyone welcomed the reprieve from the Cubans-returning-to-Cuba debate. In the newfound calm, Mami focused on the obstacles to my college goals: our paltry savings and Papi's demand that I attend a local Catholic college.

This case of Cubanosity proved especially stubborn. Each time the subject arose, Papi's posture stiffened, just like his opinions about college. "How can I let her live somewhere else when she's not even married yet?" he asked, facing a wall of women with other ideas.

Tía took me aside one day. "Your mother will take care of this. Don't worry. You go where you want to go."

I was a little surprised, remembering her steely attitude during my first days as a new *señorita*. Of course, *this* need for freedom and independence was for furthering my education, a cause she championed for all "her" children.

Even Abuela, who worried every time one of us went out of the house, supported my dream of going away to college. She comforted me—when Papi wasn't around. "Your mother knows how to handle him. You know that."

These two hyper-traditional women always left a few open spaces where their children's dreams could live. I never knew where those holes were, but I knew that they existed and that the only way to find them was to tell Abuela and Tía what my dreams were. Once they understood, they banded together in their common cause: us.

One night I came home to find Mami at the kitchen table, financial aid forms spread out everywhere. She looked triumphant. She'd gone to a talk at the high school about the college financial aid application process.

She puffed on her cigarette, exhaled and smiled. "I think we can do this. Just keep your grades up. Maybe you'll get a scholarship somewhere."

I waited for my guidance counselor outside her office. With luck, in a school of thirty-three hundred, I'd get ten or fifteen minutes of Mrs. Simoneau's time. Soon her watery black eyes would blink, blink, blink as she struggled to remember something about me.

The kids in the waiting area unsettled me. They leafed calmly through brochures, kept neat files, knew things.

Ever the striver, I wanted to get into one of the "good schools" the other kids talked about. I'd need top grades in high-level classes to have a shot at them and their scholarships. I longed to take an art class, but who could afford such a luxury? Instead, I found myself in high-level math courses, floundering at the bottom of the class.

I'd heard of Harvard, Boston College, Yale, and Princeton, but no one in my family had a clue about the application process. I relied on my competitive streak to guide me. Unlike the *viejos*, I'd developed a nose for fancy things and fancy people. "I was born poor, and I'll probably die poor," Papi would say, smiling, after a financial setback or hearing about someone's new wealth. "But I have all I ever wanted with this family." As I hunted down my elite college goal, the *viejos'* message stayed simple: love your family, work hard, live a decent life, have the *right* amount of ambition. But where, exactly, did one find that Goldilocks zone?

The word in the hall was that good schools looked for "well-rounded" students. So I got on the JV cheerleading squad and the varsity tennis team and joined every club I could—even the ones that barely interested me. I worked some nights and most weekends at my new CVS job, not only to save toward college, clothes, and have spending money but also because I thought the admissions officers at the good schools would take note of my work ethic. For someone who hated math, I calculated just fine.

I ran on dreams and the endless energy of seventeen-year-olds. Papi nicknamed me "Anita Tres Patines"—Anita Three Skates. Mami would sigh as I raced by her, late for something, as usual. "Ay, Ana . . . Spend some time in your room. Get to know yourself." Instead I'd zoom away in Papi's old brown Impala, a car that took up half the road and drove like a couch on the ocean. I felt American and free on weekend nights, windows down, my girlfriends and I singing "Born to Run" at the top of our lungs.

But the ultimate American teen rite of passage—dating—remained out of reach. The word "boyfriend" doesn't even exist in Spanish. The closest term, *novio*, means "betrothed." There was no word for what I wanted in the *viejos'* language. I was toast.

What I wanted was to flirt and go out with a boy, by myself, like all of my friends were doing. On Saturday nights, their boyfriends picked them up at their houses and drove them to Pizza Hut or to a party or to see *Star Wars*—again. But any boy who dared to visit me got the evil eye from my father, cousins, and even Sergito. My parents were shutting me out of the dating game. And if a time for dating ever were to come, they pictured a chaperone at my side—like my New Jersey cousins, Teresita and Maria Elena, had to put up with.

So not only did it look like I might have to go to a local college and live at home, my dating life would include an old Cuban woman in the back seat.

Maybe American teenagers in Cuban strongholds like Miami and North Bergen were used to abuelas attending their dances, but in nearly Latino-free Nashua, New Hampshire? It would be so wicked embarrassing that I decided I was better off staying home and waiting for visitors.

"What about this 'parking' thing?" Mami asked Alberto one night. "The girls at the store told me kids park on dark streets and—"

Alberto started cackling and I followed his lead, though I wasn't sure why we were laughing.

"Oh my God! Kids don't do that!" he said. "That's a fifties thing!"

The *viejos* were around our kitchen table for their post-dinner *cafecito* and a little gossip. They kept on talking as Mami and Alberto parried.

Alberto knew to aim his argument at Mami, the fulcrum of any big decision in the family even if Papi's swagger implied otherwise. Alberto talked about the unfairness of allowing my younger brother to go to dances with girls without a chaperone when I wasn't allowed to date unsupervised. He suggested a solution: I could join him and his girlfriend, Terri, on a night at the movies or a party or dance with a date, and *he* could serve as chaperone.

Papi finished his *cafecito* and stood up to leave. "That makes no sense," he said. "You're just a kid too."

Mami shook her head, still wrestling with the concept of "parking."

I offered what I could. "I've never even *heard* of that parking thing."

Which was true. My genuine innocence softened her up. Eventually, we won approval, with Mami warning, "One minute past eleven thirty and this whole thing is over."

Soon enough, Alberto and I found the holes in the cousin-as-chaperone model. We might start as a foursome, but then he could drop my date and me off at a party and then pick us up later, always getting me home in time.

After a year of double-dating with Alberto and Terri and relentless lobbying by me, my parents cleared me for my own car dates—only on Saturday nights, only if the boy came into the house at pickup and drop-off, and only if he talked with the Hunt Street Mafiosi in the living room.

I had an old crush—John, an older boy who'd played Little League baseball with my brother. I thought he'd survive the pre- and post-date inquisitions in our living room and my father conveying—with his stares alone—the horrible things he wanted to do to him but couldn't. Sometimes when he visited, we escaped to the basement to be alone. Within minutes, Abuela would materialize at the bottom of the stairs like a phantom. How an arthritic old woman was able to slink down a flight of rickety stairs so quietly baffled us. Abuela had a built-in sex detector, and she knew how to use it.

My fun with John ended one night when we went to a party with his Catholic school crowd. I didn't know anyone. Music pounded in the dark house. I couldn't find John. I drank a beer. Then another. I sat in a corner for a long while, waiting. I finally found him and asked him to take me home. "Not yet," he said, and disappeared. So I called home, and Mami came to pick me up.

Papi never forgot about John "abandoning" me at the party. *"Cuando yo coja a ese chiquito, le voy a sacar las tripas por la boca."*

I didn't really believe Papi was going to pull John's intestines out through his mouth—but then again, I couldn't completely rule it out.

Later that summer, Papi was at Holman Stadium on a rare weekend off from work when he recognized the pitcher coming off the mound.

"I knew I'd find him one day," he said.

I stared at my father across the dinner table, fork in hand, mouth open. Mami and Abuela held their breath, bracing for the end of Papi's story.

"I caught him before he reached the dugout. He walks like a goose. You ever notice that? He said, 'Hi, Mr. Yebra.' I grabbed him by the earlobe, pulled him closer to me, and said, 'Jyu no take home my dotter from party? I want *kick jyu*—but I no do that.'" Papi chuckled as he mimicked John's pleas—"'I sorrry, Mr. Yebra! I sorrry!'"

Seeing our horrified expressions, Papi stopped. "Don't worry," he said. "We had a good laugh after."

Mami, Abuela, and I burst into scoldings and warnings, talking over each other, as Papi finished his dinner. When I saw a grin spreading across his face I realized that he already felt absolved. He'd known the story might get back to us, so he'd outed himself. A clean getaway.

I exploded. "So humiliating—so wrong!"

Papi seemed to be enjoying his meal, untroubled by the hubbub he'd caused.

"So Cubannn!" I wailed. "And *illegal!*"

As the reprimands flew, Papi kept chewing his steak, and I saw the futility of trying to change my father. He was a block of hard, foreign stone—unyielding, proud to act differently from the other fathers. If he needed to change the world around me—even assault an ex-boyfriend—to protect his Cuban ideals, he wouldn't hesitate.

The lesson pounded in my ears: I would always be different than my friends; my family would always be different than theirs. I was permanently stuck with Papi's—my family's—bizarre beliefs and habits. Papi, especially, was an unguided Cuban missile who'd find another target soon enough. He'd follow the Cuban/macho rulebook and bring me more embarrassment and pain. He couldn't help himself.

As Mami cleared the plates and Abuela kept scolding, Papi stopped grinning. Mami was far from done with him, and it was dawning on him that there would be a Part 2: he'd have to listen to a longer version of all of this later in Mami's private lecture hall, their bed, the only place in our house where a couple could talk in peace.

Papi looked up at me, not totally contrite, the hint of a grin lingering. "I'm sorry, *mija*, but no one treats my daughter like that."

My boy problems faded into the background for a while as school, tennis—a new passion—my job, and the looming issue of college demanded more and more of my time.

When I came home from my late shift at CVS one night, I pulled out my paper bag full of college brochures and sat down to the dinner Abuela had kept warm for me, as usual. This was our little Thursday night ritual, just the two of us. She wanted to know where the colleges were, how far away from home I might go.

I looked at the letters and brochures spread out over the table. "It probably doesn't even matter. Papi's not going to budge."

"But your mother is working on him. And Tía too."

The long day at school, the worries about Papi allowing me to go away to college, and the drudgery of a slow night at CVS left me immobilized when it came to my applications. I kept finding excuses to avoid applying—anywhere. My goal of graduating in the top hundred of my class of 857 looked completely out of reach after a second C+, this time in Algebra.

"I'm tired of everything, Abuela. I don't want to waste my energy right now."

"Just start to fill out the applications, and with God's help . . ." She brought God into any problem she—or we—faced. Her "*Si Dios quiere*," a reminder that God, not us, was driving this bus, always comforted me. "Do the work and leave it in His hands" was her mantra and got her through her toughest days. She often dusted it off, polished it up, and handed it to me just when I needed it most.

25

¿Qué es un Butternut?

Nashua, Fall 1979

An easy confidence floated around my fellow class officers as we walked around Harvard that day, led by the man who was now driving us back up Route 3 to New Hampshire. He was a Nashua High and Harvard grad, now a successful businessman, who wanted to show us the campus and encourage us to apply. Janet, Tall Tim, and Redhead Tim had the grades, scores, family support, connections, and personal talents to attempt the mission. I did not. Even my role as class secretary reflected my weak position in the hierarchy.

The embodiment of American success behind the wheel asked if I was going to apply.

"I don't think I'd have a chance." I hoped my humility would draw his encouragement.

"Well with that attitude, you shouldn't," he said with a chuckle. Then he eased up. "You never know. You should at least try."

He meant well, but the sense of wrongness I'd felt all day spread through my chest, a loose ache. I looked out the window, thinking about the dark paneled dining rooms, the wonderfully cavernous library, the quiet wealth that permeated the campus. I wanted that mysterious world for myself. These were my friends—kind, funny, and whip-smart—but they seemed to have answers to questions I didn't even know to ask. I blundered back into their conversation, this time about cartoons of all things. Redhead Tim described his favorite Bugs Bunny episode, "Excuse Me, Pardon Me," where Bugs tries to get away from Elmer Fudd inside an opera theater.

"My favorite is *Yóh*-seh-mite Sam," I said.

A loaded, two-second silence told me I'd stepped in something. Then the packed car exploded with laughter. Someone coughed from laughing too hard. Heat ran up my face. I tried to laugh, but I felt exposed for what I was: a refugee-immigrant-Ivy-wannabe, reaching too high.

"I love it!" Redhead Tim said, catching his breath. "*Yóh*-seh-mite Sam! Oh, Ana, you crack me up. It's Yo-*séh*-meh-tee, like the park."

"Where is it?" I asked.

As the chuckles died down, my friends explained the connection to the park, the proper pronunciation, and who knows what else. I knew better than to hope now, having revealed my lack not just of confidence but also of basic knowledge—from lowly cartoons to iconic parks.

I bit my tongue to keep from talking. But as I bit down, I felt my embarrassment fade. Hope—or was it a hopeful vengeance?— bloomed in its place. Why not apply? No one needed to know, unless I got in. Wouldn't that be a great comeback for the clueless Cuban in the back seat?

I dumped the college brochures out of my "files," the brown paper bag I kept in the kitchen closet, and onto the kitchen table. The pretty photos scattered across the table all looked the same. The only brochure that spoke to me was Smith's. The golden glow on the women's faces as they peered through autumn leaves, the Victorian houses, the rippling pond, the promise of tea with professors—here was a real slice of American life. Tea. No more *cafecitos* for me.

Who knew what other clues such a college might offer someone hoping to infiltrate the culture? And, unlike with Wellesley and the other colleges that mailed me information all that fall, I'd had to request a brochure from Smith. If Wellesley knew about me, had sent all those letters and pamphlets, it must be the lesser school.

With application fees and time in short supply, I decided to apply only to three schools: Smith, Harvard, and Boston College. Finally, I had a plan.

I'd searched my closet that morning for something that resembled the bohemian preppiness on display in the Smith brochure. *Nada.* Now, sitting in the front seat as Mami drove to Northampton, Massachusetts, I knew the outfit I'd picked was all wrong. Black skirt, white blouse, clogs . . . I looked more like a maid or a nanny than the capable, smart student I hoped to impersonate at my Smith interview. I hadn't slept well the night before either; my bloodshot eyes proved it.

A gray drizzle hovered above Route 2's hills and curves. Mami peered through the windshield at the sharp turns ahead. "Where in the hell is this place?"

After a two-hour ride in the fall gloom, we were exhausted, tense, hungry, and lost. But the interview started in thirty minutes. No time to stop.

My hands and armpits started to sweat. Perfect.

When we got near the campus, I read out loud the directions the admissions office had sent us.

"Drive up Main Street to Elm. Pass the Art Museum. The admissions office is in a butternut-colored clapboard building." I stopped reading, looked at my mother.

"*¿Qué es un* butternut?" she asked. "*Y ¿*clapboard?"

The brick and wooden buildings flicked by us on either side of Elm

Street. I pictured all the American foods I'd eaten at friends' homes, the school cafeteria, the few restaurants I'd been to. *Butternut?*

I shook my head. "No idea."

"What kind of directions are these? Butternut? Clapboard?" Mami mumbled.

"Butter . . ." I said. "It must be some kind of yellow."

"I don't know, Anita. But this is a very fancy college if they think people understand things like that."

She had a point, maybe *the* point. The fancy-intellectual aspect of this place intrigued me even if it also made me feel different and woefully ill-prepared. All of that excited me. I had two new words to look up. And maybe a new world to explore.

The admissions office was tucked inside a cozy old house that was sheathed in long, thin wooden boards painted an orangey-brownish yellow. The dark office smelled of reserved white people and money. This was about as far from Juanelo and my loud Cuban family as I could have imagined.

My face felt slick with oil and sweat as we hustled up to the receptionist. I dabbed a Kleenex over my nose and cheeks as we checked in, but the sweat beaded up again over my lip. I imagined the interviewer's notes: *Not only was the candidate late, she was sweaty and dressed like a waitress.*

After a few minutes in the soft lamplight of the waiting area, an elegant woman walked over to welcome us. She thanked my mother for coming, asked about the drive, then led me into her office.

Within minutes, my nerves calmed and the sweat evaporated. I felt absolutely at home with her, this warm, charming woman whose perfect diction inspired me to work on the "t" sound at the end of words.

Maybe, I thought, *maybe.*

My applications mailed, the bulk of my schoolwork in order, CVS hours racked up, I stared into the spring of senior year ready for my last tennis season on the school team. The top players on the team practiced at clubs in the area during the winter months. My friend Annie—my doubles partner—always found ways to get me into these places at a discount (or maybe, I suspected, Annie's big-hearted mother arranged the "discount"), but only here and there.

There was no doubt which players spent all of wintertime hitting balls inside those big, white, heated bubbles. The smooth strokes, crisp whites, and bouncy confidence of the girls from the private schools or well-to-do towns, like Amherst, intimidated me into making what Coach Z called unforced errors. Coach tolerated forced errors, but *un*forced errors? Nuh-uh. I risked losing my starting spot each time we played one of those ritzy teams.

As soon as the outdoor courts were clear of snow, I dressed in sweats from head to toe and slammed balls against the backboard at Fairgrounds. I needed to catch up with the winter clubbers.

One morning, as I opened up a new can of balls, the *psst-crack* of the lid coming off was followed by an almost audible swoosh as it sliced my skin. A line of blood sprang up across my palm.

Amherst. That was my first thought. We were supposed to play the affluent town next. I wrapped something white—a sock, I think—around my palm to absorb the blood and tried to hit balls against the backboard. But the pain and blood got in the way, and I finally gave up and rode my bike home, pressing my palm, sore and throbbing, on the handlebar to slow the blood flow.

Later that week, my friend Danny met up with me on the bleachers after practice. As I unwrapped my tattered bandage to put on a clean one, I complained about the cut and the upcoming match against Amherst—how I knew I would lose.

He looked at my palm. The cut was healing but far from closed.

"Don't wrap it," he said, "use the pain. Make it work for you."

I looked at him like he was crazy. "The racket will slip right out of my hand when it starts bleeding."

"Get mad at the pain. I do it when I get checked in hockey. Helps."

I'd lost to every Amherst opponent for the last three years. The team represented the snobby, preppy elite that I both detested and envied. The gaffe-filled trip to Harvard, dreaming of Smith, my obsession with Amherst—all of these were grabs for a spot in that elusive American world. I wanted those two Amherst wins, in singles and in doubles. And something about Danny's strategy sounded right.

I practiced hard all that week. On the bus ride to Amherst, I unwrapped the thick bandage from my hand. The soft seam of the cut was paper-thin.

I kept wiping my hand during the match, but I stayed ahead of my opponent most of the time. Each time we switched sides, I took or handed her the ball without making eye contact or saying thanks. Other players did this sometimes, as a way to psych out an opponent, but I'd never been able to bring myself to copy them. That day, the throbbing pain kept me focused. The pain grew anger, the anger grew power, the power won points. I beat my opponent, and Annie and I beat the doubles team. We brought in the only wins for Nashua that day.

Danny's strategy of using pain to advance should have felt familiar. All along, I'd been using the pain of being different, of being the outsider, to fuel my determination to prove myself. The pain in my hand was just a physical reminder of that out-of-place feeling—and of my reach to belong. There was a secret power in the pain of being the other. It didn't always get me to my goal, but it kept me moving forward. And sometimes, like that day in Amherst, that power sure could salvage some pride.

I was trying to erase my Cuban-otherness that spring, but news about the Mariel Boatlift kept drawing it back in. Thousands of Cubans seeking asylum forced their way into the Peruvian embassy in early April 1980. In response to the growing unrest, Castro announced he'd allow Cuban Americans to come and retrieve their Cuban relatives without *permisos* from the port of Mariel, as long as they also took other, non-related Cubans who also wanted to leave along with them.

A troubling number of the added-on refugees turned out to be prisoners released from Cuban jails or residents of mental health facilities. Undeterred, Cuban Americans, or their hired boat captains, set sail on hundreds of boats from Key West, Miami, and other parts of Florida for Mariel, hoping to return with family members who were finally free to leave. My mother's tía Hortensia had hired a boat and was somewhere in the bobbing flotilla, determined to bring back her brother and his wife.

The footage of sunburned, bedraggled Cubans floating in their rafts tore through my heart but left me confused, until I realized why: my compassion was tainted by the shame I felt to be associated with them, after all my hard work burnishing a clean, whitish Cuban image. More shame chased the first because I didn't want to be the kind of person who turned away from anyone's suffering, let alone her own people's. Yet when my friends, their parents, or my teachers asked me about the "rafters," I deflected their questions. I thought, *How am I supposed to know? It's not like I'm related to those people.*

In their genuine concern for the refugees, the Americans showed me how far I was from true compassion. But the image I'd constructed of the perfect Cuban American was too frail to withstand comparisons with those desperate people on their rafts.

The white newscasters—the only kind we seemed to have in those days—conveyed the growing national alarm as hordes of brown people spilled out of listing shrimp boats on the Florida coast. Mayors in New Jersey, the next most popular destination for the refugees after Miami, convened emergency meetings to avoid "Castro's crisis turning into America's crisis."

I'd been outed by 125,000 of my countrywomen and men. They wanted what all people want: Freedom from fear and hunger. And liberty. But I wanted no part of them.

26

Mami Bags a Racist

Nashua, Spring 1980

"*Te ponchaste en Harvard.*"

I'd just walked in the door, loaded down with rackets, books, hope. Papi's words slapped me in the face, one after another, until the full body blow landed: *You struck out at Harvard.*

He held out the letter, sheepishly handing it to me in the middle of the living room.

Papi had accepted the idea that I would be going away to college, thanks to Tía and Mami's relentless campaign. The sad embarrassment on his face added more pain to the news. I didn't want him to see it.

"It's *illegal* to open other people's letters!" I shouted.

He looked hurt now. "But . . . you're my daughter. It's not the same."

"Arghh. I'm still a *person*—with the right to some privacy."

"Okay, I'm sorry. I just wanted to know—"

"*I'm* supposed to be the one who knows first!"

I remember the exact spot in the living room where I stood, exposed in my failure, as Papi confirmed just how impossible my dream had been. I thought of all those hours spent on that application, the little spell I'd put into the envelope when I mailed it. How stupid to dream of something so out of range. Now Papi felt sorry for me, a pity that only sharpened the ache of rejection.

A few days later, he brought me to the kitchen table when I walked in from practice. He pointed to an envelope on the table—from Smith—nice and thick and unopened.

"Thank you, Papi."

Abuela dried her hands on her apron and sat down as I opened the envelope. "It's big, so that's good," she said.

Is it possible that confetti dropped out of that envelope when I tore it open? Or that red balloons floated out and sailed out the picture window?

Like that, I was Smith-bound, with guaranteed work-study and a yearly scholarship that brought our family's out-of-pocket contributions within our reach. A more possible impossible dream, now possible.

Often, during those happy days full of tennis matches, senior play rehearsals, and dreams of having my own room for the first time—I hoped to get into one of the houses that had only single rooms—stories about Cuban rafters popped up in the background.

Each time, I turned away from them . . . until I couldn't.

My parents had been talking about sponsoring a couple out of the mob of refugees now filling up the Orange Bowl.

"We've been so lucky," Mami said. "It's the right thing to do."

Approximately sixty thousand refugees would be processed there before being released to family or other sponsors. Reports that Castro had released criminals from prison onto boats didn't bother my parents. Our Miami and New Jersey relatives, armed with firsthand accounts of some rough characters mixed in among refugee families, called often, full of warnings.

Mami and Papi ignored them.

"You wait and see," Sergito said as we talked in his basement bedroom about Mami and Papi's plan to sponsor a refugee couple. "This is going to land on me."

"What are you talking about?"

"Where do you think those people are gonna sleep? I'll get kicked out of my room, and they'll get the basement. You wait." Sergito loved his bat-cave bedroom, even with his one hundred canary roommates.

"Maybe the Miamians will turn them around."

"No way."

Mami started buying new sheets and pillows, a little coffee table for the TV area in the basement. She filled a basket with shaving supplies, lotions, and deodorant and left it in a corner by the bed. "If this happens, I want them to feel at home," she said.

Tía, Tío, and Abuela were less enthusiastic, but as long as Mami and Papi took full responsibility, they would welcome whoever landed on our doorstep too.

I stopped complaining about the plan and concentrated on the whirlwind of my last semester at Nashua High.

Sergito was never the best-behaved kid in school. He learned early not to complain at home if a teacher punished him—even if they pushed, hit, or yelled at him. "I'd just get in more trouble," he said later about his "don't ask, don't tell" philosophy.

Because he so rarely talked about school, everyone listened the night he came home and began to rail about Mr. M., a gum-chewing, hippie-dippie, "cool" teacher whose shaggy bangs and bowl haircut were meant to evoke Paul McCartney. I thought he was cute. Sergio had never liked him.

That day in class, Sergito explained, he and Frank Pérez, one of the few other Latinos in school, were sitting by the door when Mr. M.'s lecture meandered into dangerous water.

"He's talking about racial discrimination today and starts listing names—epithets, he called them," Sergito said. "He says Blacks get called 'niggers,' and Jews, 'kikes.' Never heard that one," Sergio said. "Then he goes, 'And Spanish people'—and he smirks and points across the room at me and Frankie—'are spics.' He's laughing a little, but not too many kids laughed. Even they knew he was out of line, but everybody was just looking from him to us, from us to him." He was practically spitting now. "So I stand up in the aisle and say, 'Hey, watch it! You don't do that.' And Mr. M. just says, 'Siddown. You guys have got to lighten up. Take a joke.'"

By the time Sergito finished venting at dinner, everybody around the table wanted to rumble—no one more than Mami. She pursed her lips and got a look in her eye that worried everyone.

"You're not going to go in there, right?" Sergito asked, clearly regretting bringing her into the situation.

But Mami did go in. With the Mariel crisis and whatever injustice was left over from the few but persistent racists at Papi's factory, Mami's *chiminea* was nice and full. She took an unheard-of day off and marched into the principal's office with a nervous Sergito in tow.

Within a few minutes, the principal had pulled in Mr. M. for questioning.

"She was lit up and hot," Sergito said, afterward. "And I stopped feeling nervous. Finally, a teacher gets his ass kicked! She wagged her finger at him. He even pulled back a couple of times!"

Mami ran up one side and down the other of the suddenly contrite history teacher. "You don't point to students in the middle of a class and single them out, call them by a racial slur—not for the purpose of teaching or joking, or whatever your excuse is. Unacceptable. Would you like that done to you? Is that a way to teach the injustice of discrimination? By humiliating young minorities you're supposed to be educating? You're a dishonor to your profession, but more important, you should be ashamed of yourself as a human being. I've worked hard to teach my children to be proud of their heritage. You're not going to destroy that with your abuse. No sir!"

Mr. M. apologized, using exactly the reasoning she'd imagined— he was joking, he said. He attempted earnestness, but Mami wasn't finished.

"And what about Frankie?" she asked. "What about the other students? Don't you think it's right to apologize to them too? Isn't an apology to the boys, in front of the entire class, the only way to repair—*somewhat*—the damage you caused?"

The principal and Mr. M. looked about fried by then, according to Sergito, and he agreed to Mami's proposal. That afternoon in class, Mr. M. apologized, and Frankie and Sergio recovered a bit of the dignity he'd taken from them the day before.

The Cuban pride in the family continued to grow with the arrival of the Marielitos.

Pedro and Elisa, a couple in their early thirties, were emaciated, tanned to a crisp, and so dried out it looked like they might crack if they bumped into something.

They also chain-smoked—which Mami, tired of us hounding her about smoking, appreciated. She shared her Merit Menthol 100s, happy to look like a lightweight next to our Cuban guests.

Both Pedro and Elisa were jumpy. Even when the two sat still, they gave the impression of movement, a low-level vibration you couldn't ignore. We expected them to complain about Cuba, but instead Elisa's list of complaints about the United States grew by the day: the crowded stadium, the bland food, the paperwork for refugees, the factory work Tío had gotten for them, and . . . Americans.

She scratched that last item off her list when Mami snapped at her, "Then why the hell did you come, Elisa?"

The rest of us held our breath, mouths and eyes open, waiting for the cranky Elisa to explode. Instead, she stood up from the couch, head held high, huffed, and left the room.

Mami, sitting in her yellow armchair, exhaled a plume of cigarette smoke and rolled her eyes.

Elisa. She looked at you so directly in the eye, even when she wasn't talking with you, that you felt assaulted. Pedro was lively, happy, but he startled easily. His hands shook. He laughed at the wrong time and for too long. They were slightly offbeat. And their stories didn't always match up.

"Something's wrong," Tía said one afternoon, when the newcomers were still working at the shoe factory.

Papi nodded. "All I know is Elisa has about a hundred thousand miles on her chassis."

"You two, always so suspicious." Abuela liked the couple and enjoyed their Cuban chatter.

I wondered what Papi meant about Elisa's "mileage." I didn't understand until after Elisa and Pedro moved out—he to Los Angeles, she to Miami. Only then did the *viejos* speak openly to all of us about the couple.

They'd met in the Orange Bowl. They knew they'd have a better chance of getting sponsored if they said they were married. Papi had started unraveling the mystery after he caught a discrepancy in one of Elisa's stories. He'd asked her outright if they were married. "Yes," she said. "It's just that Pedro gets confused. He suffers from nerves—always has."

But when Elisa wasn't around, Papi had gotten Pedro to flip by bringing up her comment about his "nerves." Pedro didn't like that. Told Papi everything.

Papi and I spoke about the couple years later, sitting on the porch of my parents' house in Merrimack. "He looked so guilty I stopped being mad at him," Papi told me. "He was a good guy." After Papi reassured him, Pedro told him that he'd been in a hospital due to a mental illness and that Elisa was—well, she might not be as "decent" as he'd have liked. "I think he loved her, though," Papi said. "He wanted to make things work."

As he talked, I remembered his lie to the Jewish woman at the Opa Locka refugee center, when he tried to pass as a Jew to gain a few extra dollars, and reminded him of that day.

Papi smiled. "You're right." He stared at the pink dahlias in his small garden for a bit. "People do all kinds of things when they're desperate. And when you have kids, that's a whole other level of desperate."

Mami fumed over the deception for a few days, but her desire to help the couple overrode the insult. The plan to move them out gained urgency as Elisa's complaining increased, however: Nashua, the factory, the French-Canadian ladies on her assembly line, the rain, Pedro, winter.

Pedro, in contrast, remained ebullient. He'd gained weight yet seemed lighter. He worked nonstop at the boot factory and looked for part-time work wherever he went.

The winter clobbered Elisa, and she left for Miami. A year later, Pedro left for Los Angeles. He called us regularly at first, and we cheered his successes. He bought an ice cream truck, then another, then another. It made sense: Pedro, kids, ice cream, 72-degree weather—a world of smiles.

My parents considered their Marielito Mission a success despite the surprises. They'd helped two refugees begin their Cuban American lives by bringing them into our home and pointing them in a good direction. The rest of the journey would be up to them.

27

Did Someone Wash This Food?

Northampton, Massachusetts, Fall 1980

I embarked on my own journey that fall, a hundred-mile trip that might as well have taken me to Mars. In the history of Smith College, no first-year student had ever had so many family members helping her move into her dorm. Three cars full of relatives joined the mission that day. Before I knew it, the floor was scrubbed, my bed was made, the bookshelf was full, and my clothes were hung in the closet.

We might not be quiet, but we were efficient.

Soon after my clan left, I found myself in the middle of the most orderly crowd I'd ever seen. About six hundred of my new classmates filed into Smith's Sage Hall and took their seats. We faced the paneled stage, where college faculty and staff would be welcoming us for the first time as a class. President Jill Ker Conway's mellifluous voice floated down to us like a very intelligent, kind kiss. She spoke in a wide Aussie accent and seemed genuinely thrilled about the beginning of our Smith journeys. I loved her at first sight.

I think Tammy, a housemate sitting next to me, noticed the demographics first. Her glossy black hair swished from side to side as she looked around the hall.

"Everybody's blonde," she whispered.

Yung Ju and I swiveled in our seats. Girl was right. Rows and rows of blonde heads surrounded us on all sides. For a Jew from Long Island, a Korean from Brookline, and a Cuban from New Hampshire, a brunette minority demanded a moment of silence. We blinked at each other and felt a sisterhood forming.

"I remember my first year," our class dean, a petite woman with a Harvard PhD in English, was saying. "I didn't know anyone, of course. Painfully shy . . ." She chuckled, almost to herself. "When I come to think of it, all I did was stay in my room and masturbate."

Wait. Did I misunderstand that?

Nope. The boom of six hundred women laughing at the same moment exploded through the hall but faded fast as we noticed the other speakers' stricken faces. Our dean, bemused by her own story and our reaction, continued on, unconcerned by her colleagues' reactions. She was there to help us face our new adventure, clear-eyed, fearless.

Her story melted some of the apprehension I'd felt since arriving on campus: The college had made a mistake—I didn't belong here. These women were too articulate, sophisticated, and well-read to be my peers.

The dean's earthy humor suggested I might be able to find a home here.

Smith threw new experiences at me faster than balls in a batting cage. Lesbians, Marxists, my own room, Yorkshire pudding— although most of the American food tasted like it had been washed first—so much reading and writing that my eyesight petered out by 9:00 p.m.

I barely missed the *viejos*. I was too busy. Learning, discovering, finding a new home in a world of butternut-colored buildings full of curious women, generous professors, books, music, theater—the cookies that Marga, our German cook, wheeled out to us in the living room of Laura Scales House for Friday afternoon tea.

I met my first Hispanic friend ever—Toni, a skinny, super smart Nuyorican in her junior year. We fell for each other fast, kindred spirits in a house of seventy-two mostly white women from mostly well-off backgrounds. Walking into that friendship was like walking into Hunt Street on a Sunday afternoon.

I searched for and found more Tonies. We formed a new group, Nosotras, with help from an advising professor: Patricia R., a tiny Colombian leftist hiding from her right-wing government and bent on awakening us to each other.

At our first meeting, we struggled with not just our mission but also how to describe ourselves: Latina, Hispanic, Chicana, or some kind of hyphenated people? We ranged from freckly white to delicious dark brown, and had ties to Mexico, Panama, the Caribbean, LA, New Hampshire. We were former refugees, third-generation immigrants, daughters of migrant workers, scions of Puerto Rican business empires. Some of us wanted Spanish-only meetings. Some only spoke English. We couldn't even decide on the correct word for a banana—*plátano*, *guineo*, *banano*? But we stuck together, a confused, verbose subculture mounting alt dance shows, bake sales featuring *buñuelos* and *pastelitos*, and performing twisted versions of García Lorca plays.

Nosotras led to a new pride in being Cuban and the reassurance that I belonged to a much larger family. I was no longer Sole Latina of the North. We were as complex as all families, but we recognized in each other the unmistakable trace of home.

Even with my growing Latina pride, I tried to steer clear of my Cuban links in general conversations. But my name drew questions about my heritage, and political conversations and debates about Cuba followed. With the leftist Sandinistas in power in Nicaragua and a brutal right-wing dictatorship in control of El Salvador, the decidedly liberal Smith community was focused on Latin America and tended to consider Cuba a shining example of equality and liberation. Some members of the economics department attended Cuba's five-year economic planning summits. They talked about the strengths of Cuba's system and why they considered it a worthy alternative to our market-driven economic model. The opinions of some of those professors, who usually introduced themselves at the beginning of the semesters as Marxists or Marxist Leninists—so we'd understand their biases—helped fuel the pro-Castro/Cuba sentiment I found everywhere on campus.

One night at dinner, a housemate's guest clamped down on my Cuban background and wouldn't let go. It was a Thursday night, when we invited student and faculty guests to join us at the long wooden tables in our dining room for a family-style, candlelit dinner, white tablecloths and all. The woman was one of Smith's Ada Comstock scholars, older women who were returning to their undergraduate studies after working or raising families.

With short black hair, fair skin, shiny black eyes, this woman was smart, forceful, and armed with facts that supported her pro-Castro opinions. By the end of dinner, we were deep into our debate about the validity of the revolution. Was it worth the costs? Most of the other people at that table had left us to our self-destruction, but a handful remained, eager to see who'd eat whom.

I kept coming back to the lack of individual human rights, the basic freedoms each human being deserves. I was tired but almost shaking with the need to convince her that losing those rights wasn't worth the gains the revolution had made in some areas of health care and education.

"What about the basic freedom of knowing you'll have food on the table each night?" she said. "Homeless or starving people don't care about freedom of the press." Her eyes glistened in the candle-light, intense.

She responded to anything I said with a question, putting me on the defensive. I started to return the favor. "But don't you think a free press helps ensure that homeless and starving people get the attention they deserve? Shouldn't people be able to choose their leaders, be able to leave their country if they oppose their government—or for any reason—without the government's permission? Cubans lost that right with the revolution. If you want or need to leave this country, you can. You get a passport, buy a ticket, and leave. What economic gain is worth losing that freedom?"

"But I am *not* free to leave my country!" she said. "What if I don't have enough money to buy a ticket, because I'm a waitress, poor, and don't—can't—earn enough? You're so privileged—bourgeoisie—you can't even see inequality." She pushed away from the table and stood up.

I stood too. My hands trembled. "Then you can look for other work or work extra hours. You have a way—at least a chance—to eliminate the financial obstacles. Your government doesn't stand in your way. Freedom of movement. It's a basic human right."

We were in the hall by then, our small audience clustered around us. She swung from my side and stood in front of me.

"Listen to you! You have no idea how poor people struggle. You're obsessed with Castro. Every Cuban exile is. He restored dignity to Cubans, gave them back their power—freed them from foreign exploitation, colonialism. He delivered free education and health care, and provided jobs and homes for every citizen. If all of those life-saving changes cost a few civil liberties, so what? So the wealthy elite left, so what?" She stood in front of me in the long hall of floor-to-ceiling windows, her feet spread, hands clenched. Her backpack swung wildly on her back as she gestured. "Study your own history!"

She turned around and walked away. Got the last word. Whooped me good.

Worst of all, she was right, on one point at least: I needed to learn more, to learn to look at things from the other side.

I was willing, but I was surrounded by students and faculty who shared the Ada's point of view about Cuba. Why bother to fight this battle? I'd only end up like this: shaking with frustration and haunted by failure.

But I knew why. The *viejos*. Their story needed to be told. Even if no one changed her mind, I'd honor the *viejos'* story.

Later that night, a question nagged at me. Why had I left my most powerful arrow unused? I could have described our barrio origins, our own working-class story, the hardship we endured after the revolution—*because* of the revolution—in both countries. Was it a deliberate choice or an oversight in the midst of grappling with the hard-fighting Ada? Was I so insecure about my place at Smith that I couldn't reveal my family's humble roots—that we knew what it was like to live at the bottom of a society, to lose your home, to live with hunger of all kinds?

28

Silvia, This Isn't Living

Juanelo, 1965

One year into their lives as *gusanos*, my parents' situation looked hopeless. Other families who'd drawn higher numbers in the *permiso* lottery had received their exit visas. Had their paperwork been lost? Maybe a bureaucrat who had an old grudge against our family was stalling the process. The day they'd applied for the *permiso*, Papi had recognized one of the Ministry workers, a former baseball umpire he'd clashed with at games. Was he the reason behind the delay?

There'd never been a guarantee that they'd get out, but my parents had never expected to see families with higher *permiso* numbers leaving before them.

My parents were jobless now, and, as *gusanos*, prohibited from earning money in any way. They'd saved a little before applying to leave the country, but they were burning through those reserves. They relied on their families' donations of food, money, and clothes during the three years of waiting. They worried about food, in particular, constantly. Where would there be a delivery of meat, or potatoes, or eggs? Would they reach the front of the line before the *bodeguero* ran out? How would they pay for their rations?

With five mouths to feed—my brother Sergito was born soon after my father worried about the defective Russian condoms—Mami, Papi, and Abuela grew more daring in their search for food. Papi started selling anything he could on the black market, including the rubber gaskets and parts his father, Abuelo Manolo, made with his rubber press. With the severe shortage of parts for cars and buses, the government allowed Abuelo Manolo to make the parts for the regime. Papi took full advantage of that press. He knew that if one of his buyers denounced him, he'd be jailed and our *permiso* application mostly likely revoked. No one understood the exact rules surrounding an exit visa process that was completely hidden from view.

Abuela and Mami learned to stretch every ingredient and dish to last as long as possible. They watered down every soup, pottage, even milk—especially milk. Only children under seven were allowed milk rations, and both my brother and I guzzled the stuff.

Abuela also learned to cheat—altering the shopkeepers' tallies in our ration book so we could return to buy more than we were allotted.

The daily struggle to survive didn't make my parents immune to the erosion of civic freedoms. They knew of homosexuals who'd been sent to government rehabilitation camps to be "cured." The irascible Chíviri was serving a three-year sentence in the notorious La Cabaña prison for trying to escape by boat. He was joined there by another neighborhood friend, Dr. Roche, the doctor who'd supplied my mother with medicine and supplies for the rebels during the revolution. No one knew what he'd done, exactly, but some said that his name had appeared on a list found on the body of another "traitor."

Of all the government's abuses, one stood apart from the rest for my parents.

My mother first heard about her cousin Omar from her godmother Hortensia, the conduit to her paternal family. Mami had been looking forward to visiting her godmother, but she came back to Juanelo that day shaking with anger.

Omar was sixteen, an excellent high school student, and a devout

Jehovah's Witness, like the rest of his family. At the end of one school day, instead of Omar walking through the family's front door, several of his friends burst in, breathless but spitting out details and anger. Officials from UMAP, the regime's reeducation labor camps, had arrived in their class that afternoon and accused Omar of failing to register for military service. Omar had admitted to not registering, citing his religious beliefs, including the restriction from wearing a uniform, saluting a flag, etc., and the officers had taken him prisoner and dragged him away as his teacher and classmates looked on. His mother had gone from one police station to another and to detention centers and prisons, asking for information about him, but gotten no answers from the officials.

Several weeks passed before someone told Omar's mother he was in one of the rehabilitation work camps in Camagüey, more than three hundred miles from Havana. She managed to get there and was granted a short visit with her son. She waited a long time before they brought him out. They presented him to her completely naked. He was skeletal, his face so empty of expression that for a moment she thought they had the wrong boy. She looked at the guard in horror, and he told her, "Well, his religion prohibits him from wearing a uniform."

Abuela and Tía tried to calm Mami as she finished telling them about Omar. My mother didn't want comfort. The tension of everyday life, the worry about the *permiso*, the harassment on the street, Tía and Tío's support of the revolution—all of that disappeared as she thought about Omar who was surviving on the occasional rotten egg they fed him, filthy water, and what was left of his faith. She bit back rage and fought her innate urge to fight injustice, stupidity, cruelty. Such a fight would not only be futile for Omar but also disastrous for our family.

Omar's story stayed with Mami through those brutal, hungry days, a searing example of the regime's lack of humanity.

Radio Bemba said the conditions in the camps were a horror, but it would be years—well into our American lives—before my family would learn details of the regime's programs to realign people considered to be counter-revolutionary or sexual deviants. In all, thirty thousand young people were interned, working in the fields cutting sugar cane from day to night, fed foul food—when they were fed at all—given contaminated water, and housed in cramped, rat-infested barracks. How poorly they fared depended on the guards' moods and their own rebellious spirit.

I imagine Mami haunted by the details of Omar's story as she stood in food lines with us. I remember the curbsides where Sergito and I played as the women stood waiting for their rations. Usually we lined up at our assigned bodega, where Antonio el Bodeguero, as he was known throughout Juanelo, dispensed what he'd received in the last shipment of food and noted the amounts in each family's ration book.

Sometimes, we'd end up at other, distant bodegas in line for surprise deliveries of anything from cooking oil to lentils. The women from our barrio had an extra worry on those days: Would the *bodeguero* favor the local families in his measurements and distribution? Mami played games with us as we waited, to keep us from fighting or running off. In one, we competed to see how long we could wrap our arms around our bodies and stay still. Mami would start the game with the call: "*¡Amarrense los brazos, a ver quien gana!*"

Tío Manolo used to say in those days that there are many kinds of hunger. The one that crawled into our stomachs that summer of 1965 clawed at us in a way we would remember for a long time.

For Mami, the worst stretch of hunger started with a dropped bag of lentils. We'd walked to a neighboring barrio and were in a line at an unfamiliar bodega. We'd been standing more than an hour and were nearing the front of the line when a woman began to complain loudly about the quality of the lentils. The *bodeguero* looked too tired to care and continued with the next sale. The woman threw the wormy lentils on the sidewalk and stormed away from the food line, but Mami swept the little beans into a pile with her feet, pushed us to the ground, and told us to scoop them into her purse.

Back home, she reported the good news to Abuela: we had a bounty of lentils for a pottage. Mami dumped the lentils from her purse into a pot, then opened the large bag she'd just bought. She and Abuela jumped back at the same time. Worms wriggled through the lentils. Black dots of something, maybe another kind of insect, covered every one of them.

But there was nothing else to eat—so they washed the lentils repeatedly, cooked them as long as possible, skimmed more bugs off, and served them to Sergito and me. Mami, Abuela, and Papi didn't eat that night, or the next, but by the third night, tired of the stale bread and the desiccated yams they'd scrounged up, they dug right in. "*Estábamos peor que las putas en cuaresma*," Mami said of those days. Maybe we *were* worse off than whores during Lent.

Abuela and Mami faced another problem around that same time. Blanquita, the stray who'd never left our porch, was heavily pregnant. Several of the puppies in her last litter had been stillborn, which had made the job of finding homes for the others easier. Now they worried that Blanquita, who'd proven to be a selfless mother, would die during the birth or trying to nurse another litter. Abuela described how it hurt to see Blanca walk, her hip bones protruding like blades, the vertebrae and ribs gliding under her white fur.

Mami listened to Blanca's claws clicking across the tiled floor in the middle of the night and knew. Earlier that week, she had used old rags to make a bed under the laundry sink in the alley behind the house. Blanquita had already taken to resting there. Mami sat by Blanca, stroking her side, as her puppies were born. Then, barely able to see through her tears, she picked up each puppy and drowned it in the pail of water she'd set next to Blanca's bed. Some, she was almost sure, were already dead, but she couldn't lie to herself about the others.

As Blanca rested, Mami wrapped the puppies in rags and walked to a sandy lot at the end of our street, where she buried them. When she was done, she carried Blanca inside and set her down next to her bed on some clean rags, hoping they'd both fall asleep.

At some point the next day, Mami walked into her bedroom and felt her heart drop. Blanca lay at the foot of the bed panting. She'd found her puppies, dug them up, and placed them in a pile on top of my parents' bed.

Mami felt she had failed us all—her children, and now Blanca and her puppies too. She saw nothing hopeful on the horizon, only struggle and a life that was stifling her. She'd always been optimistic by nature. This new, bleak mindset felt foreign and useless. The negative thinking only made things worse, but every time she dug for something good, she came up empty.

Of all the ongoing worries, one rose high above the others: If Tía didn't apply for her *permiso* by the time we got ours—*if* we got ours— would Abuela break her promise to leave with us? Abuela was already shaky about leaving Cuba, and if Tía was not planning to join us, Abuela would have to choose between her two daughters.

When I picture Mami grappling with all of these problems, I wonder how she persevered.

"What choice did I have?" she said. "A mother does what she has to do for her children. That's it."

29
Push Me, Pull Me

Hunt Street, Spring 1981

The six or seven old Cubans sitting in our living room weren't used to answering questions one at a time. They looked miserable, like school children kept in for detention. I was trying to collect their first-person accounts of life after the revolution for my twenty-page economics paper on the rationing system, but they kept veering off topic. They wanted me to tell my professor about the public denunciations, the strong-arming of the *comités*, the arbitrary arrests.

"They threw me in the stadium," Fernando said. The always smiling, rotund sixty-year-old smoked nonstop, an ashtray always perched on his thigh. "It was during Playa Girón—Bay of Pigs. Everybody knew I was a bad revolutionary. I hated volunteering. In I went. It was packed. We were in there for twelve days."

"I know. Awful." I turned to one of the women. "Now, Elena, you were telling me about the *libreta* . . ."

Fernando's wife was just as round and cheery as her husband. She slid her glasses back up the bridge of her nose. "Ay, Anita, I can still see that ration book, each page of it, in my mind. What was in it? Every basic necessity you can think of. Open up one of your grandmother's cupboards. Every little can, bottle, pouch, spice, was in that book. Cooking oil, sugar—imagine, sugar rationed in a country full of sugar cane—coffee, rice, soap, detergent, even matches."

"No. Matches weren't rationed. Were they?" Armando, the carpenter, said.

Elena shook her head. "Of course they were. What would you know about the *libreta*? It was the women, Anita, who dealt with those problems."

I told the old Cubans what my professor had said in defense of the rationing system—that we have our own rationing system in the States, which is that we have to pay for items on store shelves.

"The problem with that explanation," someone said, "is that Cubans have a *double* rationing system. They have to pay for their rations—they're not free."

The *libreta* discussion bored my father. "Imagine," he said, "some of her professors actually go to Cuba for those economic planning sessions!" His arms were crossed over his chest, stunned disbelief all over his face. "I'm paying them to educate my daughter, but look what they believe in. That school—well, at least you're not drawing naked men anymore." He looked around the room. "Did I tell you about that?"

Papi was still trying to understand how a college would expose young women to naked men in a drawing class.

"Imagine," he said, "a completely naked, saggy, old, skinny *viejo*, walking around with his thing barely covered, talking to these young girls. What kind of country is this?"

"It's a free and open one," Tía said from her chair. "You should be proud, Anita, to be sketching a nude man. Think of the centuries that it's been the other way around, men drawing naked women. It's about time."

My father smirked. "I'm not sure what offends me more, the naked man or the communist professor. I'll think about it."

One day in the middle of my last semester at Smith, I found myself sitting between two friends, Nancy and Ellen, in the back row of their economics lecture. They'd invited me, concerned that the talk about post-revolutionary Cuba the professor was slated to give would be highly biased.

I raised my hand repeatedly as Professor X skipped or misrepresented key parts of that day's topic, the Bay of Pigs Invasion.

"The United States bombed Havana . . ." he said.

This was inaccurate, at best. To his credit, after I spent a few minutes with my hand in the air he called on me. Nancy and Ellen shifted in their chairs.

"Professor, the invasion force was made up of Cuban exiles," I said. "A few bombs were dropped on a military airstrip on the outskirts of Havana. So to say that the US bombed Havana misrepresents—"

"Well, I think it's close enough to paint the picture," he said, and continued proselytizing, scrubbing a nuanced story into a simple David-vs.-Goliath, Heroic-Castro-against-Imperialist-America fairy tale.

I lost it again when he described pre-revolutionary Cuba in the '50s under Batista.

"In those days," he said, "Cuban women had two choices of occupation: seamstress or prostitute."

I looked around as the Smithies bent over their notebooks, pens flying, capturing his words. I perched on the tip of my chair. My heart knocked around in my chest. I waved my hand in the air like I was drowning. I thought of Mami, Tía, Abuela—all the barrio women who had worked in factories, in stores, in schools. *Prostitutes!?* I wanted to scream about the robust Cuban economy of the '50s, the country's high economic development rankings, the factories in Juanelo where so many of the strong women in our barrio had worked. But the professor had heard enough from me. He invited me to come talk to him after class.

More than angry, more than frustrated, I felt betrayed. Smith celebrated critical thinking, taught us to question everything, to dig behind accepted truths. We had been staring at the crux—and told to look away. What was the point of debating the professor in his office if the other students missed the exchange and the chance to ask their own questions?

After steaming for a day or two, I decided to visit a senior member of the economics department who specialized in Cuba.

People said he was brilliant but arrogant, dedicated to his field and his political views. Cuba was his baby. I thought I had my facts and numbers together as I walked into his office.

The handsome bugger sat behind his desk in the small office and listened as I described Professor X's lecture. What could be done to correct the inaccuracies and obvious bias?

He stretched his arms up over his head, laid his hands on his thick black hair. "What did your father do in Cuba?"

"My father?" Where was he heading? "He worked in a factory."

He thought for a moment. "You said your mother worked?"

"Teacher. We were working class, if that's what you are getting at."

"Well, they had jobs. That in and of itself put them ahead of a lot of people during Batista. Your father worked for an American company, you said?"

"Continental Can."

"So he benefited from American business."

"Can we get back to Professor X's lecture?"

He smiled. "You know, you really shouldn't worry about him corrupting students in a forty-eight-minute lecture. After twenty years of privileged living, Smithies can benefit from that kind of talk." He rose, thanked me for coming, and showed me to the door.

I actually shook his hand on the way out. It happened so fast. All that time preparing for a debate that never developed. He had knowledge, power, credentials, and I didn't. What had I thought would come of my bone-headed crusade? Why was I battling their point of view so passionately?

I walked back across campus in my borrowed businesslike shoes and blazer, angry at myself for wasting time and energy and looking like a fool in front of Mr. Economics himself. Worst, though, was feeling I'd again failed to tell the *viejos'* side of the story—Juanelo's side, *my* side.

I didn't have time for impossible missions. I was correcting papers for Spanish professors, hunting for jobs in New York, finishing papers, studying for exams, and trying not to think about how I was going to pay off my college loans.

Going into the last stretch of senior year, Mami dropped her own little bomb on me. I'd been excited about my job interviews with New York bankers on campus. I dreamed of getting into one of their training programs and moving to Manhattan, where several Smith friends were headed. Mami suggested another path: stay in the Boston area.

She was apologetic, understanding that she was asking me to let go of a dream, but she was also insistent. "I want you and your sister to really get to know each other, to bond," she said. "You've been gone for so long. The eight-year age difference seems big, but the older you get, the less that number will matter."

I couldn't remember the last time Mami had stood in the way of any of my goals. My heart broke as she went on.

"In life, a woman needs a sister—especially later in life," she said. "You'll need each other one day, more than you can know right now. And a bond doesn't just happen. You have to make it happen."

I made promises about visiting often, that eventually I'd end up in Boston. But even I could hear the hesitation in my voice.

How could I ignore Mami's gentle plea? She and the *viejos* lived with family at the core of their lives, had fought to stay together, had protected that bond. That clear, simple value shaped everything I cherished too.

I let the image of me walking around Midtown in a business suit fade away into the warm nights of that senior spring. I needed to stop belittling Boston, looking down on it like so many of my New York classmates, and try it on for size. I'd interviewed with a Boston software consulting firm. Maybe that would be the answer, if they offered me anything.

I waited inside the phone cubby in the middle of my dorm hall. How many Sunday nights had I spent in this tiny space, rattling away in Spanish to Tía, or Mami, or Abuela during our weekly call? With graduation just weeks away, this would be one of the last calls.

I held the phone close to my ear, knowing I'd never forget this moment.

"Are you ready?" I asked Mami on the other end of the line. "Is Papi on?"

"I'm here." He sounded far away.

"I got it! The Boston consulting job! I start the first week of June!"

Shouting and hoots came over the line. I heard voices cheering in the background as Mami filled them in.

As the hubbub died down, Papi asked the most important question for him: "How much is this computer company going to pay you?"

"They're giving me eighteen thousand dollars and two weeks' vacation—and health insurance!"

"*¡Qué premio!*" Mami said.

I waited for Papi's reaction but only heard a heavy silence for a long beat.

His voice was low and quiet when he finally spoke. "*Mija, te felicito.* Congratulations. You are earning more than I earn. Your mother was right to let you go to that school. I'm so proud."

The sadness in his voice surprised me. I knew he was thrilled for me, but what would that feel like—to know that your daughter, just graduated, earned more than you, her father? Papi was seeing the fruit of his labor, my education and what it brought me, but also how far from the starting line he had been—would always be.

"Anyway, Mami, looks like you'll get your wish," I said quickly, wanting to change the subject. "I'll be back in the house, at least for a while."

"Mija, you're going to save so much money and time, believe me. What apartment comes with an *abuela* cooking and doing laundry for you? I've got numbers for a couple of vanpools that go into downtown Boston every day." I could hear her smile.

"This isn't for too long, Mami," I reminded her. "Maybe a year, no more. I'm going to live in Boston eventually."

"We'll see. You might realize how great it is to live at home."

She was already trying to tie me to Hunt Street. Exactly what I'd feared. I knew I'd have to break her heart sooner or later, and Tía and Abuela's too. Wasn't it enough that I had agreed to go back for a while? They'd always want me to stay at home, the Cuban way. I'd already given up New York City and living with friends in Boston. Now Mami was raising the bar.

I shook off the urge to argue with her. This would be an ongoing battle. I should save my strength.

Papi jumped in, sounding more like himself again. "Let's get a softball game going when we're there for graduation. Get the *chiquitas* together. I'll bring balls and gloves."

"They'll love that! I'll reserve a field. Maybe we can get the grandmothers out there."

We chuckled at that idea, but Mami's comments stuck with me. They showed me that even though they'd loosened up, the *viejos* would always want me to hew to the old world more than I ever could. At some level, I'd always disappoint them by choosing values and priorities that were foreign to them. Now, I'd set an unrealistic expectation by sticking to Boston and living at home.

Instead of heading out to create my own first home and starting my own life, I was walking right back into the confines of a Cuban home. Breaking away again would be a wrestling match between my three mothers and me—I could see that already.

Mami and Tía should have understood. Hadn't they left everything they knew for freedom? What if Tío Manolo, or Tina, or the rest of the family had tied them down instead of letting them choose for themselves how to live—*where* to live?

To stay or to break away? That question had shaped the *viejos'* lives after the revolution, when the Cuba they'd known crumbled around them, forcing them to choose one life or another. And just as I doubted my choice as I graduated from Smith, the *viejos* had doubted theirs, in varying degrees and for different reasons.

Especially Papi, who, doubting our *permiso* would ever arrive, had for a while considered another way out of Cuba.

30

Chucho's Plea

Güines, Cuba, 1965

I studied Chucho's fingers out of the corner of my eye. His hands gripped the steering wheel, but some of the fingers didn't make it all the way around—the fat nubs sat on top.

Chucho had come for Papi and me early that morning for a visit to his family's farm—twenty miles southeast of Juanelo, at the top of the Loma de la Candela—and now I sat wedged between the two men in the front seat of Chucho's ancient "Olmobí" (as Papi still pronounces it). Chucho and my father had worked together at the cannery, Chucho on the die cutters, Papi on a forklift, but they hadn't seen each other in a while—not since my parents had applied for their *permiso* and Papi had lost his job.

Most of my father's friends from the factory had chopped off a finger or two over the years. Their mangled nubs—some rounded and smooth, some lumpy with leftover flesh—looked naked to me. They terrified and fascinated me, and given my height, I often found myself at eye level with the monstrosities.

Sitting next to Chucho that day, I faced one of my worst nightmares: brushing up against *fábrica* fingers.

Chucho was in trouble. He chafed under the control of the new revolutionary bosses at the factory. They knew little about running the factory, carried guns, and demanded more than just fingers and sweat from the workers: they also needed volunteers for armed night guard duty, marchers at parades, people at Fidel's speeches, sugar-cutting brigades. Chucho simply refused, time and again, in his quiet, stoic way. So they harassed him—followed him around the factory, and outside it as well. Chucho, like our irreverent neighbor Chíviri, retaliated with skillful sabotage. No one ever caught him. All they found were the hammers that had been thrown into machines, the screwdrivers stuck inside assembly belts.

Chíviri had escaped punishment for his anti-revolutionary attitude for a long time, purely because he was such a good mechanic, but he was locked inside La Cabaña prison now, serving a three-year sentence for having tried to escape Cuba by boat. His "partners" in the escape had turned out to be undercover policemen. He was arrested as soon as he arrived at the launch site in the middle of the night. Now, Chucho was on his own.

Papi admired Chucho's courage, so when he offered to take Papi to his family's farm on his day off, Papi had accepted. Plus, Papi would get points for taking me off my mother's hands and have a shot at bringing home a few vegetables for dinner—as long as the government's *comisario* wasn't at the farm and our *comité* president didn't stop Papi to inspect the bag when we got home.

Chucho's farm centered around two *bohíos*. The thatched-roof, dirt-floor shacks were tucked close together near the road. They only had an outhouse, which I refused to enter until I saw there was no other option. As a reward for my bravery, Chucho's mother gave me one of best things I have ever tasted: perfectly ripened *mamey*. She cradled the *mamey* in her hand, sliced it neatly in half, and fed me spoonfuls of the sugary red fruit.

As I savored each drop, a rambunctious white dog skittered around me on the dirt floor. When I was done eating, I dedicated myself to wrestling and harassing that poor animal. Years later, I learned that what I'd thought was a dog had actually been a baby goat, and Chucho's mother had been feeding me goat milk chasers all day long.

When Papi kissed Chucho's mother hello that day, she scolded him gently. "Why would you bring your *niñita*? You know he's always taking chances."

Papi wondered what she meant. Maybe Chucho was causing trouble with the *comisario*?

"The police could show up any minute," she continued. "Maybe they'll take the farm from us once and for all or throw us all in jail . . ."

The old woman's sorrow weighed on Papi for a long, long time. That afternoon, though, his mind filled with other worries as Chucho complained about the shortages of everything and the dwindling options he saw for himself in the new Cuba.

At one point, the two men found themselves talking about steak. They couldn't avoid the topic as they leaned against a fence, admiring the family's last few cattle roaming in the small pasture. The animals' humped backs swayed as they kicked at the dry grass. The men's mouths watered as they remembered steak dinners full of garlic and lime, black beans and rice, sweet fried plantains.

"All this meat walking around and no way to enjoy a steak without the government's permission," Chucho said.

Papi turned his back to the animals. "Let's talk about something else. We're torturing ourselves."

Chucho walked Papi toward a shed full of tools and old machinery. They worked together, organizing equipment, oiling rusty tools, trying to forget their steak fantasies. For Chucho, the factory generated plenty of other topics.

"Guess how many workers we've got now?" he asked.

Papi considered. "Weren't we at four hundred when they threw me out?"

"Now it's eight hundred."

"*¡Coñó!*"

"What's happening with that—with your *permiso*?"

"Not a damn thing. It's been . . . a year—no, a little more." Papi thought about the number on our *permiso* form, and how many of our *gusano* neighbors with higher numbers had received their exit papers. "That can't be good, *verdad*?" he said. "Maybe they passed over us."

Chucho must have seen the despair on Papi's face. "It'll come, you'll see." He turned back to the safer topic. "We're bumping heads at the same machines all day now. Three of us at the same station: one doing the training, one doing the work, and one watching to make sure no one sabotages the line."

As they laughed, Papi remembered Chucho's armed guard duty problems.

"They keep harassing me," Chucho said, "and I keep refusing." He grabbed more tools off the shed wall, handed them to Papi. "It's not just that I don't want to help them. *Mi vieja* needs me here on weekends."

Chucho set a box on the floor and pulled out an old fishing net. Papi helped him spread it over the ground.

"They're not going to stop until I do the guard duty." Chucho stared at the worn net for a long moment. "I don't know how much more I can take . . ."

Papi heard a new gravity in Chucho's voice. He tried to lighten the mood. "*Coño*, Chucho. Look at this thing. There are more holes than net."

Chucho didn't laugh. "Radio Bemba says they'll give my shift to a 'good revolutionary' unless I volunteer for *some*thing," he said as he wound rope around a big wooden spool. Then he turned to the problems under the regime's new rules. "My mother can only sell her pigs and tomatoes to the *comisario*. The government sets the prices, buys what it wants, when it wants." He churned through restriction after restriction, each one adding tension to his voice. "And the *comisario* has an inventory of everything. If we sell anything on our own— he finds out." The words boiled out of him. "Seeing my *vieja* battling all of this . . ." He threw the spool into a box. "We're drowning!"

The look of desperation on Chucho's face scared Papi. Chucho was normally measured, calm, even when the new bosses harassed him. "Think of your family, Chucho," he pleaded with his friend. "You have to do things the safe way."

"Who do you think I'm thinking about?" Chucho leaned toward Papi. "I have to talk to you about something. Listen to me carefully . . ."

Later that afternoon, Chucho drove us over dirt roads and paths to a beach on a river. Papi's heart dropped when he saw the boat floating in the shallow water. He studied the boat as I settled in to dig in the sand.

"That's not the boat, right?" he asked.

"It's my old man's," Chucho said. "It's solid. Trust me."

Papi walked up to his knees in the water, ran his hands along the boat's wooden hull. "Paint's peeling. It doesn't even have a roof!" He pictured Chucho out on the ocean on this thing, and it hit him: this was going to happen. Papi knew of people who'd escaped by boat, but this was his friend. He felt helpless, knowing this was the reality they both faced and there was no end in sight.

Then a new fear snuck in: Would he be driven to this same desperate act if things didn't work out with the *permiso*?

Chucho knocked on the splintered hull. "The motor's strong. It's going to get me out of here. When I get to the United States, I can work on getting my family out. It's the only way."

Papi's eyes widened. "You're going to row this thing by yourself? You've got to get out a couple of miles before you turn on the motor . . ."

"If you were with me—"

"Me! *¿Tú estás loco?* You know I'm waiting for my *permiso*."

Chucho was taking a major risk not just with the plan but also by telling Papi about it, bringing him here. Now Papi knew too much about an illegal plan, one that likely would end with Chucho drowning, in jail, or executed—not living free in Miami like he thought. But in a corner of Papi's mind, he was turning over Chucho's plan and wondering if, with the two of them on that boat, it could work.

Chucho lifted me up onto the boat and let me walk around, pulling me back when I went too far. "And what if you never get the *permiso*?"

"*Coño*, didn't you just tell me back there to be patient?" Papi had two conversations going on in his head, one trying to dissuade Chucho and one wondering if he should join him. "Look, I know you'd die for me . . . but my kids are younger than yours. I can't leave them. And Consuelo already said—no child of hers goes out on that ocean. I'm waiting for my *permiso* and flying out of here with my family." But the more Papi spoke, the more seaworthy the boat looked.

"I'm getting out," Chucho said. "I'm taking a little gold jewelry to get me started over there. And my father gave me a revolver—for sharks, of course, I'm not going to—"

"A gun! And gold? They catch you with either of those, and trying to escape on top of it—think, Chucho!"

"I *am* thinking, *¡coño!*"

The two men stared at each other for a minute.

When he spoke again, Chucho was quiet, resolute. "I'm leaving."

Papi was done arguing, at least with his friend. In his own head, the doubting continued. He heard the worry in his friend's voice, saw the question still filling his eyes. He wanted to ease Chucho's mind. "I'll think about it."

"I have to solve this soon, Sergio."

Papi shook his head and pulled me out of the boat, and we walked back through the sand to the car.

We drove home in silence, the caimito and *flamboyan* trees encircling us on both sides of the road, almost shutting out the sun.

The whole way back to Juanelo, Papi wondered if he'd just passed up his last chance to get us out of Cuba.

No one in Papi's circle ever heard from Chucho again. The rumors were always the same, though: They caught him right away, not far from where he launched his boat. Alone. People said he ended up in La Cabaña prison and that he was executed not long after he got there.

"You didn't try to visit his family to find out what happened?" I asked Papi decades later.

"*Ay*, Anita." Papi looked at his hands, gnarled fingers spread wide. He rapped them on the table. "When someone got caught like that everybody turned into Peter denying Christ. Out of fear. No one went near the family. I was avoiding going out on the street by then. We were already targets. Revolutionaries and the secret police roamed the streets looking for men during the day. They'd ask for work IDs. If you didn't have one, they knew you were a *gusano*. They'd accuse you of treason or *peligrosidad*—dangerousness—whatever the hell they wanted. No. I didn't go back to his mother's house."

Forty years later and fifteen hundred miles from Juanelo, I heard something catch in my father's voice. It was more than just sadness. It was shame.

31

Who Do You Think You Are?

Boston, Massachusetts, Fall 1984

King's Chapel's two hundred-year-old cemetery was just below my office window, its tilting, eroding tombstones apt emblems of my new job. Most of the other college hires in my training group took to programming like hungry little puzzle solvers. They tucked their pencils behind their ears, flipped through scrolls of printouts, delighted in elegant, nested if-then statements. I scrunched down and flailed away, a blind woman bumping her way through a room full of pointy furniture.

I made up for my lack of coding skills with the steely work ethic I'd inherited from the *viejos*. I came in early and stayed late. Client billing was the name of the game in a consulting firm, so I billed away and prayed that my bizarre code wouldn't bring down some unsuspecting insurance company. The *viejos* were never far from my mind—their quest for overtime hours, extra shifts, second jobs. *Look what they had to put up with*, I told myself. *Lucky girl.*

The firm's higher-ups tsk-tsked when they found out that not only was I living in another state, I was also vanpool dependent. "Why should they care where you live?" Mami said when I told her. "Or how you get home? What does it matter, if you get the work done?"

But Mami's honest, practical thinking was from another world.

I'd learned by then that the owner of the firm had deliberately hired new college grads from out of town—and often state—to guarantee fewer ties to home and more to work, and to him. He was pulling in the opposite direction from the *viejos*. The office reeked of his power plays. He stoked rivalries and broke up alliances, creating a corporate minefield for rookies like me. But I was grateful for the prize I had in front of me as a first-generation college graduate and former refugee: I was both paying off my loans and helping my family a bit by living at home.

The *viejos* puzzled over my long hours without pay, but not over the hard work. They cheered my commitment and supported me in different ways. Abuela had breakfast on the table when I came down every morning at five thirty. She ironed my blouses and suits and put them on hangers each night. Tía and Mami debriefed me every night, pointing out the positives and laughing off the negatives.

I'd known from the start that I'd appreciate Abuela's meals and laundry help, but the impact of those nightly morale boosts by the formidable women who'd raised me surprised me. I thought the lack of privacy and independence of living at home would be suffocating; instead, it was sustaining. This hidden jewel was tipping the scales in the *viejos'* favor and making me doubt—sometimes—my plan to move out as soon as possible. Hunt Street had become a haven from a corporate world that baffled me on good days and flattened me on bad ones.

Cuba kept coming up with my new colleagues and clients. When my unusual last name or deep summer tan drew questions, I was happy to identify myself as Cuban American. Finally, the *viejos'* decades-long effort to nurture pride in our heritage and hold on to our language, my evolution at Smith, and the commitment I felt to tell the "other side" of the Cuban story had all aligned.

When my name or color didn't lead to talking about Cuba, the headlines often did. Cuba remained the little mouse that roared in the mid-'80s. Mariel was still in the news, at least in Florida. Cuba's militarization and involvement in foreign conflicts—it had stationed personnel in more than thirty countries and had a military presence in dozens more—drew a lot of debate. Coast Guard cutters, cruise ships, and weekend boaters still plucked Cuban refugees out of the Florida Straits regularly, as they had ever since the revolution. And Cuba's heavily USSR-subsidized economy attracted frequent analysis by the international press.

Americans' general curiosity about Cuba energized me—at times maybe too much. I started to notice a distance that a few people in top management put up when I talked about my link to these topics. A slight change in tone, a sideways look, a repressed thought or emotion that lurked beneath the white collars.

One afternoon, a top executive showed me what that emotion looked like when it seeped out. We were alone in his office, wrapping up a meeting. My Cuban background came up, or I referred to it somehow. He stopped talking and looked at me for an uncomfortably long moment. He leaned over his desk, squinting.

"Why do you *insist* on referring to yourself like that?" he demanded.

"Like what?"

"Like you're a minority. Why do you call yourself Cuban American? You're American. Look at you!" There was no mistaking it; even though he was grinning, Rick was angry.

"Because. I am—"

"Oh, come on! Don't tell me you consider yourself a minority. Or Cuban."

"But . . . those are facts, Rick. I'm both of those things."

"You've lived here practically your whole life!"

The surprised confusion on my face shook him away from his

questioning. He leaned back in his chair and laughed. "Whatever. I don't see you that way. I really don't know why you do."

I left his office stunned, almost reeling. His aggression proved he'd been bothered about my self-identification for a while. Just as at Smith, when some students reminded me that I wasn't white (because I am Latina) and others that I wasn't dark enough to understand the challenges faced by people of color, Rick was telling me how to fit his notion of what Hispanics were like. But I didn't want to play, and he didn't like it.

Rick outranked me in every way—age, status, experience, wealth. I'd seen the irritation on his face; it scared me, but I felt I'd held my own little piece of ground, and the more I thought about it, the happier I was that I'd pushed back.

That night, when I told the *viejos* the story, Tía and Mami paused for a minute to consider the executive's point of view.

"But you are *both*," Tía said. "You are Cuban, and you are American." She was using the plain logic she lived by. "I don't see the issue."

Mami shook her head. "You don't fit his idea of what a Latina is. That's his problem, not yours."

Tía's face hardened. "Don't ever let anyone tell you what it takes to be Cuban. That's what the revolution tried to do to us."

32

Hand Me That Microphone

Juanelo, 1966

When Mami walked into the *comité* meeting that night, everyone knew three things: she was not a revolutionary, this was not her *comité*, and people still respected her in the barrio.

She'd just stormed out our front door, leaving Papi in charge of putting Sergito and me to sleep. We'd all been in bed together, my parents begging us to close our eyes for the night and the two of us fighting to stay awake—easier than usual that night, since angry shouts kept pounding through the open window above our bed—when she decided she'd had enough.

The *comité* of a nearby block had attracted an oversize crowd to a special meeting that night, and they'd moved the gathering to the courtyard next to our house to accommodate the numbers. The meeting was to denounce the principal of a local grammar school.

As the accusations blasted out of the loudspeakers, Mami had muttered her own responses, each one louder than the one before. She knew the principal. Conchita had been kind and fair to her when she worked at her school.

As Mami tossed on the bed, Papi tried to calm her. He knew what she was thinking, but our family didn't need more attention. We were already branded *gusanos*. If Mami managed to get a hold of that mic and the crowd turned on her, he'd have no choice but to run over and stand with her. More than just stand. He didn't trust his fists to stay at his side.

But Mami couldn't be calmed. Suddenly, she popped off the bed, put on her shoes, warned him not to get up, and rushed out the front door.

People were piling up at the mic when she walked into the courtyard. The loudspeaker rattled as another parent shouted that Conchita was an impediment to the revolution, completely uncooperative, suspected of anti-revolutionary beliefs, devoid of revolutionary zeal. How could she lead the school? Above all, they didn't want their children taught by Makarenkas—the very young student teachers who were replacing the experienced teachers who'd left Cuba. The principal was forcing these inept teachers on their children.

The accusations grew ridiculous. People were competing for revolutionary status and grandstanding as they excoriated the *directora*.

Mami caught the *comité* president's eye and raised her hand. Mami was a *gusana* now, but everyone knew she had fought for the revolution—and that she was Don Manuel's granddaughter, a third-generation Juanelian, and a teacher. The *comité* leader signaled her approval and Mami stepped up to the mic.

Mami introduced herself, described her revolutionary past, and delivered a long speech defending the *directora* and turning the table on the woman's accusers. The parents, Mami said, were the ones who were impeding the revolution by not accepting the reality of a teacher shortage and the only solution available: young but capable teachers working under close supervision. And the *directora* was a true professional, a fair leader, the perfect mentor for the young teachers. They were lucky to have her.

When she finished, everyone applauded.

Papi was waiting for her at the front door when she came home.

"*Estás completamente loca*," he said, wrapping her in his arms. He thought if he held her tight enough, she wouldn't notice he was shaking. "Only you could insult a hundred people and get them to applaud."

Mami had put us all at risk, but my father felt only pride. She was utterly fearless and at times stubborn beyond reason, dangerous traits in the new Cuba. But he knew that night that she was the best partner he could have chosen—not just as a wife and mother but also for the fight that lay ahead for our family.

33

Too Much but Not Enough

Hunt Street, 1985

The tangy smell of garlicky black beans greeted me like a hug when I stepped onto the porch. If I'd hit it right—I hoped I had—Abuela might have *maduros* warming on the stove.

That cold winter afternoon, the house was thrumming with the typical Sunday activity. A TV blasted in the living room, a boom box thumped somewhere else, voices fought for airtime in the kitchen, 110 canaries sang in the basement. The condensation dripping down the picture window told me the thermostat was set in the mid 70s.

The *viejos* and a few Cuban visitors were admiring a chubby baby one of the guests had plopped on top of the kitchen table. Papi rolled a tennis ball across the table and into the V of the baby's splayed legs. The little crowd cheered as the baby wobbled, reached for the ball, and picked it up. Papi was always scouting for future shortstops.

"You're never too young to field a grounder," he said, rolling the ball toward the baby. "See how he watches it as soon as it leaves my hand? Never takes his eyes off it."

Papi's eyes lit up as the baby swatted the ball and it rolled back to him. He looked like a kid himself.

"When are you going to give me one of these?" he asked, turning to me. "I don't want to be so old that I can't play ball with my grandkids."

The chatter stopped. I didn't know the visitors well. My face grew hot. My father had never said anything like that to me before.

I don't recall how I answered, but I remember the others scolding Papi for embarrassing me, then laughing it off, as I'm sure I tried to.

I heard something so pure in my father's voice—a painful earnestness, a wish deeply felt—that the moment stuck in my mind. I had plenty of childbearing years ahead of me, but Papi was watching another clock. I was late for a party I didn't know was happening.

Elliott Key, Florida

"*You* are going to need a very, very strong man," Tío Andrés said. "You're just like your mother and your aunt—opinionated, strong. You Fernández women like to argue. You need a man who will stand up to you. It'll be better that way."

The New Hampshire Cubans and the Miami Cubans were floating on the Miami Cubans' boats at Elliott Key, just outside Miami Harbor. Showered up after a day in the salt water, some people were scampering from boat to boat—visiting, listening to music—and some were dancing on the dock. The night sky was packed with stars. A warm breeze blew around us, carrying the scents of talcum powder, lotion, cologne.

I let Tío Andrés's authority hang over me, but I didn't like it. I scanned the faces of the cluster of uncles and male cousins surrounding me. They worried that at twenty-five I showed no sign of settling down. I knew they loved me, and they meant well. But I didn't need their advice.

Tío Andrés wanted the best for me, he said. "Your problem is that you're too independent. You need a man who will put parameters around you . . ."

A part of me wanted to laugh at their worries about my status as a single workingwoman, happily dating around. Another part of me wanted to smack the *machismo* out of them.

This branch of the Miami family had been worried about me for a while. I didn't wear enough makeup or believe in manicures. I acted too American and wore my clothes loose and comfortable. They saw the typical well-groomed Miami Cubana as the embodiment of refined femininity. I saw her as a beautiful, lacquered, high-heeled, walking Latina Barbie. And now my nonconformity had stretched into a happy single womanhood that unsettled the Miamians.

I listened as the *tíos* and *primos* told each other how right they were about my future. I thought of the exec in Boston, of my father's pushing for grandkids according to his timeline, and now these male relatives in a tizzy over my freewheeling unwedded-ness. Maybe it was the rum and Coke, or the beautiful night, or the safety of knowing my uncles and cousins loved me, but the demand to fit other people's definition of what it meant to be Latina suddenly overwhelmed me.

I tossed off my good girl mantle just as a couple of the male cousins were winding up for another round.

"*¡Un momento!*" I shouted.

The men stopped talking.

"I have *absolutely* no intention of being dominated by or dominating anyone. Maybe I won't even get married—who knows! And you"—I pointed at the younger cousins—"you guys were born here, or you came when you were little, so you have no excuse for this old-man Cuban thinking!" I felt the heat of that day's sun radiating off my skin.

"*Oye*," one of the old men mumbled. "I'm not old . . ."

"Okay, okay," Tío Andrés said, chuckling. "But you see what I mean about you Fernández women?"

I couldn't help but laugh, just like everyone else.

A new Cuban song poured out of the speakers on one of the boats. The Miami Cubans of all ages sang along to lyrics I didn't know. The couples stepped flawlessly to the beat, spinning away from each other, reeling each other back in. I couldn't touch that kind of dancing. I swayed from my quiet spot on the dock, content to watch from afar what could never be mine. No matter how charming their world looked at times or how well I sometimes slid into it, I knew I didn't belong.

At Smith and in New Hampshire I was a Super Cuban, but in Miami I wasn't Cuban enough. Without a Cuban American community in the North to rein me into its middle, I ran around what turned out to be its fringes. So I stumbled in Miami when I visited family, and I was always stunned to discover that I felt like a foreigner in a place that was supposed to be like home. I was out of step at both dances.

My friend Wendy and I were in our twenties; we should have been out clubbing on Saturday nights. But we were usually too exhausted to venture into Nashua's smoky discos. We preferred hanging out with the *viejos* and watching *The Golden Girls* in my parents' living room.

The old Cubans watching us lounge away our youth had other plans for us. Mami came downstairs one night after her shower and stopped on the stairs to take in the scene.

"Girrrls. You're never going to find your hosbands in here. It's nine o'clock. Put on some lipsteeck and go to that new club—the Bounty, right?" She resumed her walk around the stairs, turned off the TV, and went into the kitchen.

"Consuelo," Abuela piped up, "don't make them get up now. It's too late. Plus, like I always say, 'You meet your husband when you're at the bus stop and your hair is up in curlers.'" She nudged Tía, who got up and turned the TV back on.

Mami poked her head back into the living room. "Go! It's nine p.m., for God's sake!"

Wendy and I yawned, shook off the throws, and got up, complaining. My liberal American side, the Smith-feminist side, finally woke up. "We're not hunting 'hosbands,' Mami. We don't need—"

"And put some color on those cheeks," she called from the other room. "Have fun out there! You're not going to be twenty-five forever."

"Most guys like the natural look anyway," I mumbled.

Tía looked away from Dorothy's latest misadventure on *The Golden Girls*. She'd been listening to us after all. "*No sean come-mierdas*," she said. "If a well-dressed, well-made-up woman walks in front of a man, he's not going to think, 'Too bad she doesn't look natural.'"

My eyes narrowed. "You guys have this old Cuban view of what women—"

Mami popped back into the living room. "Now it's 9:20. Get out there, be twenty-five and dance. Paleeese."

No American mother I knew said such things. They might think it, but they just didn't go there. Tía and Mami, however, were stuck in the '50s, and no amount of debate was going to convince them. I racked this up as another Cuba vs. America battle that I'd pass on. They weren't all worth fighting. And now that we were up off our butts, dancing did sound pretty good.

Hunt Street, 1987

Abuela turned out to be right about how you meet your hosband—sort of. I met Andy when I least expected to, at a going-away party for a colleague at the Scotch and Sirloin in downtown Boston.

Within six months we were wondering if a Jewish guy from Connecticut and a Cuban girl from New Hampshire could maybe make a go of things.

I brought him up to Hunt Street to meet my family the weekend of Wendy's wedding. She'd met Rob on one of those forced Bounty Club nights, thanks to Tía and Mami's bullying. Andy, I was learning, was fearless about most things. "As long as there's a TV where I can watch the Patriots, I'll be fine," he said. I reminded him he'd be alone a fair amount while I helped Wendy get ready. "No problem."

23D Hunt Street that Friday night felt more like rush hour at Park Street Station than a post-dinner family gathering. Andy fell into the noisy groove immediately. He answered the questions flying at him from all directions and in two languages. He needed interpreters, of course, but he pulled out enough of his high school Spanish to score some extra points.

After a while, Mami looked at him with pity.

"Andy," she said, taking him aside. "Go down to the basement for a leetle while. The birds are loud, but this up here"—she swept her hand through the air—"can be overrrwhelming."

Abuela kept her Bible open on a table in the dining room my parents added onto the back of the house. Her red crystal rosary stretched neatly across the open page where she'd left off that day. Her Catholic faith had saved her—pulled her through the colossal depression after we left Cuba, out of those black winter days. She decorated her bedroom with dried palm fronds from past Palm Sundays on the walls, tiny crucifixes on the dresser, a large wooden one centered above and behind her bed. I wondered how an old traditional Cuban Catholic would accept a Jewish grandson-in-law, even one she'd grown fond of. She opened up one afternoon.

"Tell me why you two aren't engaged," she demanded. "This

Jewish business can't be as bad as what happened with your cousin Iliana and the Jehovah's Witness. We all got over that."

I described how Andy and I were still learning how the other saw the world because of our faiths—how things like crucifixes, for example, didn't mean the same thing to each of us. "So for you and me the cross, our rosaries, the little statues of la Virgen—they bring us comfort, right?" I explained. "But, for Jews, not so much. They're symbols of a group that persecuted them."

Abuela nodded and thought for a long moment. I knew that the rosaries Tía brought back from her field trips to Spain and Mexico, the vials of holy water, the tiny bottles of sand from pilgrimage sites, were handholds to her faith. Her God, her Virgin, her Cristo had given Abuela profound comfort and strength, all her life, but especially in the new world where she knew she'd be buried one day. I thought about us praying in bed, how she had taught me to turn to Cristo in times of fear or suffering. Abuela didn't just read her Bible, she brushed her fingers over its pages with a lover's touch.

Finally, she smiled. "I think I understand."

During our next visit to Hunt Street, Andy came down to breakfast stunned by the changes in Abuela's room, where he slept when he visited.

"Hippie Jesus is gone," he whispered. "The palm fronds, the painting of that bleeding heart thing with the thorns, gone. The big crucifix isn't there . . ."

After Andy left that day, I sat Abuela down. "You didn't have to do that."

"*Ay, chica.*" She patted my hand. "I don't want Andy to be uncomfortable when he's here. Now that I know how those things make him feel, I understand. Don't worry, I'll put everything back tonight."

Abuela continued to show her embrace of Andy's Judaism in the years to come, including at our wedding, where she danced the hora the mariachi band trumpeted during the cocktail hour.

I'd thought this rosary-praying, hardcore Cuban *vieja* would at least drill me with questions about the souls of our future children. Instead, she opened up her old heart. I hadn't understood until then how much that heart had been shaped by immigration, another culture, the decades of incremental adjustments needed to create a new life in a new world.

34

All the Windows Smashed

Juanelo, June 1967

When my parents heard the mob turn down Castillo, they shut off
every light in the house. As a *gusano* family, we were targeted whenever one of Fidel's speeches riled up the pro-revolutionary groups,
the *comité* gangs, the assorted, bored teenagers longing for the sanc-
tioned violence accorded during these "acts of repudiation." In our
dark living room, Sergito kept hollering and Abuela Fina kept shush-
ing him as the gang rattled their cans and waved their Russian and
Cuban flags just outside our house.

I'd never seen my parents hide behind furniture before. I thought
it was a game, but they got angry with me when I tried to talk. They
were terrified.

Some of our Jewish neighbors also hid in their homes that day,
unsure of how what would become known as the Six-Day War would
affect them. The conflict brought Fidel, who always allied himself
with the Arab countries during these conflicts, to the airwaves. He
railed against Israel for hours. Cuba was one of the first countries to
recognize the PLO after it was founded and denounce Israel's defense,
calling it "armed aggression . . . in the Nazi manner." The PLO's soldiers also came to Cuba for training. Fidel's speeches against Israel

fired up the gangs that carried out *actos de repudio* against anyone considered counter-revolutionary: religious people, gays, *gusanos*, and others who fell short of the regime's standards.

My parents knew these gangs harassed and beat people in the streets, egged people's homes, broke windows. The barrio remained a relatively safe haven for us due to my parents' long histories in Juanelo, but these gangs often formed elsewhere and marched through other barrios, freeing reluctant members of connections to the targeted community.

As she tried to quiet us, my mother thought about Irela, her close childhood friend who'd taken vows as a Catholic nun. She wasn't sure if Irela—Sister Lourdes, as she was called now among the Benedictines—was still visiting her family on Ulacia. What if the gang caught her on the street wearing her habit? The government had recently driven more than a hundred priests to a ship in the harbor—at gunpoint—and forced them out of the country.

The mob was just outside our house now, chanting, banging on their drums and cans.

My father peered over a chair in time to see a man run up onto our porch. We heard windows shattering. "He's just outside," Papi whispered to my mother, ashamed of the fear in his voice.

The man on the porch called out to another one to join him, yelling something about a lamp. Papi watched as the second man boosted the first one up and he pried our ceiling lamp off its base. The men banged on our front door for a few minutes, and then left to join the gang marching down the street.

My father never forgot Fidel's long rants against Israel. Years later, he would rage against my plans to travel to Cuba with Andy and our son. He worried that with Gaza heating up again that summer, anything could happen in the Middle East, which would bring out the anti-Israel speeches in Havana and all that came with them.

At the end of our last heated argument over that trip, Papi banged his hand on the table. "*¡Ya!*" he said. "*You* go. Take your chances. But leave my Jewish grandson here."

35

Confessions and Announcements

Nashua, Summer 1989

Sister Irela met me at the front door of the duplex wearing her gray habit and a dazzling smile. I'd driven up from Boston, eager to meet this old family friend whose name came up constantly in the barrio stories. But I was worried about how she'd react to my relationship with Andy and had decided to avoid talking about religion as much as possible.

Irela had risen to a prominent position among the Benedictines and had been allowed to travel outside of Cuba to work in Rome. She'd made excuses to both the Cuban government and her order and arranged a stopover in New Hampshire. For twenty-five years, Irela and the mothers had written to each other regularly, but to touch the face of a lost friend and neighbor transformed them all. My brother had called me with a report. "Mami's completely different," he said. "She's kind of . . . goofy."

After a surprisingly powerful hug, the tiny, rotund nun sat me down on the couch. She blanketed me with questions about my life. She was spectacularly up-to-date. "I wasn't surprised to hear you'd moved out," she said. "Everyone was worried about you driving home late."

When she started to zero in on Andy, I squirmed, and she noticed.

"Look. I don't want you to worry about the fact that Andy is Jewish. God doesn't care about whether people are Jewish or Christian, only that they're good people." She smiled and hugged me again.

I thought of Abuela's reaction to Andy's faith and marveled at the flexibility of these old Catholic women. They could follow their faith to the letter, yet leave enough room for people to be human.

Suddenly, Irela looked at me as if she'd remembered something important. "Anita, forgive me, but your mother says there's an ice cream parlor near here. I am having such a craving. And I could use a break. I've been talking and talking to these old women for days and days!"

We hopped into my new Corolla and headed for Hayward's.

Irela was overwhelmed by the range of flavors and toppings on the chalkboard and needed help. I'll never forget her face as she beheld her cone. I sat across from her at one of the picnic tables, watching her black eyes sparkle. She licked her ice cream and smiled, her eyes half-closed. We ate our treats in silence, understanding the sanctity of the moment.

When we finished, I asked her if I could interview her. I'd been planning to write an article about Cuba. She agreed—but when I pulled the tape recorder out of my purse, her face changed.

"But are you going to use my name?"

"No, no. It's just for me right now. I'm not sure it'll ever be published. I just want to capture what's happening there, especially through the eyes of religious Cubans."

"You're as nosy as your mother. You're a sponge."

She smiled and began to talk freely. I could feel the weight of what she was describing and how sharing it relieved and hurt her at the same time. She described the severe food shortages and the toll, physical and spiritual, of daily life on everyone. The government had always looked at religious people, and especially the remaining active congregations, with suspicion, hewing to Marx's belief that religion "is the opiate of the people." Religious Cubans endured greater hardship than average Cubans. Irela and her fellow nuns depended almost entirely on food donations from congregants and neighbors.

Sometimes, as the most senior nun in El Cobre, where the cathedral to the patron saint of Cuba is located, she received unexpected visitors searching for spiritual guidance. All but the oldest and most religious people in the community knocked on the convent's back door to avoid being questioned by the *comité* or unfriendly neighbors. Irela described the many women she had counseled in recent years—some religious, some not—as they faced new pregnancies. She linked the long stretch of severe scarcity in Cuba to a rise in these kinds of visits and the abortions she knew often followed. Irela shared their anguish. "Some were skin and bones," she remembered. "To bring a child into such a world . . . They had horrible doubts, fear."

Many times, the visitors were young revolutionaries who came to ask about God and faith and all the "whys" that we all have when confronting hardship. "Those kids asked great questions," she said. "They challenged me at first, but they saw that I wasn't trying to persuade them of anything and they relaxed." Often, in response to their questions, she simply opened the Bible to a random page and read, or had them read, a passage. "So many times, the passage spoke directly to their questions. We'd just stare at each other, a little in awe, a bit more comforted."

Irela ended with a thought that was a wish, a question, and a worry all at the same time: "This will end soon, Anita. It can't go on much longer."

"I'm sure you're right," I said, but didn't believe it. My parents had said the same thing for decades.

As we drove home in silence, I remembered that Mami had asked me to pick up dog food. Irela said she'd never been to an American grocery store and would be happy to accompany me.

She asked a million questions and marveled at everything on the shelves. When we finally turned into the dog food aisle, Irela stopped and reached for a shelf to steady herself. Her mouth was open, her expression complete disbelief.

"All of this? For just dogs?"

I was tossing cans into our cart when she spoke. I looked at the shelves loaded with not just food but also collars, toys, leashes, treats. I saw that aisle, and the store itself, as if for the first time.

"It's—some of it's for cats—and birds."

I sounded ridiculous. All that she had just described to me about the difficulty of everyday life in Cuba, and now this, an almost indecent display in the Land of Plenty.

"Are you okay?" I asked.

But Irela wasn't okay. She looked at the floor as a few tears fell down her cheeks. I put my arms around her, but I had no words for that moment.

Hosting Irela prepared us for our next Cuban visitor. Tina, Tío Manolo's wife, had been Mami and Tía's second mother. She and Abuela had raised their children—Abuela's two daughters and Tina's son, Alfredo—together in Don Manuel's house.

Tina was not a nurturing woman. Somber, strict, quick-tempered, and harsh, most people didn't like her, and a good number feared her. I was nervous about meeting her. I remembered her pinching me with her toes when I played on the floor in Don Manuel's house. She thought it was a funny game, but I was terrified of her pincer toes back then, and they lurked in my mind when I met her again.

Still, the women of Hunt Street were indebted to her. She'd cared for Don Manuel in his last years, until he passed at ninety-five. Tía, Mami, and Abuela had sent money and support in their letters and phone calls, but the daily burdens had fallen on Tina. The mothers knew what it meant to live with shortages of every basic good. The difficulty of caring for a bedridden old man, often unaware of time and place, without easy access to essential supplies—linens, laundry detergent, soap, bandages, suppositories, bleach—surpassed any of their worst days in Cuba. They owed Tina more than they could ever repay.

When she came they treated her like a queen—took her on excursions to Boston, to the White Mountains, to the homes of the few other Cubans in the area. As the weeks passed, Tina relaxed and smiled more often. The light mustache she'd arrived with vanished one day thanks to some products Mami got at CVS. Suddenly, Tina sat up taller; her high cheekbones and sharp features became more apparent. I realized she must have been terribly beautiful in her youth if in her late sixties, after such a difficult life, she was still this striking.

One night, as Tina was getting ready to return to Cuba, Mami called me. She sounded off, distanced from whatever she was saying, as if she didn't care about her own topic. I knew she'd eventually get to the problem.

"I wasn't going to tell you. What's the point? It'll only make you bitter, and there's already enough bitterness right now." She described the conversation she'd had with Tina, Abuela, and Tía—how Tina had steered them to the topic of Don Manuel's care.

"She needed to confess, apparently. Said she'd lost patience a few times. Abuelo had wet the bed just after she'd bathed him and changed the sheets—at least once it was that. She slapped him across the face, yelled at him. The three of us just sat there stunned, feeling like she'd just slapped us. We were silent at first, but then the anger came. Tina—you could tell she was sorry, but I don't think she ever actually said it. That's not her way. She needed to get it off her conscience. But she dumped a tremendous weight on us."

The mothers took a long time to recover from Tina's confession. They understood how she must have felt, how easy it must have been to become overwhelmed. But their forgiveness could only go so far. Abuela, in particular, carried new images of her father's last years that were very different from the ones she'd created to comfort herself. "I was right to worry about him," she said to me one day. "How I wanted to take care of him . . ."

The cost of leaving Cuba always popped up like this, the sudden awareness of an injury you'd kept hidden from yourself. Now here it was again—announcing itself, demanding redemption. By this point—the early '90s, more than twenty-five years after leaving Cuba—the *viejos* understood that grief faded somewhat with time. They just needed to remind themselves of the many reasons for leaving their families, their homes, for needing to build new lives. But some of the losses were stubborn. They found their way to the surface again, sprouting fresh wounds on tired flesh.

I hadn't learned to look at my own losses from that time yet. I'd focused most of my attention on the *viejos'*. What could a well-loved-and-cared-for six-year-old girl have suffered compared to them?

It would take having my own child of six before I could hear that question.

Not long after Tina left for Cuba, unburdened and imperfectly forgiven, I announced the news that our Cuban family in three states had been waiting for: Andy and I were expecting a baby in October.

After the baby came, I'd keep working at the software company where I was managing support for international affiliates. I was speaking Spanish every day and working with businesspeople from all over Latin America and Spain and the rest of Europe. I loved my job, and we needed my income. With a good nanny, we could make it work.

The entire family exploded with joy when we told them—except Tía, who tempered hers with a warning: we should move to Nashua so the family could care for my baby, as they had cared for *all* the new babies in our family, when I went back to work. This "nanny" business made no sense to Tía—at all.

36

Blindsided

Needham, Massachusetts, January 1993

Mami's rapid Spanish poured out of the phone and into my ear, but I didn't want to tell her what I was feeling that January, fresh from our first holiday with our sweet baby girl.

I'd expected such happiness after giving birth. Now, a feeling of profound isolation and loss followed me through my days and nights. I didn't recognize myself or my life. I was in a different universe, and I didn't know how I'd gotten there. Even worse, I couldn't tell anyone. Andy and our families were overjoyed with Baby Natalia. The mothers called regularly with advice, visited often, and dug into anything that needed tending. On Noche Buena, the *viejos* had fought over who would get to hold our baby girl. I was swimming in blessings.

Each time I visited Hunt Street, the sadness that had grabbed hold of me let go for a while and I could enjoy the baby, motherhood, with a sense of relief. But when I left Hunt Street, I had to push down a grayness that grew the farther I got from home.

What *was* home, I wondered? Our little house in Needham— just the three of us, two clueless parents and their baby? That kind of household bore no resemblance to the kind I had known all my life. I felt alone, unequipped for parenting, even though Andy was a hands-on dad from day one. Natalia's October birth meant short days and long, dark nights. Strolls in the carriage were few and far between. No one was outdoors anymore; when we went out it was just the baby and me, bundled up and rolling along, the sound of the wheels rustling the fallen leaves as we passed.

One afternoon, I looked down at my sleeping daughter. She'd fallen asleep in my arms—she'd been so tired—and I'd laid her down in the bassinet we kept in the sunroom. Now, I saw the absolute peace on her tiny face.

This vulnerable creature depended entirely on me. And I knew nothing. *I* was her mother. A wave of pity for her overwhelmed me.

I was startled by the power of those first sobs. I walked out of the sunroom quickly, hoping Natalia would stay asleep. I sat on our cranberry-colored couch, under the front windows, and cried, let tears and sobs do what they needed to do to me.

Now, as I listened to Mami's cheerful voice rippling out of the phone, I noticed that she sounded too happy, and I realized: even though I hadn't told her much about this sadness that I just couldn't shake, she was trying to lift my spirits. She knew. She'd told me about her own postpartum depression—how it had eased after a few weeks, how mine would too.

That wasn't happening.

"I think I need to see a psychiatrist," I blurted out. Silence. "I've been so sad, every day, every night. It only lifts when I'm with all of you, but then it comes back."

There was another beat of silence before I heard her sigh.

"*You* are going to be fine. This takes time. Besides, Cubans don't go to psychiatrists." I knew how much my mother wanted to believe this, even if she'd once been so worried about me that she'd broken our culture's anti-shrink taboo. "You don't need one," Mami said. "You've got me!" She sounded upbeat, but I could hear the effort in her voice.

I followed my mother's advice—waited it out, toughed it out. Other than Andy, and now my mother, I didn't tell anyone how I was feeling. Never told my doctor, never got any help. In early summer, my mood finally lifted. A hole opened up in that gray world, and I walked through it.

I see it so clearly now—summer, sunlight, but more important, other mothers around, other women to talk to on the street, in the parks, to share problems and solutions with. And the *viejos* visited me more often, too, once the ice had melted away.

The mothers brought me more than support and wisdom. They helped me see that Needham *was* home. It would never be like Hunt Street, a Cuban home with lots of other women around, women who drove you crazy by telling you what you were doing wrong but always had your back and helped you find your footing in a mother's rocky world.

I'd been searching for a gift I wanted desperately to give to my children, and myself: the world I'd known, the world of many mothers in which I'd felt absolutely protected all my life. Now those same mothers were telling me to create another kind of gift to give my kids, one shaped by my hands and love. First, though, I had to accept, accept, accept.

I hired Maria, a young Guatemalan nanny, and went back to work, but Tía and Abuela worried that Maria wouldn't do a good job—"What if she's just propping a bottle and letting the baby sleep like that? What do you really know about her? She's so young."

So, Mami sent me Abuela, who slept in the spare room and kept an eye on Maria while Maria took care of Natalia. I had a nanny for my nanny. Abuela loved chatting with Maria during the day, but she seemed to be on alert, sniffing her out to make sure she was who she said she was, did what she said she was doing.

With Maria and Abuela in the mix, I finally had a household I recognized: three women everywhere, working. At night, after eating the Cuban meals Abuela prepared for us, bathing the baby, and putting her to sleep, Andy, Abuela, and I huddled in our tiny living room to watch TV. To accommodate Abuela and help Andy learn more Spanish, we tuned in to *Televisión* most nights. Abuela rocked away in her chair, keeping us company and giving us much-needed backup with this parenting thing. Relief.

But a power struggle between the nanny and the nanny's nanny was inevitable. These weren't related women, just daytime housemates. They couldn't tell each other exactly what they felt or thought, as my mothers always had. They had to hold all that in, wait it out, and then complain to me about it later.

The phone rang in my office in the middle of a crazy-busy spring day. Noontime was always hectic. European affiliates were wrapping up their software cases with us and trying to get home at the end of their workday. Latin America was running at full tilt, and the Asian affiliates were waking up and reporting new problems.

"I think it's your grandmother," Meg said when I picked up. Something dropped in my stomach as Abuela's voice erupted from the speaker. She sounded angry and terrified at the same time. I had to ask her, again and again, to repeat herself—she was speaking so fast I couldn't understand.

Finally, her words came through: "I said . . . I think Maria stole the baby."

I let the words pound their way into my brain.

"Wait. What? That's ridiculous!"

"*Mira, chica* . . . Maria didn't drive today, like she usually does. Someone in a station wagon dropped her off. She took the baby out more than two hours ago, and there's no sign of her. How well do you know this woman? You should move back to New Hampshire so we can take care of the baby. Do you really have to keep working?"

I flew down the stairs and was in my car in a flash. My heart knocked around in my chest, a wild thing trying to escape. I slowed down only when I got to our street.

Pulling up to the house, I saw Abuela standing on the sidewalk in front, her hand over her mouth, her housecoat and white hair blowing in the warm breeze. She was wearing her slippers, fuzzy scuffs that stood out against her white ankle socks.

I lowered the passenger side window. "I'm going to drive around and look for them."

"There are baby kidnapping rings all over Latin America," Abuela said.

"Get back inside in case she calls! Go!"

I drove slowly, swiveling my head from one sidewalk to the other, hoping to catch sight of Maria on a visit to one of the neighbors. My heart felt like it was being squeezed. I couldn't catch my breath. It was one of those perfect New England spring days, the sunlight clear, the cloudless blue sky soft and friendly. Could something horrible happen on such a beautiful day?

I drove up one street and down the other. Nothing. *Could Maria be part of a kidnapping ring? Why* did *a car drop her off this morning? Was it waiting for her and the baby somewhere nearby?*

I found them in the park, both fast asleep—Natalia in her stroller, Maria curled up on a bench next to her. The beautiful day had seduced Maria, a woman who still missed her sunny country. The warm bench, the background noise of toddlers playing in the sandbox, had lulled both baby and nanny into a deep sleep. I was sorry to interrupt their bliss.

When we walked into the house, I signaled to Abuela, with a swipe of my thumb across my neck, to stay silent. She rolled with it, all the drama of the previous two hours forgotten.

The Guatemalan Baby Kidnapping Scare annihilated me. The crisis marked the end of an era. I hung on to Maria and sent Abuela back to Hunt Street, where she and her cooking and cleaning skills had been missed desperately. I was ready, I told her and the other mothers, partly because of Abuela's help, to take this motherhood thing on by myself. Something in me grew up, accepted the fact that the household I'd grown up with was not in the cards for me. I would be raising my children the American way: in a simple nuclear family, with some help, and with relatives somewhere out there in the distance. I'd have to bump my way through this process, even more than a new American mother. I needed to make myself brave, draw a new map, and store the one I knew by heart somewhere else, for reference only.

Without the scaffolding of a Cuban household, another loss loomed ahead. Andy had promised to study Spanish so our kids would be bilingual. But I knew how hard it had been for us to maintain our Spanish even with five *viejos* wrangling it out of us every day. Would Spanish die on my watch too—like the extended family household had—or would I persist enough to hear it flowing out of my children's mouths one day? Could the Mother Tongue survive without the mothers? Would assimilation take that chunk of Cuban territory too?

I grieved over this. I'd lost something—and stood to lose more— that I hadn't understood was at risk. Another case of the culture we left behind reaching out to us, demanding recognition and bearing a message: *This was who you were. Who are you now?*

37

On the Open Ocean

Hunt Street, Summer 1994

Cuba pulled me toward her that summer more directly than it ever had before. What Fidel had named el Periodo Especial was wreaking havoc in the country. The Soviet Union had fallen. Without Soviet subsidies and with the weakening of its Soviet Bloc trading partners, Cuba's economy was collapsing. Ships in the Florida Straits were picking up record numbers of refugee-rafters. The images of inner tube rafts full of skinny, weather-beaten Cubans spread across newspapers and TV screens every day. Another dramatic exodus was underway again, almost fifteen years after Mariel. This time we'd have skin in the game, and we'd learn what it's like when the news leaps out of the screen and into your own living room.

Tía read Tina's letter out loud to us. Mami and Abuela kept asking questions, which Tía ignored, lifting a finger up in that schoolteacher way. The thin blue pages in Tía's hands were crisscrossed with Tina's handwriting. She'd written in the margins after she filled the page horizontally. (Tina wasted nothing. You had to admire her frugality.)

My aunt turned each sheet of paper a full 360 degrees as she read, keeping up with Tina's scrawl.

Tina described a new level of desperation in Havana. After more than thirty years of post-revolutionary life, she was used to standing in long lines for almost everything. But now she was walking up to six miles a day in order to find a line for sweet potatoes, cooking oil, a bag of beans, rice. For the first time, people were shoving each other while they waited in line. Tina, skinnier than ever, worried she'd be knocked down in the now-common scuffles.

People carried little bags with sugar to add to water so they'd have enough energy to get through the day. Some were eating cats. Others were making ground "beef" using ground-up plantain leaves. *It's actually not bad if you put a lot of garlic powder on it. But who has garlic?* Tina wrote. Buses often failed to show up, leaving people stranded. When Tina did make it onto a bus, it was packed with passengers, the leftovers from the previous bus and the would-be passengers from other routes. All of it under a hammering sun.

"She's eighty," Abuela said when Tía finished. "How is she walking from El Cerro to La Habana in that heat?"

Tía and Mami worked to put a call through to Havana. But the call came in our direction instead.

Alfredo, Tina's son and Tía and Mami's *primo hermano*, sounded scared. His seventeen-year-old son, Adriano, had left Cuba on a raft, like thousands of others. Fidel had announced that for the time being, anyone who wanted to leave the island was free to do so. He was releasing the steam that had built up during el Periodo Especial. Tens of thousands of Cubans moved quickly, fearing the government would change its mind. They rushed out to sea on anything that could float. Eventually, about thirty-three thousand Cubans climbed onto patched-up rafts and repurposed trucks and cars and floated out to sea, hoping for rescue.

Alfredo's voice broke. "Consuelo, I gave him a bag with sugar and a note with your name, address, and phone number."

Mami couldn't speak.

"Try not to worry," Tía said from the other phone. "With all those people on the ocean, lots of ships will be out looking. Someone will pick him up. We'll call you as soon as he calls us."

Days passed without word from Adriano, and Abuela started to unravel. Her seventeen-year-old grandnephew was out on the ocean. Her arrhythmia worsened so much that Mami took her to get checked. The expense of international calls didn't matter anymore. In Havana and Nashua, we reached for each other for support and ideas about how to solve the problem.

A week later, I answered Abuela's daily dinnertime call.

"He should have been picked up by now." She was sobbing. "Why haven't we heard anything?"

The news reports showed hundreds of rafters being picked up by US Coast Guard ships, cruise liners, and pleasure boats. I'd noticed new terminology in the news. These Cubans were "rafters," not "refugees." Some reports described them as "migrants." How could people fleeing one of the only countries in the world that denied its citizens the right to leave be migrants? Weren't they just as much refugees as we'd been? Cuba hadn't changed, but somehow the way the United States saw the people fleeing it had.

"Can you do something?" Abuela asked. She'd just described how the tough-as-nails Tina had whimpered the last time they spoke.

Abuela's desperation reached right through the phone and into my heart.

"I'll try . . . I'll try. He's going to be fine, Abuela. He's strong. He's young . . ."

I started calling 411 "Information" operators and got the numbers for government agencies that might know something. All my attempts failed in dead ends—wrong numbers, useless recordings, clerks pointing to other clerks—until somehow, I managed to get a phone number for a barracks on the Guantanamo base, where the refugee-rafters were being "processed."

I dialed with little hope but heard a young man's voice on the other end. I explained our story as quickly as I could, sure he'd hang up on me. I emphasized Adriano's young age, that he'd never been away from home, how worried we all were. But the sailor refused to help me. Said he wasn't allowed even to talk with anyone about the "situation."

"Look," I said, "there are two old Cuban women, one in Havana and one in New Hampshire, and they are hurting. You can end that."

A long silence, then—"Awright . . . But you never talked to me . . . And I never talked to you. Call me tomorrow night at nine. I'll try."

He answered the next night after the first ring. He seemed to be covering the receiver with his hand. I could barely hear him.

"Your cousin was picked up by the Coast Guard cutter *Tampa*," he muttered. "He's here, in Oscar 2 Camp, Tent 3. And remember, you never called this number."

"Oh my God! Thank you, thank you! You don't know how happy you've made me—my whole family. Those grandmothers can breathe now! How can I ever thank you?" I would have done almost anything for this sailor. "Do you like chocolate chip cookies?"

A completely different voice answered, "Are you kidding? I love 'em!"

He gave me his name and address, and I think he would have given me his social security number if I'd asked. I put every ounce of appreciation I had into that double batch of cookies. I don't know if he ever got them. I hope so. He saved two old women and their children a great deal of pain.

Adriano spent his days in the refugee camp sketching, artist that he was, scenes of his time at sea—the creatures he saw, the Coast Guard cutter that rescued him. Fidel's image appears in a few drawings. There are chains and locks and thorns. But the motif that repeats the most is a sword impaling a tongue, cutting it in half.

As Guantanamo filled with 30,000-plus refugees, the United States flew some of them, including Adriano, to a naval base in Panama. We worried about Adriano's spirits. His letters had grown less optimistic, were full of doubts.

Tía stepped up. "I'll go to Panama, talk with him, make sure he stays calm and doesn't lose hope."

When Tía returned, she was convinced the boys—Adriano's raft mates were still with him—would be alright. Her photos showed Adriano and his friends inside their tent, their arms linked over each other's shoulders. She brought back Adriano's drawings and the baseball cap he'd worn on the raft. "I'll hold these for you until you get to us," she'd told him. "The Americans respect good behavior. Follow their rules. Stay honest and keep away from any trouble. Stay together. This may take a while, but it'll all be worth it."

Months passed with little progress. We watched in confusion as the United States reversed its thirty-year-old policy toward Cubans found at sea with a new agreement between the two nations. Cuba promised to prevent mass migration from its shores, and the United States promised to stop automatically paroling Cubans found at sea into the States—unless they proved a credible fear of persecution upon return to the island. There was a loophole. If the refugee reached US soil, the United States would parole Cubans into the country. Known as "Wet Foot, Dry Foot," the new policy made Cubans' escape by sea more dangerous than ever. Now instead of looking for rescuers, the asylum seekers tried to avoid them. Only by touching US soil could Cubans be assured a chance to enter the States.

The bleak tone of Adriano's letters worried us. The boys had been returned to Guantanamo by then, as some of the refugees had been cleared to enter the United States and space had opened up at the base. *He'll be okay*, we told each other, still dreaming of the moment when another family member would join us. Tía and Abuela smiled at the memories of five-year-old Adriano begging them to bring him to the United States in a suitcase. He would finally get his wish.

One night, we got a collect call from one of Adriano's raft mates. *He* was still in the camp, he told us, but the situation had grown extremely tense for all of them. After six months, with—still—no official guarantee of getting into the United States and refugee tempers rising, officials had announced that a portion of the electric fence surrounding the Guantanamo base would be deactivated and the mine field beyond cleared. Any refugee who wanted to return to Cuban territory would be allowed to leave.

Adriano's friend confirmed what we had sensed in Adriano's recent letters and calls: Adriano had given up hope. His friend had tried to convince him to stay, but Adriano had gotten upset. They'd fought, and his friend had backed down. Adriano had made up his mind.

He didn't have anything to pack, his friend told us. He and a few others said goodbye to their companions and their dreams and simply walked back into Cuban territory.

After Tía recovered from that call and trying to console Abuela, she set up a call to Havana. She needed to prepare the family for the shock of Adriano's unexpected return.

Eighty-year-old Tina answered. "*Espera, espera,*" she said when she heard the news. "My legs won't hold me. Let me find a chair."

At one point during that call, Tina said to Tía, "His life is over."

I remember thinking her prediction was too bleak. Adriano was seventeen. He had time to recover. But twenty years later, when I met him in Havana, Adriano told me about the troubles he'd had off and on over the years, many of them linked to his attempted escape. I brought up his drawings, told him how I cherished them. Adriano just said, "*Fue una locura volver.*"

Returning to Cuba had been a crazed act, but so was launching an inner tube raft into the Florida Straits with nothing but a plastic bag filled with sugar. The same rebellious, artistic seventeen-year-old heart led to both desperate acts. He'd done what he thought was best at two very different moments in his life.

Some of the old Cubans I knew, the same ones who'd given everything up when they left their homes forever in the '60s, scoffed at Adriano and the other rafters who had walked back into Cuba. I heard a group of them talking in our kitchen on Hunt Street not long after Adriano had returned. They were enjoying the café Cubano Abuela had served in tiny Dixie cups when Adriano's story came up.

"They must not have really wanted freedom very much if they gave up that easily," one of the older men said.

"They're different from us," someone else said. "They only know that system. They don't know what it's like to lose the freedoms you had . . ."

As often happens when Cubans are talking together about politics, a vigorous debate broke out. I hovered in the dining room, listening and wondering, *How can they have forgotten what it was like to be young and terrified, facing a foreign government, a wildly uncertain future?* I remembered the man Papi had fought with in the refugee center when we first got to the United States, the one who had accused him of lacking principles because Papi had described the hunger we'd endured. "You're just a glutton," the man had said. "You're only coming here for food, not for freedom." His accusation had cut my father so deeply that he'd lost control and plastered him with punches.

Were we really so different from the latest group of Cuban refugees—or was it simply that too many years had passed for us to see ourselves in them?

I keep Adriano's drawings in a plastic portfolio behind our china cabinet. I need them close at hand, these artifacts of a life almost lived. When I look at them, I can almost hear him saying what he told me when we met in Havana: it *was* crazy to return. I feel the loneliness of a seventeen-year-old boy, far from his family, scared, caught between his dreams and an unchanging reality, hungry for home. I see how easily that hunger and desperation could build up, spin him around, and propel him toward the one place he knew would take him back— home. Barbed wire, minefields, and governments be damned.

38

What Trauma?

Lexington, Massachusetts, Summer 1998

Tina's letters, which detailed Adriano's miserable prospects now that he'd returned to Cuba a traitor, a branded *gusano*, filled Abuela with anguish. The worrying worsened her irregular heartbeat. She ran out of breath often, tired easily. Mami warned her not to go up and down the stairs when she was alone, but she forgot one day and tumbled down. She suffered a stroke soon after.

I felt strange that summer, and I knew it stemmed from more than Abuela's ailments. Nothing felt right or easy. I couldn't pinpoint the reason. Sometimes when I spoke, my voice sounded far away, a foreign sound that belonged to someone else. Other sounds felt so sharp they hurt my ears. I was agitated, expecting the next assault at any moment, my hands ready to cover my ears.

I moved through those August days like a ghost—not really there, but functioning somehow. We'd grown out of the Needham house after Sam, our second child, was born, and had moved to Lexington. A year had passed, but I still missed the old house and the close-knit neighborhood we'd left behind. And with a new baby and Natalia about to start kindergarten in the fall, I saw a more complex life ahead for all of us, the end of another era.

I knew something else lurked behind the homesickness and my uneasiness. I just couldn't name it.

I sat on the stairs of the deck, the cordless phone in one hand, taking notes as Mami talked. A scrum of little kids ran loose through the sprinklers I'd set up. Their shrieks tore through me.

I tried to focus on what Mami was saying. She and Tía were loading up the next package to Cuba and needed a few more things for sick friends from the barrio. Ensure—vanilla, if possible—adult diapers, wet wipes.

"Aren't those too heavy?" I asked.

"The wipes? Absolutely. They're not going to eliminate a problem, but at least Otilia's daughter won't have to wash clothes for a couple of days. Imagine cleaning a bedridden grandmother with rags, then washing and drying them for the next round. Those wipes are going. You know what? Get three packages."

"I'll go to CVS. Bring them up this weekend." One more to-do for the day. Otilia wasn't even a relative, just Don Manuel's front-door neighbor. It wouldn't take long, but the idea of getting the kids in the van, hauling them out, collecting the items—I felt stupid being overwhelmed by something that simple.

Maybe Mami heard something in my voice.

"Should I go get them?" she asked. "I want to get everything to them as soon as possible."

"No . . . we'll be up."

"*¿Qué te pasa?* Something's wrong."

I felt the ache in my heart bubbling out.

"I don't feel right. Haven't been right for a while. I'm sad, I miss Needham, and I'm worried about Natalia going off to kindergarten."

"She's going to be fine! And it takes a long time to get used to a new place. You'll do it."

Her optimism reassured me. I *could* do it. This would pass. "Yeah. I know. I know."

Natalia's excitement about school sometimes lifted me up that summer. But I saw new troubles ahead: schedules, expectations, books, homework—mean kids. As fall approached, I worried even more. Was she really ready for kindergarten? My bright, Tiggeresque five-year-old bounced through the world full of joy and energy. How would that play out next year?

Other parents we knew had brought their kids for readiness evaluations by a well-known child psychiatrist in town. Natalia's preschool teachers thought she was ready for kindergarten. A second professional opinion would quiet my doubts.

The psychiatrist met with me first to learn about our family. She spent a little time with Natalia in another session and asked to meet with Andy and me the following week. We sat in her perfect white Pottery Barn living room, pretending to be relaxed.

When she told us that Natalia was delightful and ready for school, we both released sighs. But the doctor wasn't finished.

She looked directly at me. "I'd like to hear more about *you*, and what you've been worrying about."

This confused me. Weren't we done? *Ah, these doctors. They never want to let you go.*

Let's see. I felt completely at ease now. "Well, I just want her to be okay and to . . . blend in." But that wasn't it, was it? Something bigger sat behind that, hiding. I thought about how to capture that, but before I could answer, a sudden force—a wave of sobs—bent me in half.

The cries shook my body. I fought to breathe. I stared down at the rug, my head over my knees, my hands tucked under my chest. Embarrassing, primal sounds tore out of me. I buried my head in my hands, shaking uncontrollably. I felt Andy's arm around me, saw the tissue he passed me through a watery lens.

For the five minutes of this mini breakdown, the doctor sat quietly. When I stopped crying, I looked up, mortified. What was wrong with me?

Her eyes were kind. "I think that some of this has to do with the trauma you experienced when you were Natalia's age."

What was she talking about? "Wha—what trauma?"

She explained how sudden exile, the loss of your home—being kicked out of it—losing your family, culture, world, in the span of hours was trauma, especially for a child.

My mouth hung open as she talked. I thought *she* was the crazy one now. What happened to us hadn't been a trauma. We had escaped Castro, flown to freedom, and rebuilt our lives. We'd won! We were the lucky survivors who'd stuck together, even in the frozen North, and landed on our feet. That was our origin story, our legend. We were superheroes.

The doctor thought I was clinically depressed and had been for a long time. I disagreed. How could I have functioned so well all those years if I was so depressed?

She smiled. "Gifts."

She strongly advised an antidepressant and therapy. I refused both. I had plenty of friends and family to talk with. I wasn't crazy. Just a little sad. Now that I knew the cause of my blues, I'd figure things out myself.

I hobbled away from that conversation in an exhausted daze.

My mother was quiet on the other end of the line when I told her the news. I heard a little gasp when I mentioned the antidepressant idea.

She had to have struggled to say what she said next: "That's a long time to have suffered. Maybe you should think about the pills."

Even with that 180-degree turn by Mami, I stuck to my anti-psychiatry bias. I wasn't going to be one of those poor souls on meds and a couch for the rest of my life. How many times had I heard the *viejos* whisper about *locos* going to *siquiatras*? The shame helped me dig in, but what I fought most was seeing myself as a victim of trauma. I wanted to have won, not lost. And yet the depression clawed at me, bleak and unrelenting.

Andy couldn't understand why I refused the solutions that were right in front of me: therapy, medicine, and more. But the real problem was I didn't think I had a problem. Accepting that I did meant losing the tough refugee warrior identity I'd inherited. Even worse, I realize now, was acknowledging an injury I'd covered up for decades, one that Andy had glimpsed for the first time the day I broke down.

I couldn't articulate any of that at the time, but somehow Andy pulled enough truth out of my denials to open my eyes a bit.

"Why can't you have both things?" he asked one day after I'd meandered through my excuses. "Why can't you be a badass Cuban refugee *and* get help for the ass-kicking you got as a kid?"

Something about that storyline—the myth of the win-win—appealed to me. But ultimately it was Andy's gentle, unceasing questioning that led to change. One afternoon I stood at the kitchen sink, staring out the window into the yard, for a long time . . . lost. I didn't want to feel this way anymore. I began to let go.

Soon, I was back in that Pottery Barn living room crying my eyes out with the kind doctor across the room. I started taking Prozac. Within a few days of starting the medicine, I felt a change in the sunlight. The doctor said it was too soon to credit the meds for this change. I disagreed. Everything was brighter.

I began to sleep again at night and woke up rested for the first time in years. The rattling of silverware and plates no longer pierced my eardrums. The air around me thinned. I walked undisturbed through a new landscape. With greater freedom from anxiety and depression, a new space opened in my mind, and I considered the possibility that the doctor's word choice, "trauma," might be correct.

What did I remember? I'd been writing a bit—short essays, journal entries. Writing helped me understand what I was thinking. One afternoon in our guest room, I typed away, capturing early memories of Cuba and our first months here in New Hampshire. The memories started to take shape. I remembered my mother running around the living room as the guard interviewed Papi, how Papi hung his head over the table, the look in his eye, the guard sealing the door, the sense of floating up into space when I burst out crying after saying goodbye to my teacher.

I had blocked so much out. Until that moment, I had buried all of the nighttime memories. How Abuela had cried in bed, how sad she had been every day. And the voices—I could almost hear the metallic tension again. I considered myself a thinker, a close observer of my and other people's feelings. But at some point, something had triggered a protective mechanism. I'd locked the pain from those days away in another room, tossed the key into a river. And it had taken me until now, at thirty-six years old, to wade into the water to retrieve it.

One night, as I wrote about Amherst Street School and how I loved studying the ants in our yard, Bernice strode in and tore down the last part of the wall. I paced the room as the details returned of when I attacked her. I remembered Bernice's face, the feel of her flesh under my nail. I was on the guest bed now, crying into the pillow so the kids and Andy wouldn't hear. I don't know how long I cried that night.

I should have taken the doctor up on her recommendation to keep seeing her, but after a few months of therapy, I didn't see the point.

I'd found myself again. She believed I'd been clinically depressed for a long time; I didn't agree, but did it matter? I understood now that this would be a pattern, maybe had been a pattern all my life. Sadness seeped in, even in happy times. I'd have to watch out for that and prepare. Most of all, I needed to pick up each fuzzy refugee memory and blow away the dust so I could face what I now saw as a traumatic time.

I spent hours flipping through Mami's photo albums, asking the *viejos* questions, going back with more. I scrawled notes on scraps of paper that collected at the bottom of my purse, in the backs of drawers. I snatched my own memories out of the air as the *viejos* told me theirs, each one a butterfly that I greedily pinned down with words, so I'd have it forever.

I was restoring—imperfectly but tangibly—something precious that had been taken from us. I was healing.

That January, Andy and I celebrated my renewed mental health and my thirty-seventh birthday in an Indian restaurant in Harvard Square. We shared a robust sense of hope in our future as we drank wine and savored the chicken tikka masala. We talked about going on a family vacation now that our bank account had stabilized post-move.

At first, we couldn't think of any one place in particular.

Then, suddenly: "You should go back to Cuba." Andy's face lit up. "This summer! Diana could help me with the kids."

I stared at him. Why hadn't I thought of this? Cuba had shaped my thoughts and experiences all my life, but the policies of both countries had made it almost impenetrable in the past. Now, the Clinton administration had lifted some travel restrictions on Cuban Americans returning to visit family.

With total clarity, I knew I needed to go back, that returning would help me repair the damage of the night we were ripped away from our old lives. It was one of those moments in life where the light changes, sparkles. Maybe it was Cuba's brilliant sunshine that I sensed—the light of so many memories. My body vibrated. I was going home.

"Mami has to come," I said. "She's my link to all of it."

We found a pay phone just outside the restaurant. I couldn't stop smiling as I told Mami the plan.

"I need to talk to your father," she said. "He's not going to like it, but it's been too long. I want to see Alfredo, Tina, all of them."

I was oblivious to what a trip to Cuba would cost my mother, not just in cash but in the coming conflict with my father—but she knew what lay ahead with Papi. Even now, when Tía and Abuela's trip back to Cuba came up, he let them have it. I'd heard some of our Miami relatives blast Cubans who'd returned—*After all we went through to get out! Now they go back and put money into Castro's filthy hands.* Papi echoed them.

The irony was that, of all the *viejos*, Papi was the one who talked about Cuba the most—his youth, his baseball days, outings in Havana, the crazy characters of the barrio. Yet he swore that until Cuba was free of Castro and communism he'd never return.

Mami's relationship with my father suffered as a result of our trip. They stopped talking to each other for a time—an incredible act of will in a house full of chatterboxes.

Tía and Abuela filled the quiet with their own opinions. "It's easy to not go back when there's nobody to go back to," Tía would say, reminding Papi how lucky he was to have his entire family in the United States. But after one look from Mami, Tía or Abuela would shut right up.

Mami complained to me about the tension in the house. "You can't go against a man like your father head-on," she told me. "Your aunt and grandmother just can't get that in their heads."

Her advice helped when I got dragged into these arguments—the trip was my idea. But whatever guilt I felt vanished the second I thought of walking down Castillo again.

While Papi stewed, the women began shopping, beginning with shoes for each relative and some of the neighbors.

Sizing was tricky. We kept paper outlines of each person's foot in a drawer and took them with us to the store, drawing curious stares from the other shoppers as we stuffed the paper into shoes and discussed the fitting with each other. We knew the rest of the shopping list by heart: first aid supplies, vitamins, lacy bras, and undies in a range of sizes, Ensure and Carnation Instant Milk—of course. Was Alfredo still a 38-inch waist now that he wasn't drinking? Would Esther like that pocketbook from JCPenney? She'd always been so fashion conscious in pre-revolutionary Cuba; we worried she would think it was too cheap looking. But the airfare was expensive, and our shopping list kept getting longer. She'd have to settle for a Penney's purse.

With the torturous visa process, the trip took months to plan. In the meantime, we weighed and re-weighed our suitcases to avoid the extra baggage fees.

Thirty-plus years later, and we were still weighing items going to Cuba.

Months passed before Tía, Mami, and Abuela deemed the contents of our suitcases satisfactory. Different *viejos* took turns getting on the scale with and without the suitcases to confirm we wouldn't have to pay extra baggage fees.

The most important item we were bringing wasn't packable: a new walker for Tina, who'd broken her hip trying to kill a cockroach in her apartment. We found a lightweight model at the local pharmacy and saw it as the crown jewel of our cache. We planned to leave everything behind. We'd leave Cuba like we left it thirty years before—light as feathers.

Havana

All the weighing of suitcases proved pointless when we hit customs inside José Martí Airport in Havana. We were recovering from the harrowing flight on a Cubana jet with duct-taped overhead compartments when two customs agents pulled us aside.

The US embargo meant we couldn't use checks or credit cards in Cuba. I had $2,000 in cash in my bra, in my purse, and under the insoles of my sneakers. With our dollars, we planned to buy the household items we knew our family needed, if we could find them. All of that raced through my mind as the two uniformed agents corralled us in front of a table and asked for our passports.

"*Buenas*," Mami said, handing hers over.

"*Buenas*," the short agent said.

They weighed our suitcases on the other side of their table and conferred for a few minutes, their backs to us.

The tall agent shook her head. "You're over the weight limit."

Mami's mouth dropped open. "That's impossible. Those bags weigh just under fifty pounds each. We've weighed them over and over. You're mistaken." She stood ramrod straight while the agents flipped through our passports again.

"Well," the tall agent said, "you'll have to pay five hundred dollars if you want these bags."

Mami was huffing. "And how would we be able to do that? We're here to visit family. We don't have that kind of money! It's not like we're staying at a hotel and brought all that cash."

"We can't let you—"

"Look, your scales obviously need to be recalibrated. I'll bet my life that the bags are under the weight limit. Bags don't gain weight during a flight." Mami started to smile the way she did when she caught us in a lie. "And since *when* is a suitcase weighed coming *into* a country? Your own airline weighed them leaving the Bahamas and didn't have a problem with them then."

I was sweating, thinking about all the money I had on me. I was sure they'd search us if this kept going.

And it did, for about fifteen minutes, long enough that even I found the courage to speak up in defense of our shabby suitcases, stuffed full but respectfully underweight. Each time I joined the point-counterpoint with the agents, Mami gave me her *don't-say-another-word-or-I'll-kill-you* look.

The agents kept repeating their request for the $500, calmly, reasonably. Their tan-and-green uniforms were starched so stiffly that I could smell the fabric from three feet away.

Mami started to raise her voice, and the tall agent came out from behind the counter and asked her to step aside. The other agent walked toward me and began asking about our plans while in Cuba and then, suddenly, "How much can you pay us?"

"What? We don't have—"

"You have to give us something. That's our supervisor over there." She pointed to a cluster of uniforms across the room. "She's been watching. If she comes over, you'll end up paying the full amount."

Mami had her back to me, but I could tell from her stance that she wasn't budging. Suddenly, she turned around. "You know what? Keep the bags. We'll just leave them."

She tried to get past her agent, but the woman put her arm out and stopped her.

"*Señora.* You are confused. We cannot store these bags here. We don't have the facilities—"

My agent, meanwhile, kept going: "You don't want to leave that walker here."

I'd forgotten about the walker. There was no way I was leaving it behind.

I worked my agent down to a hundred dollars and kept at it until she finally accepted the thirty dollars I stuffed in her hand. Just like that, she waved us through. I hooked the walker over my arm, grabbed my suitcase, and walked with pride toward the exit.

My self-congratulatory mood vanished when Mami realized I'd paid our way out of the mess.

"They are nothing but *sinvergüenzas*," she said after a good round of scolding and swearing. "They'll keep doing this to all the Cubans who come back. Thirty dollars! That's more than a month's pay here. It's criminal."

Alfredo interrupted my mother's rant with bear hugs for both of us. He had been waiting just outside the main doors. He smiled and wiped his eyes as he embraced us again and again.

Mami patted him on the back for a while like she was burping a baby. When she told him about the confrontation with the agents, Alfredo's smile twisted. "*Hijos de putas*."

We got a taxi and headed off to his apartment in El Vedado. As we turned onto the main road, a farm truck cut in front of the cab. It had five-foot-high wooden sides, but the back flap was down. We could see its cargo: a massive mound of purple and yellow asters that filled our cab with a clean smell, like hope.

Our journey took us back to Juanelo, to the four magical streets whose names Abuela and I would say together as we drew maps of the barrio in Nashua: Castillo, Serafina, Ulacia, Blume Ramos. Those incantations left us smiling and feeling as powerful as sorceresses— we'd recreated the land we'd been uprooted from. But the magic never lasted long. In the end, they were just pretty words and scraps of paper. No spell could fix the brokenness underneath it all.

Yet here I was, walking down Castillo, my mother by my side, our old house just ahead. It felt like something between a hallucination and a daydream. I knelt in front of our porch to collect stones and sand, a few weeds I saw growing in the broken sidewalk. I needed something tangible to prove I had been here, had heard the sounds of kids playing on Castillo just as I'd done decades earlier. I stared at our white door, half expecting to see remnants of the Property of the Revolution banner, my father at the kitchen table, the *guardia* across from him.

As I put the little relics in a baggie, the woman who'd been given our house came out to the porch. She asked what I was doing, and I mumbled a little explanation. I saw pity in her smile. She invited us inside.

Everything was pristine and orderly, the scent of bleach somehow comforting, familiar. White eyelet curtains were nailed around a window; a bowl of plastic fruit sat on the Formica-topped table. Could Abuela be in the kitchen? Was Blanca by the stove? I floated through the rooms, remembering and rebuilding a world, one wall at a time.

39
Elian

Nashua, January 6, 2000

Andy and I flipped through the photo album, stopping now and then when I remembered a new detail about our trip to Cuba. I stopped at a photo of a woman looking up in shock at the camera.

"That's Neri. We caught her off guard in the alley behind our house. Look at that face." Neri had been pulling clothes off her line when we called to her from the back of our house. Her laundry sink was behind ours, a few steps lower and separated by a wall. Our old sink was just as I remembered it: perched on top of a slab of chipped concrete. This was where I'd watched Abuela a million times as she slapped our clothes against the washboard and tried to clean them with a big yellow cake of useless Russian soap. *¡Chaca, chaca, chaca, ploof!*

This was also, I realized, where Mami had drowned Blanca's puppies.

As Mami and I peered over the stucco wall, Neri looked up, her face stricken with confused shock. She saw my mother's ghost leaning over the wall, where she'd leaned so many other times. "Consuelo?" she whispered. "*¡No lo puedo creer!*"

I wasn't sure Andy remembered her. "She was the neighbor my mother passed our family photos to the night we left."

He ran a finger over the image of Neri's incredulous face. "I'm glad these old women keep their photos."

Mami had given me the small album as a birthday gift, a collection of the best photos from our Cuba trip. Her meticulous albums brought our family's past back to life. The photos blossomed across the pages in strict chronological order. Her elegant handwriting dances happily under the images, reminding us of the babies' ages, the names of the neighbors at the picnic table, the winner of that night's wrestling match on the living room carpet. She kept the albums dated, titled, and lined up chronologically. My sister always said that Mami's album fetish was her way of restoring the loss of our family photos when we left Cuba. Mami wanted to capture what she'd almost lost and leave it at our fingertips.

Instead of photos, I relied on my notes to recall the details of our trip. We visited a few famous sites, like the colonial-era cathedral and Havana's famous Hotel Nacional, but we spent most of our time talking with family and friends and rushing to and from one of the government's US dollar–only shops. The shops pulled in the dollars, francs, and pounds that circulated on the black market. Without that hard currency, which was always scarce in the post-revolutionary economy, the government couldn't purchase most international goods.

The outrageous prices in the dollar-only shops didn't keep Mami and me away. The shops were packed with visiting Cubans from overseas or Cubans who'd received dollars from family abroad. These were the best-stocked stores by far, and the fastest way to buy basic supplies to help our family accommodate us during our trip. Jam, crackers, bologna, soap—nothing we brought back from the shop lasted long in Alfredo's apartment. The family fell on the snacks and devoured everything within hours.

After one of our shopping trips, I watched Alfredo enjoying the saltines and orange marmalade we'd brought back.

"There are many kinds of hunger," he said, licking the orange jam off his fingers. "We have food here—not always enough, and almost never what we really want—so I guess you can't say we're starving. But, definitely, we have other kinds of hunger."

Pain flashed across Mami's face as her *primo hermano* finished his thought.

"Here, *primo*," she said, passing him the new kitchen towel we'd bought that day. "You sound like your father when you say things like that."

The image of Alfredo licking his fingers and waxing philosophic rushed back one night while Andy and I were watching news reports about Elian Gonzalez's rescue. We were celebrating my birthday with pepperoni pizza and red wine, but Elian's tragic story and the memory of Alfredo marred the happy mood. I'd been telling Andy about the marmalade, Alfredo's dreams of attending MIT, how he'd waited all his life for a change that never came.

"Forty years waiting for fresh food, peace, and freedom," I said, watching the images of the little boy, now with his father's family in Miami. "And that's just one life."

I felt a profound hopelessness as we talked. Nothing seemed to change for Cubans. Cuban refugee-rafters had been making the news throughout 1999, but the topic had boiled over in November with the story of the five-year-old Cuban boy rescued off the Miami coast. Elian's mother and nine others in their group had drowned trying to make landfall on US soil. Elian and two adults had survived. The father's family in Miami wanted to keep the boy in the United States, but his father, estranged from his wife and still in Cuba, wanted him returned. The tragedy ignited a legal and diplomatic debate that topped the news for months.

"Funny—Three King's Day today," I said as reporters described the custody battle. "We could use King Solomon for this one."

I slipped into a long commentary after that. Americans were only seeing a sliver of the full truth. It was too easy to laugh at the overheated Cuban exiles marching to keep the boy here. They were depicted as excessively emotional, too dramatic, unhinged. Their passion was hard-earned, but their history was too complex for the evening news.

"Why don't you write about it?" Andy said. "Try the *Globe*."

I'd had some luck getting some pieces about Cuba in local papers. "There's plenty already being written."

"Not by somebody who was a refugee kid herself. Go. I'll clean up."

Deep into the night, the words flowed out of me and onto the screen. I couldn't imagine the horror of Elian's escape from Cuba, but I could share my child self's recollections of sudden exile, the mix of anguish and joy that followed, the confusing journey of recovering your life, the Cuban American lens on Elian's story.

The *Globe* didn't take my essay, but the *Focus* editor's encouragement gave me the confidence to call the Boston NPR affiliate, WBUR. They were interested. I faxed it, and within a short time they had me in a studio recording what would turn out to be the first of twenty or so commentaries for the national broadcast of *All Things Considered*.

"Good job, Anita," Mami said as I walked into Hunt Street. "It turns out a lot of people listen to that strange station." Mami had never heard of NPR, but she loved knowing that neighbors and friends had heard our story on the radio.

We were at Hunt Street to celebrate Angel and Susan's daughter Audrey's birthday. We ate cake off paper plates and drank Coke from plastic cups, somehow managing to lob opinions about Elian's case as we dug into vanilla-on-vanilla sheet cake, Audrey's favorite.

"How can you give the father custody of the boy if the father doesn't even have custody of himself?" Mami shrugged. "Really. Makes no sense."

"That little boy should be with his surviving parent," Abuela said. She looked stern. "He saw his mother die. The father was always good to him. He should live with him."

"What about the mother's wishes? Doesn't sacrificing her life mean anything?" someone asked, triggering a new flurry of comments.

"Fidel's forcing the father to say he wants the kid back. Since when does he care about the poor bastards trying to escape?"

"¡Coño! Remember when they sank that tugboat full of kids?"

I'd forgotten about the sinking of the *13 de Marzo*, a tugboat carrying an extended family that tried to escape from Havana harbor in July of 1994 during one of the worst stretches of el Periodo Especial. Survivors said that government boats had caught up with the tugboat about seven miles out, rammed it, and shot water cannons, sweeping people off the decks and into the ocean. Thirty-five people had drowned, many of them children.

I thought about those lives lost, the ongoing debate about Elian, the long, hard road of the Cuban people. "*Gracias*," I said to Tía and Mami, who were sitting near me at the table.

They both looked confused for a moment. Then Tía smiled.

"Ah," she said, understanding my gratitude. "You would have done the same thing for your kids—not going out to sea. I still think that's insane."

I'd thought a lot about their choice to leave everything they knew behind and throw themselves and all of us into an unknown world. "I don't know. I'm not sure I could have done what you did."

Tía smiled, shook her head. "No one knows until the moment is in front of them. Now that I think about it, I'm not sure I could rule out the ocean completely. I don't know what Elian's mother faced."

The Elian drama didn't do Abuela's heart any good. Her arrhythmia continued its fluttering decline. One night, as she and Mami sat on the couch watching *Sábado Gigante*, Abuela passed out. Mami said she just toppled over, and her false teeth fell out of her mouth.

Mami checked for a pulse and felt nothing. She listened to her breathing—nothing, so she grabbed Abuela by the neck, slapped her face a few times, shook and shook her. When her "Cuban CPR" didn't work, she ran next door to get Tía.

As Tío called 911, Mami and Tía ran back to Abuela, and Mami resumed her strange resuscitation efforts.

"That's too much! You're going kill her!" Tía said, immediately understanding how ridiculous she sounded. Abuela was dead already, she was sure of it.

Mami ignored her and kept shaking Abuela.

Just as the paramedics arrived, Abuela mumbled something.

"Did you hear that?" Mami asked Tía.

Abuela tried to sit up as the EMTs started treating her. Her skin color—a lifeless gray—scared everyone. It would take days to fade away.

Abuela got a pacemaker, and we all breathed more easily. But over the next several years, three strokes, more heart problems, and a few minor ailments would land me over and over again in the same terrifying scene: zooming up Route 3, gripping the steering wheel, pleading with God to not take Abuela from us or to at least let me see her alive one more time.

Each time, the ER was packed with my cousins, the *viejos*, and whichever grandkids were currently visiting or sleeping over at Hunt Street. The staff got to know us and understood we all needed to be there, even if we had to take turns coming into the room. "Cuban weirdness," we told them. "We need to be together."

With all of us taking turns, Abuela was never alone during the day in the hospital. We helped with her bathing, took her to the bathroom, provided the kind of hands-on help she'd always given us. We sang her the Cuban nursery songs she'd sung to us to help her learn to walk again. The physical therapists learned one of them—*Andando, andando, la niña va caminando.* We got used to hearing the tune coming from other rooms as the PTs sang it to other patients.

We all rallied behind her, but during this period we understood Abuela's fragility for the first time. It shocked me to suddenly see just how old she was, to understand that her death, the enemy I'd pushed against for so long, was at our door. This shouldn't have surprised any of us. Abuela was one of those people who seem old even when they are young—everyone who'd known her all her life said this. She'd always been sick, with real or imagined ailments, but she always popped back up again. But now, suddenly, her ninety-plus years had swooped down on her and were holding her down.

I felt panicky at the thought of losing her—the panic of a six-year-old, not of a full-grown woman who should have been preparing for her grandmother's death for quite some time. Abuela was the incarnation of home and family for me. More than that, this ancient woman was the emblem of our family history and survival. She'd lost the most when we left Cuba, and she'd been the foundation—shaky, but enduring—in the States as we'd built our new lives.

As we talked about Abuela one night, I told Diana about a movie we watched together one night as a family, just after we arrived from

Cuba. A little orphaned boy is cared for by his grandfather, but the old man dies. All the boy has left is their dog. The movie ripped my heart out and drove me upstairs, where I hid and cried hard for a long time. I remember shaking on the bed, grieving the grandfather *and* Abuela. That night, I understood for the first time that, one day, I would lose her.

That time was coming. I didn't want to get there too soon, so I prayed each night, as I had since childhood—a greedy petitioner still asking Papa Dios to protect Abuela, to keep her safe and healthy so we could all be together for just a little bit longer.

40

Mami's Torment

Hunt Street, 2002

The mother of the mothers watched the melee of Hunt Street from a corner of the living room, in her wheelchair, completely silent. Abuela's last stroke had left her almost mute and partially paralyzed. I longed to hear one more full sentence spill from her mouth. Was she worried, sad, scared? Those emotions had shaped her entire life.

I wondered if we could ease her anxiety. We owed Abuela this small mercy. An antidepressant could help her. I pitched the idea to Mami.

She shook her head. "Old people have bad reactions to new medicines. It's tricky."

I searched Abuela's eyes and saw something I recognized, something Mami didn't fully believe in or understand. "Some of us really need that medicine."

I remembered how calm Mami seemed when I first told her that the psychiatrist had diagnosed my depression. But when I called her again a few hours later, Papi said she'd left right after our call. Immediately, I knew where she'd gone (a parking lot somewhere) and why (to cry in private about my pain and how she hadn't been able to make it go away). She hadn't seen the power of depression during those years. She wasn't seeing it now.

I doubled down. I enlisted Diana and we tag-teamed until Mami gave in. Abuela's doctor prescribed a low dose of Prozac, and, soon, the darkness I'd seen in Abuela's eyes was gone. She looked younger, even, with her new, lopsided smile.

With Abuela's needs met, I turned to Mami's. Besides taking care of Abuela, she watched Diana's toddlers, Lily and Nick, and Sergio's youngest, Mia, each day. Next door, Tía and Tío looked after Angel and Susan's two kids, Audrey and Dennis, and Alberto and Mary's older boys, Brandon and Andy. The duplex vibrated with kid energy again, but everywhere you turned someone needed saving. I popped in here and there to help, but with Natalia and Sam in tow, I only added to the body count.

In that tiny house, the best place for Abuela's commode was in the middle of the living room. Every so often, the kids would turn away from *Barney* or *Blue's Clues* and touch the outside of the basin. "Tata finished!" they'd announce when the basin was warm, and Mami and I would wipe Abuela down, put her back in her wheelchair or recliner, and clean out the basin.

How did these arthritic, aging women, with their own busy schedules, run such operations out of their houses? Eight people under their care, and yet I rarely heard them complain. Tía and Mami saw their roles as natural. This was what they wanted to do in their retirement: care for their children's children and their own mother. None of my friends' parents chose this path. But to Tía and Mami, the American ideal of achieving carefree independence after retirement looked like an empty proposition.

Driving back to Lexington after those visits—depleted of all energy—I wondered if I could ever match their awesome devotion to family.

I was afraid of the answer, so I pushed away the premature

guilt and focused instead on the pride that Mami and Tía earned every day.

I walked into Hunt Street one day and found Operation Bathe Abuela underway, complete with a visiting nurse, a bunch of kids, and a physical therapist gawking from the living room.

The *viejos* moved the kitchen table into the dining room. They brought in the collapsible blue kiddie pool from the yard and put it on the kitchen floor. They folded down the sides of the pool and wheeled Abuela into the middle. As Mami and Tía lifted Abuela up and undressed her, Tío replaced the wheelchair with the commode, the whole time averting his eyes from his naked mother-in-law. Tía and Mami lowered Abuela onto the commode, lathered her up with flowery soap and shampoo, then rinsed her off with a short hose they'd connected to the kitchen faucet. When Abuela appeared from behind the huddle of *viejos*—freshly bathed, in her pajamas, and smiling crookedly in her wheelchair—her fan club cheered.

"It's really ingenious," the nurse whispered. "But what about her privacy, her dignity?"

I looked at Abuela's regal expression. "I don't think Cuban grand-mothers worry about privacy."

But how long could Mami keep this up? The *viejos* were all looking tired, especially Tío, who'd recently been diagnosed with Parkinson's. Even so, whenever we suggested hiring help, Mami changed the subject.

Sometimes she'd reveal her greatest fear: that Abuela would end up in a nursing home. Nursing homes might be okay for old American people, but not for Cuban *viejos*—no sir.

Mami's stubbornness scared me. Hadn't she taught us to withhold sweeping judgments just like these—to never say, "I'll never do X"? If she caught us judging another person's difficult choices, she'd intone

an old Spanish saying: "*No hubo boca que habló que Dios no castigó.*"
I hoped God wouldn't punish her for judging nursing homes by forcing her to put Abuela in one.

I helped Mami whenever I could, but no amount of pitching in
could erase the weariness on my mother's face. Mami's body was
folding inward, even though her spirit refused to notice.

Diana and I sat next to Mami's bed in the post-op area of Lahey
Medical Center. Mami was still in a deep sleep, but every few minutes, she'd belt out a song. We tried not to laugh as her woozy "Jyu
Are My Sonshine" bounced off the walls. We needed a laugh that day,
after months of worrying about her health.

She'd had a relatively simple heart procedure: a catheterization
to force open a closed heart valve. The doctors thought the so-called
PFO, a congenital defect, had caused Mami's mini-stroke a few
months earlier.

Since the mini-stroke, Mami's doctors had been advising her to
slow down. Mami had fought back at first—but very slowly, she'd
accepted what we'd all seen coming. Abuela needed more care than
she and the *viejo* team could give her.

Tía had moved Mami gently through the decision, and Mami had
finally resigned herself to the facts. What she'd dreaded was straight
ahead: Abuela would live her last days in a nursing home.

I felt my mother's torment every time I was with her, even when
we weren't talking about Abuela. Her typical serenity was gone, and
that scared me even more than seeing Abuela in a nursing home. I
wanted to help her find a solution. But if Mami, with all her gifts
and strengths, had failed to achieve her crucial goal, what hope did
I have?

I reminded Mami that that she'd done her best. But none of that
mattered to her.

As everything fell apart for Mami, Tía had focused on finding Abuela the best nursing home possible.

Miraculously, a bed had become available in the nursing home right across the street. The home had gone up where the woods had been, where we'd scrambled over thirty-foot-tall pine trees despite Abuela's pleas to stay earthbound. At least she would be just a short walk from the duplex.

For Mami, that didn't soften the blow.

"I have to accept that I failed," Mami had told us before going into surgery that morning. "I wanted something for Abuela. I couldn't make it happen. Your aunt keeps talking about the positives. There aren't any."

As we listened to Mami singing in her sleep, it was easy to chuckle, but Diana and I couldn't forget the hollow sound of her voice earlier that morning.

Mami switched suddenly to a new song. "Like a Candle in the Weend" lifted our spirits and demolished them at the same time.

Abuela's nursing home roommate was clearly out of her mind, but it didn't make her racism any easier to take. Molly raged at us each time we spoke in Spanish. Fortunately, Abuela didn't fully understand Molly's swears, so she was spared their full impact.

Molly especially hated Papi. She flipped out whenever he walked in—*spic this* and *spic that*. Papi would laugh it off, go over to the chair by Abuela's window, and make the cuckoo sign until Abuela gave him that half smile we were always after.

Papi was in his usual chair trying to get Abuela to eat when I walked into her room one day—making rumbling motor sounds and waving the "airplane" spoon gently in front of her pursed lips. She was angry about the nursing home. Even with her limitations, every night, as Mami was getting ready to leave, Abuela managed this heartrending question: "*¿Mi casa?*" Refusing to eat was the best way for her to protest. Repeatedly, she turned away from the hot puree Papi had brought over from Hunt Street.

I saw my father's frustration growing, so I stepped in and used the same technique Abuela would have used on us—ruthless, effective. I held the container in front of her.

"Mami is going to get really mad at me if I bring this back full. And I can't lie to her. She's going to get *so* mad at me . . . *Por favor?*"

Abuela opened her mouth like a baby bird, and I popped in a spoonful of puree. Then another, and another.

Papi smiled. Abuela smiled. She had helped me. And that felt good.

Tía charged through the new nursing home reality with a determined cheerfulness that incensed my mother.

"She acts like it's a good thing," Mami complained to Diana and me one day. "How can she pretend like that? No. I think she really *is* happy about it."

"Jeez, Mami," Diana said. She was taking the brunt of Mami's anger these days, since she saw her every afternoon when she picked up her kids after work. "Tía is just trying to make this as positive as possible. For all our sakes."

Mami's expression was hard, but you could see the hurt in her eyes.

"Diana's right, Mami," I chimed in. "You're always telling us to accept what we can't change. Tía's just trying . . ."

The look of pain on Mami's face shot through me. Nothing I said could comfort her.

The only positive family news in those days was Alberto and Mary's new house in Merrimack. Palatial and pristine, with a sunny in-law apartment in the basement, the house felt like a prize well-earned for my hardworking cousin and his wife. And one day, they'd agreed, when Tío's Parkinson's worsened, Tía and Tío would move in.

The idea of Tía and Tío moving out of Hunt Street haunted Mami from that moment on. If they moved, Mami and Papi would have to move also—leave a house that was completely paid for and probably take on debt to find a new home.

Mami argued constantly with Tía, often listing the advantages of staying together: "We'll be able to take care of the grandkids together; everyone will help each other because the kids will always be coming and going. All ages, all the time, like always."

Sometimes, the arguments turned ugly.

"*Tranquila,*" Tío said to Mami one day after a particularly rough exchange. "We're not going anywhere for a very long time. Silvia's just excited about a brand-new start someday. But not now. You'll see."

I tried to shift Mami's thinking about a possible move. The neighborhood had turned. A smaller house and a first-floor bedroom made sense. But my heart wasn't in it. I was only trying to defend Tía and calm Mami. The idea of losing Hunt Street felt as remote as Pluto.

We got into it again one night as I helped Mami bathe Abuela. She never let the staff bathe her. "No stranger is going to bathe my mother," she said when I brought up the risk of both of them falling. So four times a week—late at night, when no one else was around—Mami wheeled Abuela into the open shower room, moved her onto a commode, lathered her up, and went to town with her washcloth.

I watched Abuela rocking, naked and slathered in foam, as Mami swabbed her. Mami complained, as she ran the washcloth over every crevice and curve of Abuela's body, about the possibility of moving, about acquiring debt in retirement, about Tía throwing logic out the window, about being forced to leave her home. I tried to defend Tía. Mami waved away my points, the washcloth spraying suds in the air as she spoke.

All the while, Abuela rocked on the commode to the rhythm of Mami's complaints, a round ball of tired but very clean flesh, fully at the mercy of her frustrated daughter.

I watched as a pile of suds slid off Abuela's head and down her face. She sighed, winked, and gave me the wisest and most weary smile I'd ever seen.

41

Just a Little Bit Longer

Nashua, June 2004

Natalia and Sam ran ahead of me through the nursing home hallway, drawing slow smiles from the residents in their wheelchairs.

I entered Abuela's room at a jog—and almost bumped into the kids. They'd stopped hard in front of Molly's bed and were quietly taking in the scene. Papi sat in a chair between Abuela and her cranky roommate and was spoon-feeding each of them their dinners.

The kids sidled up to him, and he put down the spoons and napkins. Molly took her eyes off the TV and tracked the kids as they kissed Papi. She grumbled something unintelligible. Papi raised his eyebrows at me and shrugged. He picked up Molly's spoon and resumed his feeding. When he leaned over to wipe mush off Molly's mouth, I shook my head. Papi feeding the cantankerous racist Molly just didn't compute.

He told me later he'd simply gotten tired of seeing the staff take her tray away, completely full of food. "I'm already here feeding your grandmother, so I just started with Molly, and it worked. *Qué cosa mas grande, ¿verdad?*"

Molly's plate was almost empty, but Abuela's was still full. She had been refusing food even more than usual lately. The *viejos* took turns crossing the street to the nursing home during mealtimes, carrying Tupperware containers full of warm Cuban food and prepped with new stories to share with Abuela. They coaxed and cajoled, but Abuela clamped her mouth shut in defiance.

I took over Abuela's feeding while Papi finished with Molly. Sam scrambled up on Abuela's bed and Natalia held her hand. She opened her mouth almost immediately when I leaned in with the spoon. "*Descarada*," I said, smiling. She truly was cheeky in her favoritism, not that I didn't enjoy my advantage.

But Abuela's hunger strike scared me. Was it a sign she had given up, even though we—and the staff—had done all we could to make her as comfortable as possible in her new "home"? Even Mami, who still barely tolerated the situation, put on a brave face and an optimistic attitude whenever she was with Abuela.

I tried to convince myself that Abuela would be okay for a while longer. But each time I saw her she looked weaker, a candle flickering. I prayed for the millionth time—*Please, not yet.*

I believed in prayer; Abuela had taught me well all those nights together in bed. I was ripping out Spanish Hail Mary's and Acts of Contrition in rapid succession each night, and my prayers had worked so far. How many times had Abuela crawled back to safety after teetering over the edge? I'd never thought of myself as an optimist, but my hopefulness about Abuela proved otherwise.

"You'd better prepare yourself," Diana said one day, irritated by another one of my hopeful comments. "You're not seeing this situation very clearly."

"I see it," I insisted, "but why can't I hope?"

She sighed. "I'd rather be ready than skipping around thinking she's going to be fine."

"Yeah, but then I've suffered that much sooner than I needed to."

Hopefulness is a stubborn thing, I guess. It was in the air that early June night as Mami and I watched Natalia's softball game in Lexington. We sat on a blanket, eating cookies, and as the girls chanted for their team I chattered away. I'd served as treasurer on a school funding campaign that had just ended in a win. That night, we'd be taking a bunch of Sam's friends to see *Harry Potter and the Prisoner of Azkaban* for his birthday. The happy days of summer break were just ahead.

"Abuela isn't doing well," Mami said. The leaden tone in her voice broke the happy mood.

"I know. I know. She's not eating much."

"She vomited up something strange yesterday," Mami said. "Again today. Looked like coffee grounds. The nurse says it's a sign of a bowel blockage, probably. That it might be a matter of days."

I fought off her warning, offered her all kinds of encouraging words. She didn't bite.

I'll always tie images of Harry Potter's dementors to those next few days—black veils of smoke and shrouds.

We'd just dropped off the last of Sam's friends after the movie when Mami called.

"You'd better come up."

One more time, I hurtled up Route 3 to Nashua, praying all the way—in English, in Spanish, making deals, begging. I wasn't ready. Not even close. Not yet. Not yet.

The nurses, worried that the entire Cuban clan—all twenty-five of us—might show up and stay indefinitely, had moved Abuela to a private room. My cousins, their wives, some of their kids, my siblings and their families, the *viejos*—almost every member of our family stood or sat around Abuela's bed, leaned against a wall, or each other. Lots of red eyes and quiet, deep breaths.

Abuela's mouth was open and she was gasping for breath, each one shaking her chest as it entered and left her. I wrapped my arms around her, and the sobs tore out of my chest. I felt her stir and looked up into her face. Her eyelids fluttered.

I felt a hand on my shoulder.

"I don't want people upsetting her," Mami whispered. "I want her to be tranquil."

I pulled away from Abuela's warm chest. Mary took me out into the hallway and explained in her nurse's language how Abuela wasn't suffering—the miracle of morphine.

Even then, I hoped. "Is there any chance . . ."

Mary smiled, her eyes full of pity.

One by one, each of us said goodbye and left Abuela with Mami and Tía. Diana and I were the last to leave. We held back tears until we got outside, then clung to each other. No amount of preparation would have helped ease us into this moment.

We walked across the street to the duplex, showered, got into Abuela's bed, and tried to sleep.

I was watching the sky turn purple at dawn when the phone rang. Mami.

"Your grandmother just passed away."

Diana sat up in bed as I threw on some clothes and ran across the street. Mami and Tía were standing on either side of Abuela's bed. Her eyes were still open, but they weren't hers anymore.

I'd never seen death before. Its gray foreignness overwhelmed me, but I didn't need to worry about disturbing Abuela now with tears and sobs. Mami and Tía let theirs loose, too, as I wrapped my arms around Abuela and wept. She was still warm. She smelled like Abuela. But the world was different now.

I felt Tía's and Mami's hands as they brushed my back. Each of my sobs ripped more out of them.

"Just now, so softly," Tía said. "The sky had just lightened up. I said, 'Consuelo, I think Mima is gone.'"

How differently we grieved. Some looked inward and stayed still; some busied themselves with tasks: the wake, flowers, casket, phone calls. The mother of the mothers was gone, and no one knew how to move through a world that didn't have her in it. I worried that we hadn't really checked to see if she was dead when the hearse arrived at the nursing home. I kept thinking of how she had died practically in the same spot where Big Ben, the tallest pine tree in the woods, had lived. I remembered riding high up in its branches one day, whipping around in the wild wind, and Abuela's wrath when she found me, the look of angry love on her face.

Where was she now?

The funeral home was packed with our friends and relatives. Such an old woman. *Where did all these people come from?*

I saw old Hunt Street and school friends I hadn't seen in decades. They told us stories about how Abuela had fed them *café con leche y tostadas,* how she always tried to get them to stay for dinner, the times she tried to talk with them in English and they just ended up giggling together. They still called her Abuela, as they had from the first day they'd met her. The *viejos* had always loved hearing our American friends refer to them the same way we did: Mami, Papi, Tía, Tío.

I walked through those packed rooms, full of people and roses and lilies, touching the ribboned yellow coronas that Abuela would have admired. She loved yellow; it was everywhere. People knew.

Descansa en paz, the ribbons said. Rest in peace, Abuelita.

I needed to talk with the undertaker. I finally found the stooped old man in the hallway, haggard after accompanying the *viejos* during their all-night vigil the night before. They'd insisted on honoring Abuela by following the Cuban tradition of staying with your loved one until the casket is closed for the last time.

I handed the undertaker the warm, fluffy socks I'd taken from Abuela's drawer.

"Please," I said, "make sure she has these on. Her feet get really, really cold."

42

A Crack in the Foundation

Hunt Street, Late Summer 2004

We were a wheel without a hub, each of us spinning without purpose or direction in our own grief orbit, reaching for a center that was gone. We thought we had prepared ourselves. We hadn't come close. The intensity of our grief stunned us. We stumbled around and the only thing we found was each other. Except we were different versions of ourselves, familiar strangers.

We circled back to Hunt Street often, offering comfort to Mami and Tía and trying to find solace in each other. One afternoon, our generation talked cautiously in Tía's living room—wending our way through memories of Abuela, afraid of triggering tears.

A small argument broke out about a trivial detail in one of the stories. We called into the kitchen to get the *viejos'* opinion on the matter.

"I don't remember," Tía called back. "Do you, Consuelo?"

After a long pause, we heard Mami's voice—soft, quiet. *"No tengo ni la menor idea."*

She didn't have a clue about the issue—which must have been an obvious one, because we started laughing when we realized that neither Tía nor Mami knew the answer.

"You two are useless!" I said, still laughing. "You don't remember a thing!"

The silence told me just how far from funny my words were. As refugees, we didn't have heirlooms, antiques, photos of ancestors. We depended on lightweight, portable family relics: our stories. And now Abuela, who had known them like no one else, was gone.

We would have many moments like that one. We'd reach for an answer that we suddenly, desperately needed—a particular nugget, maybe about Don Manuel's sheepherding days in Galicia or exactly how Abuela cheated on our ration book to score more food for the family—and there would be none forthcoming. Abuela had been the crucial link in our family's chain of immigrant-refugee experiences, from Spain to Cuba, from Cuba to the United States. Without her, the chain was broken, the cohering perspective gone.

For a while after Abuela died, Tía stopped talking about moving out of Hunt Street. We hoped that grief had changed her mind. But after a few weeks, her campaign to move out of Hunt Street revved up again, and Mami, Papi, and Tío renewed their campaign to stay put.

In my mind, the move, if it would happen at all, was too far-off to worry about. And I still held out hope that if it happened, they'd all move in together somewhere. Our messy, multigenerational, Cuban-style family life would continue, just in a ranch-style house with two first-floor, senior-friendly bedrooms.

I couldn't see that our Hunt Street days were numbered, that our untethered world was spinning farther away from its center. I'd let my grief for Abuela blind me to everything else.

I let that grief take all it wanted from me. I shielded the kids from my pain, but when I was alone, I cried myself dry, howling on the bed, only to clean up nice before the kids came home.

Some acquaintances and friends seemed confused about the depth of my sadness. Only Andy and my old Nashua friends understood that this had been a mother-child relationship, with the added depth of the shared refugee experience. My life had been shaped by that experience, and Abuela and I had literally slept in the same bed with it for a huge piece of our lives. Abuela was my life raft and guide—an imperfect one, yes, but dependable and heroic, in her own way. And, now, gone forever.

Mami fought hard against the imminent change that I couldn't even see. The battles with Tía wore her down. The tension, even when they weren't arguing, stayed with her, just beneath her skin. She snapped every time we spoke about the possibility of Tía moving—or even the smallest things. She was furious about having to consider the possibility of such a colossal change, especially now, so soon after losing Abuela.

Tío saw her agony one day and tried to reassure her. I was washing dishes in Mami's kitchen when he walked in. He leaned over Mami as she read the real estate listings on her computer.

"Don't worry, Connie. This isn't going to happen. It can't."

Mami looked up at him. "*Ya Silvia decidió.*"

Mami's flat tone, the grim look on her face, drove that fact into my grief-numbed mind for the first time. Silvia *had* decided. The *viejos* were going to move out of Hunt Street.

Tío looked as destroyed as I felt. He'd come to offer Mami the only things he could—a bit of hope, a little comfort. Instead, Mami had shown him what he needed to see: Hunt Street was crumbling to pieces in front of us.

Mami picked up the red crocheted beret from the floor of Abuela's closet. Her eyes closed as she buried her nose into the scent. "It's *exactly* her," she said. I heard the snag of pain in her voice, and my heart squeezed tight around it. I'd inhaled my children's clothes the same way, relishing the scent of my babies. I realized that Abuela had become Mami's baby during those last years of constant tending and care.

Mami sighed, put the beret inside a baggie, and zipped it shut. "This will make it last."

We were packing up 23D. Tía and Tío had already moved into Alberto and Mary's in-law basement apartment. Each time I visited them, Tía beamed. She showed me the different kinds of birds at the bird feeder, the little gravel path and the gate to their door, the decorations in her new bedroom.

Mami and Papi had found a nice, brand-new, stand-alone condo in a fifty-five-and-over community in Merrimack, New Hampshire. Mami hated it. The mix of grief, loss, and anger had changed her. For the first time in my life, I sensed a persistent bitterness in her.

I was with her when she left Hunt Street for the last time. She stood at the bottom of the stairs, in front of the door, scanning the empty living room. She used the Cuban term of endearment for mothers when she called out to Abuela: "*¡Mima!* We're leaving. *¡Vámonos!*"

The pain of losing Hunt Street grew quietly in my heart. I'd been too focused on grieving Abuela and on Mami and Tía's problems to notice. Small moments signaled my depression returning. I'd learned to pay attention to that distant "me" sound. Nothing brought me much joy anymore.

I went into self-protection mode—kept away from sad songs, movies, and negative people. But I didn't want to start seeing a psychiatrist again. I was too busy. It was too expensive.

Maybe this is what deep grief feels like, I told myself. *It's normal. I can handle this.*

Mami listened patiently as I told her about my vivid dream. It proved something to me. Abuela was Elsewhere, but she was fine. She had sent me a message that only I could understand, something so powerful that even my skeptical mother would take comfort from it.

I wasn't sure it was a dream, actually. I had heard our bedroom door swing open and hit the wall, the familiar sound of one of the kids coming into the room in the middle of the night looking for comfort, needing something. I'd listened as light footsteps crossed the room to my side of the bed, had felt the mattress dip and spring back a few times as someone leaned on it repeatedly in a very kid-like way. I'd heard giggling. I'd moved over to let Natalia or Sam in beside me. A little body had slid in next to me. Then, a child's whisper: "*¿Cinco minutos más?*" Five more minutes?

Those were the words I always said to Abuela when she tried to get me out of bed and ready for school. She teased me about that all my life. "*¡Cinco minutos más! ¿Te acuerdas?*" she'd say, chuckling, even after her first stroke. And, of course, I did remember. But my kids didn't speak Spanish unless I hounded them.

I swept my arm toward the edge of the bed to identify which kid was messing with me. But the space was bare, nothing but sheet and blanket. I kept sweeping my hand over it, even after I sat up, fully alert by then. I looked around the room. A crack of early light slid under the shade and lit up my hand.

Mami sighed when I finished. "You're not going to believe this. Last night, I dreamed I was in the living room and heard her call me from her bed in the dining room. As clear and real a sound as you can imagine. It was her voice. 'Consuelo, Consuelo,' she was calling me—very light, not urgent. I ran to the dining room, but her bed was empty. The sheets were rumpled, though, like she had just gotten up.

I touched them. They were warm. *'¡Gracias!'* I heard her say. Then again—so happily—*'¡Gracias!'*"

I tried to find peace in that strange coincidence, but the dead weight of depression returned and took over. I fought the idea of getting help. *I can do this; I can do this,* I told myself.

The tipping point came on a girls' weekend with my old Nashua friends. We'd gone to see *Million Dollar Baby.* I wasn't prepared for the final hospital scenes, where love leads Clint Eastwood's character to end the suffering of his prizefighter in the most horrible and beautiful way. Memories of Abuela's last days sprung up in front of me, then images of the yellow duplex, empty except for the ghosts we'd left behind. My sobs must have annoyed everyone in the theater that night. I felt my friends' hands on my back as they tried to calm me. I could not stop crying, even in the lobby. The manager rushed over to see what had happened. I blubbered incomprehensibly as my friends reassured him that I'd be fine.

I saw my psychiatrist for the first time soon after. As I sobbed in her office, she pointed out what should have been obvious: I'd lost my home again. But now, Abuela was gone, the family had separated, and Tía and Mami's relationship was in tatters. Those losses had revived the wrenching dislocation and sorrow I'd felt when we lost our Cuban lives abruptly thirty-seven years before.

The long reach of trauma stunned me. I saw its handprint on Mami's rage about the forced move. She'd always been so future-facing. Now she kept looking back with unrelenting bitterness at the ending of Hunt Street, the end of another way of life, the loss of another kind of country.

43
Juanelo's Gifts

Merrimack, New Hampshire, Summer 2005

Mami and I were sitting in her new living room, unpacking boxes. I tried to cheer her up by complimenting some aspect of the new condo or the neighborhood. She didn't care about the pretty porch, the gas fireplace, the sparkling new kitchen, the gleaming wood floors. She did like the small deck in the back.

"I know you don't like it when I smoke," she said. "But I have a cigarette out there each night after dinner. I sit and look for the first star, and I talk to Abuela and tell her what's happening."

She picked up a doll from one of the boxes full of toys. "This is the end of *primos hermanos* for all of your kids," she said, looking at the doll's face. "Lily and Nick won't have what you kids had. It won't be the same." She looked at me with watery eyes. "We'll see each other like the Americans, at Thanksgiving and Christmas."

"No," I protested. "We'll still visit each other on weekends and for birthdays."

"You kids don't have time to talk on the phone half the time. How are you going to make time to visit two houses on weekends?"

Tía and Mami began to inch their way back to each other. The cautious politeness between them made all of us cringe. They were each "nesting," creating their own homes for the first time, completely independent from each other. Tía flowed happily through the decorating, Mami reluctantly, but she seemed to be settling in. I thought she was letting go of her anger until she called me one day.

"Your aunt and I had a terrible fight. It was time she heard *everything* I've been feeling."

My heart dropped as she described a shouting match that had lasted far too long. Tía had come over to Mami's new condo for coffee, but her bright mood had aggravated Mami so much that she'd snapped.

Now it was my turn. "Why do you *insist* on returning to this subject? You're destroying the relationship!"

"I'm not the one—"

"Remember your saying, '*Dos no pelean si uno no quiere*'? Well, now it's your turn: Two don't fight if one doesn't want to."

"She slammed the door when she left."

"I'm calling her right now."

"I'd give her a while to cool off."

Tía was seething when I got her on the phone, but I sensed hurt more than anger, and the defensiveness that comes with guilt.

"Your mother is a very, very hard woman sometimes," she told me.

Mami sounded even angrier the next day, an incessant typewriter, tapping out complaint after complaint about Tía. Incidents at the nursing home, long forgotten slights, some reaching to when they were kids. This was going in the wrong direction. What would this sisters' war do to our family, which was still trying to redefine itself without Abuela and Hunt Street? I wondered if after all the hardships they'd overcome together, all these years, the sisters would finally break from Don Manuel's last request of them: stay together.

I hung up, got in the car, and drove up Route 3. Mami needed someone to pound sense into her head. She never hesitated to pound it into ours.

The front door was locked. Weird. Mami didn't lock the door during the day. I rang a few times and, finally, the door opened.

Tía's hair and eyebrows were covered in brown hair dye; a stained towel was draped around her neck to catch the drips. The smell of ammonia stung my nose.

"¡Hola, mijita! I'd kiss you, but . . ." She turned and walked toward the kitchen.

I realized then why the door was locked. In her new apartment, Tía had started locking her doors during the day. Mami laughed at her, but Tía pointed to the woods all around the house and said, "You never know . . ."

Mami was at the kitchen table reading the newspaper, her hair similarly plastered in hair dye. The squeeze bottle of dye was on the table, next to Dixie cups full of Cuban coffee. I looked from one dye-smeared face to another as the mutual grooming ritual resumed.

"I thought you two had a horrible fight."

Tía didn't look up as she dabbed dye over Mami's eyebrows. "Oh, you know we say horrible things to each other. It doesn't matter in the end."

Slowly, the warriors and their husbands created new homes, one more time. For the first time in their lives, they didn't live in the same house, or next to or above each other. But the ride between their homes was short, a mere ten minutes. They saw each other almost every day, either at the condo or the in-law apartment. When we visited either Tía or Mami, usually the other sister was around, on the way, or had just left.

Their restored relationship calmed me. Life was different without Abuela, but it was moving forward and taking a new shape. I started to recognize myself again. The heavy mood started to lift. Slowly, contentment returned.

Now that Mami's anger and grief had subsided, Papi could show more of his excitement about the condo, from the green marble fireplace surround to the granite counters. He talked about adding a tile backsplash and finishing the basement. He loved the friendly new neighbors, who were as eager to create a new community as he was. Mami, cautious about any friendship that moved too quickly into intimacy, tried to rein Papi in; every afternoon, she refused to gather with the other retirees for wine and cheese, a bizarre combination of ritual and food choice for a traditional Cuban. But Papi accepted every invitation and made excuses for why Mami couldn't join him.

My parents had never lived alone as a couple in their forty-five years of marriage. They'd grown up in multigenerational, crowded households, and Abuela had moved in with them when they got married. In the United States, duplex living had meant a constant wave of people flowing in and out of the house. Now, Papi had to satisfy his people-person needs with Mami or the American retirees. But long stretches of speaking English tired him out, so Mami was mostly it.

"I never knew your father talked that much," she said, shaking her head. "Even at night, we get in bed, and he's still talking. I have to tell him, 'Shh . . . Leave something for tomorrow.' And . . . he walks around the house in his underwear! He never did that before."

I watched them rediscover each other after almost five decades of marriage. Their young-couple tiffs often caught me off guard. One afternoon, I stood between them in their new kitchen trying to lower the heat on an escalating argument. The day before, Papi had—once again, and without telling Mami—invited some of the neighbors over for wine and cheese, the novel American-style entertaining that was so exciting for him.

Mami was almost shouting. "In he walks, two couples behind him! Just before dinner. As if I have cheese and white wine!"

"You're completely antisocial!" Papi's arms were crossed over his chest.

"I don't like surprises."

Mami didn't want more friends in her life. She was still bruised from Abuela's death and the forced move. But more than that, she was enjoying the first quiet afternoons and evenings she'd ever had.

She grabbed her Cuban mop and started swabbing the floor in violent arcs. "At least ask me the day before. Give me some warning before bringing fifty people into the living room looking for snacks!"

"Two couples! Don't exaggerate. I never knew you were so cold! How are you going to make new friends if you don't accept invitations or invite people over?"

"Just tell me before you invite someone!"

"That's just an excuse. Admit it. You don't want to make new friends."

"I don't have anything in common with them! The other day, a couple of the women kept hounding me about taking care of my grandkids every single day. Why didn't I just say no to my kids? Didn't I want time to myself? They looked at me like I was from Mars."

"Listen, listen! I found it." As they argued, I'd been searching for Cuban tunes from the '50s on the Web, hoping to distract them. As Beny Moré's "Santa Isabel de las Lajas" trumpeted out of the speakers, my parents slowly turned toward me, their eyes wide as they switched to a better channel.

Mami had mentioned this song once, when they were embroiled in another fight. I'd tried to distract them by offering to find old Cuban music online. Mami had scoffed, "Our music isn't going to be on the Internet!"

But it was. "See? I told you that stuff is there."

Cuban music transformed most of the old Cubans I knew, but with Mami the change emanated from deep inside and shone in her eyes, as it did now. She started singing the old tune, and Papi swooped her into a spin. The dancing began, and the fight about surprise wine and cheese guests lost its steam.

"Find more! Can you find 'La Engañadora'?" Papi looked like a little boy waiting to open a present.

"I haven't heard that song in a million years," Mami mumbled. "How's it start . . . What are the two streets it talks about?"

"*¡Prado y Neptuno!*" Papi said.

"No. That's not right. Anita, find it."

Papi was right. He nodded as "The Deceiver," an old Enrique Jorrín song, flowed out of the computer speaker.

"A Prado y Neptuno . . . Iba una chiquita . . .
Que todos los hombres . . . La tenían que mirar . . ."

"I told you!" Papi was dancing by himself, an erratic cha-cha-cha that Mami had been trying to tame for almost fifty years.

She held his hands and helped him recover the rhythm so they could keep dancing—together.

Merrimack, Noche Buena 2005

The windows of Mami and Papi's condo rattled with noise they couldn't contain. Andy, the kids, and I were on the porch, hoping someone would hear the bell. We hunched into our coats, trying to stay warm in the freezing wind.

Someone finally opened the door. The smell of roasting pork, garlic, and lemon wrapped around us—and in that split second, the icy December night vanished. We walked into the tropical Noche Buena that Mami and Tía had always created for us in our new country, no matter how little we had or how much snow surrounded us outside.

That Noche Buena brought us all together for the first time since the *viejos'* move from Hunt Street. I counted all twenty-five of us that night and thought about Abuela. Whenever we were all together, she liked to point out how we'd grown as a family. "*¡Imagínate, chica! Eramos nueve nadamás cuando llegamos.*"

We were just nine when we arrived, that was true. And now look.

Alberto and Mary and their sons, Angel and Susan and their son and daughter, Sergio and Jada and their three, Diana and Dave and their two, Andy and me and our two. And the four *viejos*. Spanish Christmas carols played on Mami's stereo. The same few albums had been played for so many Noche Buenas that they should have been in shards by now. On a table next to the fireplace, Mami's elaborate Santa's Village, electric miniature train and all, attracted every grandkid in the room. They relocated skaters and sledders to their hearts' content in the mounds of cottony snow. A couple of dogs threaded through our legs as we cleared furniture out of the way and set up folding tables and chairs. Someone had already broken into the *turrón*, a Spanish almond bar that we sliced and passed around, usually for dessert but often well before. The Bacardí, Coke, and limes waited on the counter for the birth of Cuba Libres.

In the kitchen, the *viejos* stood in a semicircle around Mami's computer. They hunched over the screen, pointing and talking. Someone had pulled up Google Earth and zoomed in on images of Juanelo. I peered over their shoulders and wedged in closer.

"That's where Porta had his little farm," Tía said, pointing at an area of the barrio near the river.

Papi's voice was an incredulous whisper. "Look at that, that's where El Chino and I stole *bacalao* from the kiosk vendor. The little alley's still there. I can still taste those fritters."

I saw clay-tiled roofs, thick tree canopies, crumbling roads. But what the *viejos* saw, no matter how far away and removed from time, was home.

I left the crowd downstairs and ran our bags up to the guest room. Mami had decorated the room with dried sunflowers—the flower of la Virgen de Caridad, Cuba's patron saint—and framed prints of seascapes. The patchwork quilt on the bed picked up the sunny yellows and dark blues.

A photo album on the dresser caught my attention. Mami had created a new one for us to look at when we stayed over. She'd titled it, "Cuba, 1999." It was yet another collection of photos from our trip.

I needed to get back downstairs, but I had to look through the latest compilation.

I'd seen some of them before. Juanelo's schoolchildren holding hands, their red Pionero neckerchiefs contrasted against bright white shirts. A photo of my cousin Patricia with me on the back of her moped. *Just like Alfredo's*, I thought, as I remembered riding with Patricia's father, long before there was a Patricia, on the back of his moto when he visited us in Juanelo.

The moto. Tío Alfredo's was the only one I ever remember seeing in the barrio. Such a different moto than the one the guard rode when he brought the *permiso* for one of Juanelo's families. Those were the last normal nights for those families, in Juanelo, in their old lives.

Staring at my cousin's face, I saw the family resemblance that everyone had pointed out to us during our visit. I hadn't seen it then. I'm almost ten years older than Patricia. But the tilt of our heads, the shape of our smiles, are exactly the same. Don Manuel and Vicenta's great-granddaughters had found each other because of their mothers, mostly, and their battles to stay connected to each other. Those old, stubborn women.

I remembered, suddenly, where Patricia and I had been the day Mami took that photo. We were coming back from an artisan's market just to the west of Havana, near the Hotel Nacional. I had stopped at a table where an old woman was selling necklaces of beans and seeds, coconut shell bracelets, trinkets. I chatted with her as I looked through the little treasures she'd laid out. She stopped talking and beamed a smile at me. She'd thought I was just a very dark tourist who spoke almost-perfect Spanish. But now she knew.

"You're from over there, aren't you! But you're also from here!" Her eyes sparkled as she reached for my hands. "You didn't forget us! Take anything from my table. My gift. But don't ever forget us! You see, when the old women there die and the old women here die, it all ends. Promise me you won't forget!"

How could I forget the old warriors, the women who never let go of each other or of Juanelo? Over the decades and across the miles, they'd sent each other an unwritten message that saved them, again and again. *Ponte guapa.* Make yourself brave. I heard that message when I visited Juanelo and saw our baby photos in our neighbors' frayed albums, our graduation pictures on their pitted walls. And I still hear it whispering to me each time I read the old letters, soft as tissues now after years of folding and unfolding. The women of Juanelo refused to let anyone or anything break their barrio bond. Not even a revolution. They would pass that bond to us, the next generation, if we reached for it.

And we did, understanding that we were the heirs to something magical.

The barrio formed us and tied us to each other. Some of us stayed and some of us left—but no one ever forgot home.

Afterword

The twenty years following Abuela's death have brought our family great joy as well as painful losses. We've welcomed the younger generations' life partners, loved their beautiful babies, celebrated their milestones at school and at work. Angel, Alberto, Sergio, Diana, and I are now the family's *viejos*, having said goodbye to Mami, Tío, and Tía in recent years, and then to Papi on March 23, 2024. Diana, Sergio, and I were holding him when he took his last breath. I felt a rush of air down one arm and through the other, a soft whoosh of energy—maybe it was all that love spinning around us. Sergio had wedged an old baseball into one of Papi's closed hands, Mami's favorite necklace in the other. Thirty or so family members and assorted friends filled the common areas of the hospice house during Papi's time there, a last manifestation of the gratitude and love for the intrepid *viejos* who brought our family to New Hampshire, the Live Free or Die State, in 1967.

Papi gave us one of his last smiles when I whispered to him that there were towns in Cuba that had risen up in protest during those days. That I thought freedom for Cuba was at hand. A hopeful *mentirita* to sweeten his journey home.

We remain as grateful as ever for the priceless gift of freedom the *viejos* gave us. The struggle for a free Cuba hasn't ceased since the 1959 revolution came to power. Cubans continue to risk their—and their families'—safety each time they call for democratic change and freedom, as tens of thousands did on July eleventh and twelfth of 2021, when overwhelmingly peaceful and spontaneous protests broke out across the island.

The regime's crackdown after 11J, as the mass protests are known in Cuba, was brutal and well-documented. Video recordings posted on social media showed shock troops, plainclothes police, and state security pepper-spraying, beating, and shooting at unarmed protestors. International human rights groups, journalists, governments, artists, members of the clergy, and Cubans around the world denounced the arrests of peaceful protestors, military trials against civilians, forced disappearances, and sham trials that sentenced some protestors to twenty-five years in prison.

As of July 2024, Cuba's communist-run military dictatorship holds more than one thousand known political prisoners—men like longtime Christian dissident José Daniel Ferrer and artists and San Isidro members Luis Manuel Otero Alcántara and Maykel "Osorbo" Castillo. Cubans are tired of such cruel punishment, of food lines, of the incomprehensible edicts and excuses of a sixty-five-year-old, unelected, single-party system that has declared itself "irrevocable." 11J revealed this, and the mass exodus currently underway—the largest in post-revolutionary history— confirms it. According to the Cuban government itself, over a million Cubans left the island between December 2021 and December 2023— almost 10 percent of the total population of 11 million. More families torn apart, more *viejos* left behind.

To them and to the mothers and fathers, the sons and daughters, the teachers, artists, priests, musicians, journalists, and unflinching dissidents who dare to stand up to tyranny, I send my admiration, my support, and my prayers for your safety and the birth of a truly free Cuba.

Patria y Vida . . .

Book Group Guide

1. In this memoir, what is the meaning of "home"? How do Ana's perceptions of home change, or not, over the course of the book?

2. Like most refugee families, Ana's family can't return home, and they depend on letters and phone calls to stay connected to loved ones who stayed behind. How does this forced and potentially permanent separation shape the family's view of the past—and the future?

3. Mami decides early on that the revolution is turning into a worse dictatorship than Batista's and that the family must flee. Abuela, Tía, and Tío wrestle with moral dilemmas before they arrive at the same conclusion. Tío Manolo's family decides to wait things out and ends up enduring decades of hardship. If faced with an existential challenge, would you be more likely to decide and act quickly or to wait things out?

4. Abuela has an especially difficult transition to America, but so does Papi. How do they each manage their transitions? How does his former baseball career help Papi in America? Is their transition different from Ana's?

5. Ana is uncomfortable with her Cuban culture as a young person, even as she celebrates much of it. How does she come to terms with her hyphenate identity? Should refugees and immigrants have hyphenate identities, or is it better to simply call themselves Americans?

6. Later in life, Ana reluctantly accepts that she has been through significant trauma and must deal with the ramifications. How is Ana's trauma different from her grandmother's? Is the sudden uprooting of families a trauma that ever heals?

7. What family stories/myths/history keep the family going through relocation and change? Why are the distortions in some of those stories both helpful and problematic for Ana?

8. How do religion and spirituality help Abuela confront her new reality? How do they help the rest of the family?

9. Ana and Abuela share a unique and powerful bond. The old and the very young in refugee and immigrant homes are often overshadowed by the adults busy making all the decisions, working multiple jobs, and learning the new rules of the game. Could the bond between the "bookend" generations be an overlooked hallmark of the refugee and immigrant experience?

10. This memoir celebrates women family members in particular. How and why does Ana choose to highlight them? Which characters stayed with you? Why?

11. What if Abuela had stayed in Cuba, as she wanted, to care for Don Manuel? How did choosing her daughters over her father affect the family's chance of success in the United States?

12. What surprised you most about this refugee household? About the refugee experience?

13. How does returning to Cuba to visit the family and friends they'd left behind help Ana and her family? Why is Papi so vehemently opposed to their trip back? Who is right?

14. When she becomes a mother, Ana tries to follow Cuban tradition and it doesn't work. How does becoming a mother change her perspective toward her culture? Herself? The idea of family?

15. In one of his last letters, Don Manuel urges his daughter and granddaughters to "stay together." Do the sisters fulfill that wish, even though they move into separate homes later in life?

Acknowledgments

Writing this book has felt like searching through a dark house looking for something you lost—going room to room, feeling the walls, poking into corners, peering through shadows, and then, after reaching the top floor and inspecting the last closet, realizing you were in the wrong house the whole time.

I'm certain my family and friends worried about my sanity over the last five years of this project, but they hid whatever doubts they had and nudged me along, page by page, draft by draft. Shirley Vernick, Wendy and Rob Gual, Dale Sinesi, Anne Phillips, Christine Savage, Diana Merchant, and Sam Flaster were my constant, patient, and early readers. Alan Schlingingbaum served as my one-man IT department, sharing my screen and my agony as we fought computer gremlins. Brooke Warner, the force-of-nature leader of She Writes Press, saw the possibilities and green-lighted the book after other publishers had passed. Krissa Lagos, my eagle-eyed editor at She Writes, swooped in and fixed obvious—and not so obvious—problems I'd missed as we neared the final deadline. There have been daily debates about commas and semicolons, version control debacles, misplaced files, glitches at midnight. Thank you all for not giving up on me.

Ruth Bejar, Richard Blanco, Armando Lucas Correa, Marjan Kamali, and Aran Shetterly, your generosity and support arrived when I needed it most, boosting my spirits and the book's visibility as the publication date approached. *Gracias* for all that—and for writing beautiful books that continue to inspire and move me.

To my beloved New Hampshire, our snowy port in the political storm. Your beauty soothed us and your people welcomed us—with the exception of some *seborucos*. We could not have landed in a better place than the Live Free or Die State.

To the *viejos* whose stories and wisdom and courage fill these pages, I hope I've honored you here. You are our heroes. It was one of my life's great pleasures when Papi was able to read the first chapter in Spanish. "Do you like it?" I asked him. "*Claro*," he answered. "*Esto lo viví yo.*" He could not stop the tears that ran down his cheeks as he read those first scenes and relived them.

To my Cuban American clan in New Hampshire and beyond, this is for all of you and the next generation, so we'll never forget how we got here and why.

To my magnificent children, Natalia and Sam, and the source of so much of my happiness, Andy, *mil gracias* for the love you give me every day and for believing that I could and would bring this book into the light.

About the Author

photo credit: Sue Bruce Photography, LLC

Ana Hebra Flaster was just shy of her sixth birthday when her family fled post-revolutionary Cuba, in 1967, and settled in Nashua, New Hampshire. She graduated from Smith College and was a software consultant before beginning her writing career. Her essays have been published by the *Wall Street Journal*, the *New York Times*, the *Washington Post*, and the *Boston Globe*, among other national print and online media. Her commentaries and storytelling have aired on national broadcasts of NPR's *All Things Considered* and PBS's *Stories from the Stage*. *Property of the Revolution*, her first book, has won early recognition in several international writing competitions, including being shortlisted in the 2023 Restless Book's New Immigrant Writing Prize and the 2022 Cintas Creative Writing Fellowship. After forty years in the Boston area, Ana recently moved back home to southern New Hampshire with her husband, Andy, and their Havanese pups, Luna and Beny Moré.

For more about Ana and her writing, please scan the QR code below or visit her website, anacubana.com.

Looking for your next great read?

We can help!

Visit www.shewritespress.com/next-read
or scan the QR code below for a list
of our recommended titles.

She Writes Press is an award-winning
independent publishing company founded to
serve women writers everywhere.